Sacred, not Secret
THE OFFICIAL GUIDE IN UNDERSTANDING THE LDS TEMPLE ENDOWMENT

Christopher

Sacred, not Secret—The Official Guide In Understanding the LDS Temple Endowment

All rights reserved. No part of this book may be used or reproduced in any manner whatsoever without written permission of the author or publisher, except by a reviewer who may quote brief passages.

SOFTCOVER FIRST EDITION
ISBN 13: 978-0-9785264-7-4

Library of Congress Catalog Number: 2008922113

Worldwide United Publishing
P.O. Box 9617, Salt Lake City, UT 84109
http://wupublishing.com—1.888.499.9666

Printed in The United States of America

It is given unto many to know the mysteries of God; nevertheless they are laid under a strict command that they shall not impart only according to the portion of his word which he doth grant unto the children of men, according to the heed and diligence which they give unto him. And therefore, **he that will harden his heart, the same receiveth the lesser portion of the word; and he that will not harden his heart, to him is given the greater portion of the word, until it is given unto him to know the mysteries of God until he know them in full**. *And they that will harden their hearts, to them is given the lesser portion of the word until they know nothing concerning his mysteries.*

Alma 12:9–11

Contents

PREFACE — IX

CHAPTER 1 — THE CREATION OF HUMAN BEINGS — 1

CHAPTER 2 — THE CREATION OF THE EARTH — 20

CHAPTER 3 — THE CREATION OF HUMAN MORTALS — 34

CHAPTER 4 — THE FIRST SACRIFICE — 65

CHAPTER 5 — THE GOD OF THIS WORLD — 85

CHAPTER 6 — TRUE MESSENGERS OF GOD — 114

CHAPTER 7 — THE TELESTIAL GLORY — 141

CHAPTER 8 — THE TERRESTRIAL GLORY — 153

CHAPTER 9 — THE CELESTIAL GLORY — 176

CHAPTER 10 — SALVATION IN THE KINGDOM OF GOD — 194

EPILOGUE — 219

Preface

The LDS Temple Endowment is one of the most beautiful and inspirational tools for teaching the mysteries of God ever instituted among mortals. Through the use of symbolic and metaphoric illustrations of simple eternal truths, free agency is supported and protected. The purpose of life is to experience an existence *without* being governed by eternal laws and truth. By this means, we can become convinced of how important these laws are to our happiness. In this *probationary state* (mortality) we prove to ourselves what the values are that we will accept and support as eternal free-willed beings. Thus, we are allowed a "schoolroom" atmosphere, in which, through trial and error, we can determine what works and what does not in each of our individual pursuits of happiness. There would be *no purpose* for the "Veil" (a metaphoric expression of a human's inability to remember anything past one's most recent birth) if all mystery was taught and explained by those who understand these things. Just as basic mathematics lead to algebra, geometry, and calculus, finally culminating in mathematical theorems and hypotheses that always remain true, in order to help the people arrive at a proper understanding of the eternal purpose of life, *true* prophets are commanded to teach as Isaiah reports:

> *Whom shall he teach knowledge? and whom shall he make to understand doctrine? them that are weaned from the milk, and drawn from the breasts. For precept must be upon precept, precept upon precept; line upon line, line upon line; here a little, and there a little: For with stammering lips and another tongue will he speak to this people. To whom he said, This is the rest wherewith ye may cause the weary to rest; and this is the refreshing: yet they would not hear. But the word of the LORD was unto them precept upon precept, precept upon precept; line upon line, line upon line; here a little, and there a little; that they might go, and fall backward, and be broken, and snared, and taken.* (Isaiah 28:9–13)

Unfortunately, no religious ordinance or institutional requirement appears more arrogant, more esoteric, or more confusing to the understanding of a logical and reasonable mind, than the Temple Endowment performed by members of The Church of Jesus Christ of Latter-day Saints (LDS). Mormon leaders instill in their members' minds its grave importance to their personal salvation, and that it is sacred and highly revered as the most significant ordinance one can receive in mortality. Despite this, the LDS faithful do not understand the nature, significance, and meaning of the truths hidden in the endowment. Participants who receive the endowment are commanded not to discuss or reveal any part of it outside of the confines of the temple walls, which walls are becoming worldwide landmarks of Mormon belief, as many Temples (LDS Houses of God) are constructed and placed throughout the earth. Because of its secrecy, and the inability of LDS members to properly explain or understand it, the Temple Endowment has become the cause of much mockery, debate, and controversy.

Because the LDS presence is spreading and being felt throughout the world in both economic and political venues that affect all facets of human life, the purpose of this book is to reveal to the world at large, and more importantly to the LDS people themselves, the *exact* meaning of the endowment. The commentary within these pages will unfold all of the mysteries and hidden symbolism that pertain to it. In so doing, the non-LDS mind will come to an understanding of its extraordinary beauty, wonder, and glorious message. But more significantly, through its exceptional clarity and plainness, this profound and original explanation will afford the LDS people the opportunity to become aware of exactly what they are symbolically doing when performing the endowment. This insight will help them gain a better eternal perspective and comprehension of the hidden mysteries of God that they do not understand. In being made aware of its *true* purpose and intent, LDS members and their leaders can come to understand and acknowledge the insignificance of this ordinance with regard to the salvation of a soul, while at the same time, rejoice and make a proclaimation to all the world of its paramount significance in teaching the mysteries of the plan of our mutual Creators. The beauty of the temple endowment is that it is meant for *everyone* (the children of God) upon the earth, regardless of gender, race, or religious creed.

LDS members are taught that the presentation of the endowment is symbolic and that the true meaning of the symbolism is revealed only through the "Spirit of God." This teaching is one of the few real truths the LDS members understand about the endowment. They are taught that sincere and believing patrons will be able to understand the "mysteries of godliness" as they participate in the ceremony through regular temple attendance. It should be quite apparent to the general membership of the LDS Church, however, that neither they nor their leaders have a complete understanding of the true meaning of the symbolism in reference to the mysteries of godliness. This is evidenced by the fact that none of them professes to know these mysteries and cannot answer questions posed to them regarding those things presented in the Temple Endowment that are relevant to the human race. Upon gaining the essential understanding of what each and every symbolic part of the endowment represents, one will have the answer to all of life's most compelling questions concerning who we are, why we exist, and about our existence before birth and after death. The answers are some of the most comprehendible and beautiful explanations ever given to mortals, but ironically unknown by all temple-worthy LDS members who faithfully participate in the presentation of the endowment.

Mormon scripture teaches that it is possible to know the mysteries of God until they are *known in full*. The ancient prophet Alma writes:

> *It is given unto many to know the mysteries of God; nevertheless they are laid under a strict command that they shall not impart only according to the portion of his word which he doth grant unto the children of men, according to the heed and diligence which they give unto him. And therefore,* **he that will harden his heart, the same receiveth the lesser portion of the word; and he that will not harden his heart, to him is given the greater portion of the word, until it is given unto him to know the mysteries of God until he know them in full.** *And they that will harden their hearts, to them is given the lesser portion of the word until they know nothing concerning his mysteries.* (Alma 12:9–11)

If a person does not know *all the mysteries of God* in their fullness, then according to the above scripture, that person is not giving "heed and diligence" to the commandments of God. The only commandment of any relevance ever given by Jesus, the Christ, in whom the LDS proclaim belief, is: Love your neighbor as yourself in doing unto others what you would have them do unto you.

The very ordinance the LDS members believe is necessary to *save* them and their dead ancestors has brought upon them spiritual deterioration. It is a published fact that, per capita, the LDS people consume more anti-depressant prescription drugs than anywhere else in the world. The Church also has continual problems with mainstream society because of the way faithful LDS members treat their non-member *living* neighbors. The LDS people have forgotten to love their neighbors as themselves, and are more concerned with their families, education, careers, temple work, genealogy, and the dead, than they are with the homeless, naked, sick, and imprisoned in their midst; therefore, adhering to Alma's proclamation above, they have received "the lesser portion of the word until they know nothing concerning his mysteries."

The above passage of scripture comes from what is known as the *unsealed* portion of the Book of Mormon. LDS people accept this book as the word of God equal with the Bible. They claim that it contains the truth and a *fullness* of the gospel of Jesus Christ. Yet, nowhere in the Book of Mormon is any indication given of the importance of temple ordinances. The *sealed portion* of the historic plates prepared by Moroni after his father Mormon's death, however, gives great detail regarding the relevance, or rather irrelevance, of temple ordinances:

> *And I, Moroni, have seen the manner in which the leaders of this church in the latter days present the Holy Endowment unto the people. And after the people have paid their money to the church, and after the church hath taken this money and constructed all manner of fine temples and adorned them*

with the fine things of the world; yea, even after they have done all these things, they shall prohibit those who are poor and needy, even those who are unable to comply with the requirements of the church, from receiving this endowment. And they have changed the ordinance of the Lord and have broken his everlasting covenant. They seek not the Lord to establish his righteousness, but every man walketh in his own way, and after the image of his own god, whose image is in the likeness of the world, and whose substance is that of an idol that they do worship, instead of worshiping the Lord and doing the things that he hath commanded them. And I know that the Lord condemneth those who have used the ordinances that he suffereth the children of men to have in the flesh, according to the administrations of the priesthood which he hath given them, for their own gain, or for the gain of their church. For behold, these ordinances were given by the Lord freely unto all of his children. And they are given for the edification of all; and it is not important to the Lord whether or not his children can pay a tithe unto him. Behold, this is not the sacrifice that he requireth of them; for he requireth a broken heart and a contrite spirit. And all those who come unto him with a broken heart and a contrite spirit shall receive the gift of the Holy Ghost as it hath been explained previously in the words of the brother of Jared. And the Holy Ghost shall teach them all things whatsoever they need to do in order to enter into the kingdom of God. And I have the gift of the Holy Ghost, and it hath been my constant companion all the days of my life, and it doth not tell me that I need to participate in the presentation of the endowment to be saved in the kingdom of God. Behold, nowhere in the words of Christ doth he command his people to receive an endowment that they might be saved. And in this way shall the word of God be changed by the church in the latter days. And this because the spirit is not among them, and they listen to the vain words of their leaders and follow their examples, which are not the examples of Christ, but are the examples of men. (The Sealed Portion, The Final Testament of Jesus Christ [TSP] 12:36–41)

If those of the LDS Church concentrated on the living with just *half* the time, effort, and money they spend on "saving the dead," they could reduce poverty and homelessness proportionately to the number of dead souls they believe they are saving. Consequently, they would be demonstrating a compassionate love for their "living" neighbors as directed by the gospel of Jesus Christ as given in the Book of Mormon. Well did the Christ say, "Follow me; and let the dead bury their dead" (see Matthew 8:22). In saying this, Christ intended for people to concentrate more on loving others and caring for the living (the very things he taught and showed by example) than worrying about the dead.

The LDS Church's main professed missions are to Save the Dead and to Perfect the Saints. These beliefs have convinced millions that this religion is the ONLY *true* church upon the face of the earth and was set up to properly offer the human race eternal salvation. These LDS convictions have caused millions to suffer needlessly through personal guilt and family alienation because of the "worthiness" requirements that are necessary to receive a Temple Recommend. This "Recommend" is necessary in order to receive the Temple Endowment ordinance and attend to other temple work. It is made available only to those LDS members who abide by the teachings and commandments of *the Church*. Ironically, however, these "commandments of the Church" have nothing whatsoever to do with what Jesus taught the people while he lived and worked among them during his mortal sojourn.

Because of the importance placed on the endowment by the LDS Church, millions of dollars are spent and countless hours of dedicated service are rendered each day in attempting to find the names and then perform the temple rituals of receiving the ordinances in behalf of all those who have died in the human race. The LDS believe that these ordinances can be performed vicariously for those who are dead, so that the dead might also be saved.

Ironically, the practice of genealogy, which is the extraction and compilation of the names of the dead, is not mentioned in early LDS scripture. In fact, the Book of Mormon speaks against genealogy:

> *And now I, Nephi, do not give the genealogy of my fathers in this part of my record; neither at any time shall I give it after upon these plates which I am writing; for it is given in the record which has been kept by my father; wherefore, I do not write it in this work. For it sufficeth me to say that we are descendants of Joseph. And it mattereth not to me that I am particular to give a full account of all the things of my father, for they cannot be written upon these plates, for I desire the room that I may write of the things of God. For the fulness of mine intent is that I may persuade men to come unto the God of Abraham, and the God of Isaac, and the God of Jacob, and be saved. Wherefore, the things which are pleasing unto the world I do not write, but the things which are pleasing unto God and unto those who are not of the world. Wherefore, I shall give commandment unto my seed, that they shall not occupy these plates with things which are not of worth unto the children of men.* (1 Nephi 6:1–6)

Thus, in no uncertain terms Nephi explains the purpose for his work: "…*that I may write of the things of God. For the fullness of mine intent is that I may persuade men to come unto the God of Abraham, and the God of Isaac, and the God of Jacob, and be saved.*"

Baptism for the dead, one of the temple ordinances practiced by the LDS faithful, was established in the beginning as a purely symbolic ordinance instituted to reinforce to the people of the earth that whether alive or dead, all must receive and accept the gospel of Jesus Christ in order to be saved in the kingdom of God. The Sealed Portion expounds upon this perfectly. Concerning the ordinance of baptism for the dead, Moroni writes:

> *Now, I know that this doctrine hath caused some contention and disputes among you. For there are those of you who believe that the actual ordinance of baptism must be performed by all of us,*

whether we are alive, or dead, according to the ordinance of baptism for the dead, which thing we also perform according to the will of the Lord. And now, I would that ye should know, that baptism is only a symbolic ordinance that the Lord hath suffered to be given unto us to keep us in remembrance of the plan of salvation and those things that we must do to be saved in the kingdom of God, as I have previously explained them unto you. And we perform baptisms for the dead as a symbolic representation, that whether we are alive or dead, we must keep the commandments of God in order to be saved in His kingdom. And these baptisms for the dead are for our instruction and our learning. For the dead know much more than we do, and have no need for a baptism according to the things of the flesh. But those in the spirit world, who were wicked during the days of their probation, shall also be required to be baptized, but their baptism shall be one of fire, for they shall be in a state of misery for that which they have done in mortality. And many of them must return again to this earth and go through more days of probation, wherein they must prove themselves worthy of the kingdom of God. And all that have died without receiving a baptism and making this covenant with God, who would have received it if they had been permitted to tarry, shall be heirs of the kingdom of God. And also all that shall die henceforth without this baptism, who would have received it, shall be heirs of the kingdom of God. For the Lord judgeth all men according to their works, according to the desires of their hearts. And baptism availeth a man nothing, if it so be that he doth not keep the commandments of God. And if he keepeth the commandments of God, then this baptism availeth him nothing, except that he keepeth the commandments of God in receiving it. (TSP 22:78–83)

The work of this book is given in love and under the guidance of the Creators of us all through the ministrations of those who have been sent to this earth with the sword of truth. Our Creators do not condemn any human for the way in which he or she chooses to worship the god in whom he or she chooses to believe, as it is given unto each of us to worship God, or not, according to the dictates of our own conscience. Though the sharpness of this author's pen condemns the general worshipping patterns of others by the words of truth and reality written herein, his general love for all people creates a personal dissonance. Yet, however much he might be dismayed in writing this exposition because of his gentle and accepting nature of others and respect for their beliefs, nevertheless, the requirements and mandates of his calling require it. No other person alive or dead has presented an explanation of the LDS Temple Endowment, let alone made the attempt, with such completeness and profundity. The explanations and revelations given throughout this book will shut the mouths of the critic and open the eyes of the blind. No matter what the reader might think of the author, no matter what public opinion might be generated by this work, none will be able to negate the miraculous expounding of truth revealed within this book. Absolutely none!

The LDS member is just as loved, just as respected, and just as blessed as any other human being upon this earth. However, the greater responsibility rests upon the LDS people because they have been provided with many more tools and guides in order to find the *true* nature of God and understand their Creators' plan so that they might gain salvation—which simply means lasting and fulfilling happiness. Sadly, those of the LDS Church are some of the most neglectful people upon the earth when it comes to living the *true and simple* principles of the gospel of Jesus Christ. They do not understand or follow the teachings of the *true* prophets who have been called by God to teach His plan to His children. Like the ancient Jews who lived with and listened to the teachings of Jesus, their hearts and minds have been lulled into carnal security from their constant concern with temporal rewards of economic and educational success. Well did Nephi prophesy of them:

> *Yea, they have all gone out of the way; they have become corrupted. Because of pride, and because of false teachers, and false doctrine, their churches have become corrupted, and their churches are lifted up; because of pride they are puffed up. They rob the poor because of their fine sanctuaries; they rob the poor because of their fine clothing; and they persecute the meek and the poor in heart, because in their pride they are puffed up. They wear stiff necks and high heads; yea, and because of pride, and wickedness, and abominations, and whoredoms, they have all gone astray save it be a few, who are the humble followers of Christ; nevertheless, they are led, that in many instances they do err because they are taught by the precepts of men. ...And others will he* (the devil) *pacify, and lull them away into carnal security, that they will say; All is well in Zion; yea, Zion prospereth, all is well—and thus the devil cheateth their souls, and leadeth them away carefully down to hell.* (2 Nephi 28:11–14, 21)

The LDS Temple Endowment is one of these "tools and guides" and was established from the very first day that the Creators of the human race first introduced Their spirit children into mortal bodies upon this earth. Knowing that Their children are quick to forget how to treat each other the way they were taught in the beginning, and are easily persuaded to follow the natural course of the flesh (thus becoming carnal, selfish, and sensual), our Creators *suffered* a series of teaching "tools" to be instituted into our mortal lives. By reason of human nature, mortals follow their empirical senses in the search for truth by listening to other mortals (the arm of flesh). With divinely mandated "tools" such as the endowment, mortals can be gently persuaded to find their true purpose of living life, eloquently expressed by Jesus as the "kingdom of God within." The endowment is a tool that can keep one in remembrance of better ways and points the way towards a more noble and eternal existence and environment like that in which all human beings were created and lived in the beginning—the purpose and nature of this eternal existence being the experience of happiness.

In ancient Israel, whenever our Creators' plan of education was carried out properly, the results testified of its truthfulness and author(s), which were usually chosen prophets. But in many Israelite households, the training appointed through the prophets and the teachings it intended for the people was rarely followed. The fullness of our Creators' plan for mortals was usually only partially and imperfectly fulfilled. This "fullness" was that the people experience peace and happiness living and associating with each other. Because of unbelief and disregard for the Lord's directions, the Israelites surrounded themselves with temptations that few had power to resist and which led to much misery and their eventual destruction.

Many of the biblical stories concerning the Israelites are symbolic representations and metaphoric legends and myths. They originated from succeeding generations who did not follow and accept the simple message of the prophets who were sent among them to teach the straightforward truths of the gospel, which are always based on loving your neighbor as yourself. Having no practical means of reporting exactly what transpired during the early years of Jewish history, the people were left with stories and traditions passed down from other relations of long-ago heroes and ancestors whom the Jews believed were specifically chosen by a universal God. In a similar manner, the stories and traditions of all civilizations, religions, and belief systems came into existence. Most were only based loosely on the truth, thus perpetuating many myths and legends that are false.

The early Israelites began to mingle with the "heathens" and learn their works. They began to serve strange gods and worship idols. These became a snare unto them that eventually led them away from the simple truth of loving each other as one would want to be loved. Their hearts were not right with their God, neither were they steadfast in keeping the commandments given to them by the prophets. Because various factions of leadership existed among them, which taught varying forms of the same belief system, the fathers and mothers in Israel became indifferent to their obligations to God, and of worse effect, indifferent to their obligations to their children and their neighbors. Because of unfaithfulness in the home and idolatrous influences from without, many of the Hebrew youth received an education differing widely from that which was taught by the holy prophets; thus they began to adopt the ways of the heathen.

To meet this growing evil, the prophets provided other means to aid parents in the work of educating their children. From the earliest times, prophets had been recognized as teachers divinely appointed. In the highest sense, the prophet was the one who spoke by direct inspiration, communicating to the people the messages that he received from our Creators. According to tradition, the name "prophet" was also given to those who, though not so directly inspired, were appointed by the people to instruct them in the works and the ways of God. For the training of such a class of teachers, Samuel, by the Lord's direction (according to Hebrew stories), established the Schools of the Prophets.

These schools were intended to serve as a barrier against wide-spreading corruption, provide for the mental and spiritual welfare of the youth, and promote the prosperity of the nation by furnishing it with men qualified to act as leaders and counselors. To this end, according to Jewish history, Samuel gathered companies of young men who were pious, intelligent, and studious. These were called the "sons of the prophets." As they studied the teachings of the prophets, Jewish history reports that these students received God's life-giving power, which quickened the energies of their minds and souls. *True* prophets were not only versed in Divine truth, but made claim to communion with Advanced Human Beings who knew what other less-experienced humans needed to do to experience happiness. These *true* prophets received a special "endowment" directly from celestial emissaries which these prophets referred to as "angels of God." Because of their wisdom, the prophets earned the respect and confidence of the people, both for learning and for piety.

Eventually, the kings of Israel, and more especially David and Solomon, supported these schools of the prophets. Because our Creators are Eternal Beings who never change, Their plan is just as eternal and never-changing as They are. Therefore, the Holy Endowment that was given to *Adam* (who figuratively represents the very first human being created in Their image and each and every being thereafter) is the *same* endowment revealed to the prophets who set up the doctrine and teaching curriculum of the ancient schools of the prophets before Solomon's day. It is an endowment of understanding covering *all* the mysteries of God.

Because the people rejected the *true* prophets and desired kings to lead them, they eventually followed the false doctrine of their chosen and appointed leaders (many of whom were *false* prophets), and the original endowment in its pure form and splendor was soon corrupted. When it came time to build the great temple in the day of Solomon, the presentation of the endowment inside its walls became a corrupted form of the curriculum taught in the schools previously established by *true* prophets of God.

In more modern times, a group of men called Masons believe that they are in possession of the original secrets of those who built Solomon's temple (thus the moniker: Masons). These believe that the original temple masons passed down their understanding of the mysteries of Godliness to them, and they separate themselves from everyone else and set themselves up as "the elect"—those who are "endowed" with a greater knowledge and understanding of life than the general public. Therefore, they have convinced themselves that they should remain in a brotherhood of mystery and secrecy that sets them apart from the general population of the world. Appropriately, the modern-day Masonic temple ritual has some interesting similarities to the LDS Temple Endowment.

In the early 1800's, Joseph Smith (a latter-day *true* prophet) reestablished the school of the prophets and began to explain and teach the significance of the Masonic rituals and secrecy of their brotherhood. In this endeavor, he reached a significant level or "degree," as it is known in Masonry. Joseph continued with the Masonic ways until others kicked him out when he began teaching them that they were using a corrupted form of the *true* Holy Endowment of God that they did not understand properly. Joseph tried to explain the endowment in its simplicity and beauty, but the prideful and separatist Masons wanted nothing to do with a young man who did not think it was appropriate to keep Masonic rituals secret from others. The Masons believed that the revelation of the truth and the reality of the presentation of their temple rituals would take away the very essence of their power—their egos—and their own (supposed) superiority over the "unenlightened" masses.

As Joseph Smith received an understanding of the true endowment, he was inspired to incorporate many other teachings of the mysteries of God into it. Some of these truths had either been lost or were not necessary in ancient times, but were necessary in the latter days in order to come to a proper and complete understanding of *all* the mysteries of God. He was taught these truths in the manner as they have been, are, and will always be revealed to *true* prophets. Like all others before him, Joseph was taught by ministering angels sent to the earth to teach him. He did not receive *any* mental revelation, reflection, or intuition. He was taught by a resurrected and Advanced Human Being (angel) who came from another planet located in a solar system like our own and spoke with Joseph *face to face*.

When Joseph received the explanation of the endowment in its purity, he understood that its whole purpose was to teach living mortals the mysteries of God in parable, allowing those who sincerely seek to know, the opportunity to receive an understanding based upon their desire and worthiness. Joseph was commanded in the same manner as the ancient prophet Isaiah:

> Go, and tell this people, Ye hear indeed, but *ye do not* understand ; and ye see indeed, but perceive not that which ye see. ***Therefore thou shalt give unto them that for which they seek, and those things which they do not understand, for they seek to hear heavy things, and their hearts are full of excess because they desire that which maketh their ears heavy, even that which they do not understand. Preach unto them much*** and make their ears heavy ***with your preaching; yea,*** make the heart of this people fat ***in that which they desire, but*** shut their eyes ***to the truth that would heal them; For they are a fallen people who seek not the Lord to establish his righteousness so that*** they see with their eyes, and hear with their ears, and understand with their heart, and convert, and be healed. (Isaiah 6:9–10; correct translation given in bold italics.)

The practice of performing this endowment for the dead was not instituted into the modern LDS Church until well after the death of Joseph Smith. Brigham Young formally established this practice on January 11, 1877 in the St. George temple, where he acted as proxy for his dead father.

It is very important to understand that Brigham Young did *not* receive instructions from Joseph to finish or continue the endowment or to change it in any way, nor did he receive any instructions from any mortal or resurrected being to do anything with the temple ordinances. The belief that the endowment is essential for salvation was incorporated into modern-day Mormon doctrine by subsequent leaders *after* the death of Joseph Smith. These leaders wanted to convince the people that they had the authorization given directly from Joseph to do with the endowment whatever they wished. Because the modern leaders since Brigham Young have no idea what the symbolism of the endowment represents, they justify the changes they make to it because they feel they are entitled to "modern-day revelation"—in other words, they have given themselves the authority to make things up as they go along. It is important to point out that Joseph *did not* receive the true and uncorrupted endowment through any means other than the *actual* voice of a resurrected being sent to this earth to establish it. He did not receive "modern-day revelation" invented in his own head.

In innocent ignorance, the modern LDS Church uses the following scripture from the King James biblical rendition of the New Testament to justify their belief in the necessity of temple work, and its significance to salvation:

God having provided some better thing for us, that they without us should not be made perfect. (Hebrews 11:40)

What modern LDS leaders and teachers fail to point out, however, is that Joseph Smith himself retranslated this verse of scripture to read appropriately:

God having provided some better things for them through their sufferings, for without sufferings they could not be made perfect. (Joseph Smith Translation [JST], Hebrews 11:40)

Nevertheless, not even Joseph seemed to completely understand the insignificance of symbolic vicarious ordinances until as late as 1836, when he received an understanding that his brother, Alvin, would be an heir of the Celestial kingdom without ever having been baptized while alive, or having the temple ordinances completed for him after he was dead:

Thus came the voice of the Lord unto me, saying: All who have died without a knowledge of this gospel, who would have received it if they had been permitted to tarry, shall be heirs of the celestial kingdom of God; Also all that shall die henceforth without a knowledge of it, who would have received it with all their hearts, shall be heirs of that kingdom; For I, the Lord, will judge all men according to their works, according to the desire of their hearts. (Doctrine and Covenants [D&C], 137:7–9)

Joseph negates without question the necessity of the literal ordinance of baptism for salvation. Upon considering what the modern LDS Church omitted from the D&C (when received in conjuction with the rest of the above vision and the explanation that a man is saved by his own actions and deeds and not by those of another), the truth seeker can begin to understand how the truth became corrupted so quickly after Joseph Smith's death. The rest of the above vision known as D&C section 137 continues as follows:

I saw the Twelve Apostles of the Lamb, who are now upon the earth, who hold the keys of this last ministry, in foreign lands, standing together in a circle, much fatigued, with their clothes tattered and feet swollen, with their eyes cast downward, and Jesus standing in their midst, and they did not behold Him. The Savior looked upon them and wept. (History of the Church, Vol. 2, pgs. 380–1.)

Well would the Savior have reason to weep when those who claim leadership over his people have "*their eyes cast downward*" because "*they [do] not behold Him.*" Part of what they "do not behold" is that the temple ordinances have absolutely nothing to do with the fullness of the gospel of Jesus Christ.

The endowment became the perfect vehicle for Joseph to teach the truths about the mysteries of God that he had learned, which have been hidden since the foundation of the world and only revealed to the very few who do not "look beyond the mark." Joseph knew the people of his time wanted religion the same way the Israelites wanted something to worship instead of accepting the purity of the simple law of loving one's neighbor as one's self. Joseph gave to the people of his day exactly what Moses gave to the golden calf-worshipping Israelites of ancient times: these two *true* prophets gave the people *organized* religion so that they might stumble. (See scripture reference to Jacob 4:14 at the end of the Preface.)

Can one imagine what would have happened to Joseph Smith in his day had he taught what he knew? Even because of the few truths he *did* teach, he was murdered by non-believers and some traitors among his close associates who had once called him friend. Had Joseph openly taught the fullness of the truth in plainness, his own followers would have proclaimed blasphemy and hung their prophet. This is the reason Joseph said the following to those who honored him as a prophet and called him a friend:

> *If I revealed all that has been made known to me, scarcely a man on this stand would stay with me. ...Brethren, if I were to tell you all I know of the kingdom of God, I do know that you would rise up and kill me.* (Joseph Smith Jr.)

Heber C. Kimball reiterated what many had heard on various occasions from the mouth of their prophet: *Had not Joseph said many times—are not men now living who heard him say: 'Would to God, brethren, I could tell you who I am! Would to God I could tell you what I know! But you would call it blasphemy, and there are men upon this stand who would want to take my life.'* (Whitney, Orson F., Life of Heber C. Kimball. Salt Lake City, Utah: Kimball Family, 1888. pgs. 332–3.)

After Joseph Smith's death, the LDS Church divided itself into two main factions. One was led by several of the most popular and intelligent leaders of the Church who reorganized it and named it the *Reorganized Church of Jesus Christ of Latter Day Saints*. This faction believes that the proper authority of the Church belonged in the hands of the most "righteous" leaders who were personally closest to the prophet Joseph Smith, and that the priesthood authority had its rightful home in the hands of Joseph Smith's son, Joseph Smith III. Flowing down from the teachings of these individuals, this organization has now been renamed, and is currently known as the *Community of Christ*. From these men, who were closest to Joseph and who had greater access to his personal writings and explanations than any other group, there have come no special endowments or any mandate to build temples for rituals. They do not believe in the concept of salvation for the dead and thereby demonstrate a better understanding of the true purpose of the endowment that Joseph Smith originally intended.

The other main faction, and the one that has become by far the larger and more powerful of the two, was led by Brigham Young. He was a very flamboyant and charismatic apostle under Joseph Smith and led most of the poor, indentured, and illiterate members of the early church out West into what was then Mexico near the Great Salt Lake located in the present state of Utah in the United States. There he founded "The Place" where he would eventually oversee one of the most phenomenal personal dictatorships known in modern times. Brigham Young's ego and spiritual dictatorship was the perfect venue for corrupted truths to be introduced to a people full of faith in God—a people who would give their lives if necessary for the building up or defense of what they were convinced was the "kingdom of God" on earth. It was Young who inspired the LDS people to put themselves above all others and become a "peculiar and special people." They believed that they were led to the land of present-day Salt Lake City in order to establish a city of God they called Zion.

Brigham Young incorporated some of his own understanding and doctrine into the early endowment, including "blood atonement" and other spurious and strange doctrines that have since been removed from more modern presentations. It was from Young's administration, and the administrations of those who followed after him, that most of the original endowment as Joseph Smith taught it remained intact. Subsequently, however, even Brigham Young's altered presentation of the endowment has undergone significant alterations and deletions from the original form presented by Joseph Smith. Young didn't understand the symbolism of the endowment any more than the LDS leaders do in modern times; thus, its irrelevance to salvation never occurred to him, and allowed him to change it to conform to his own beliefs and the accepted doctrines of his time.

The current LDS leaders are as naive in their understanding as was Brigham Young, and in their desire to please the world and get along with those who do not believe in Mormonism (Gentiles), they have removed less palatable portions of the endowment. In fact and in very deed, they have changed the endowment to accommodate the whims of society, and with these changes, maintain a learning environment where LDS members are left "ever learning but never able to come to the knowledge of the truth" (see 2 Timothy 3:7). Whenever society steps up against the LDS Church to mock it for its secret temple rituals (which the lay person assumes are stolen from Masonry and appear to the "Gentile" as outright strange or unbecoming of a rational mind), the Church conveniently receives a new "revelation" from its self-proclaimed modern-day prophets, seers, and revelators (LDS General Authorities), who change the structure and format of the endowment in order to eliminate any misunderstanding or embarrassing part concerning it. <u>Never</u> has a modern leader of the LDS Church publicly proclaimed that he received an *actual* visitation from any ministering angel of God or any other Being to instruct him to change an ordinance that should be as everlasting and unchangeable as the God in whom the LDS believe. All LDS General Authorities do their work solely by the "personal revelations" coming into their minds.

LDS General Authorities are some of the wealthiest, educated, and most prominent business leaders throughout society. They know how the world thinks, and they act accordingly in their positions of authority to structure the church and maintain its integrity consistent with mainstream religious thought. The LDS Church has received countless "honors and glories of men" and has received an abundance of platitudes from the rest of the world. *Nothing* the LDS General Authorities experience in the administration and performance of their leadership positions reflects the caveat given by Jesus to his disciples concerning the expected treatment they would receive from the world as they preached and lived his *true* gospel:

Blessed are ye, when men shall hate you, and when they shall separate you from their company, and shall reproach you, and cast out your name as evil, for the Son of man's sake. Rejoice ye in that day, and leap for joy: for, behold, your reward is great in heaven: for in the like manner did their fathers unto the prophets. But woe unto you that are rich! for ye have received your consolation. Woe unto you that are full! for ye shall hunger. Woe unto you that laugh now! for ye shall mourn and weep. Woe unto you, when all men shall speak well of you! for so did their fathers to the false prophets. (Luke 6:22–6)

If the world hate you, ye know that it hated me before it hated you. If ye were of the world, the world would love his own: but because ye are not of the world, but I have chosen you out of the world, therefore the world hateth you. Remember the word that I said unto you, The servant is not greater than his lord. If they have persecuted me, they will also persecute you; if they have kept my saying, they will keep yours also. (John 15:18–20)

If the leaders of the LDS Church possessed the *true* "Spirit of God," they would understand His mysteries in their fullness. They would understand the symbolism of the Holy Endowment as they teach by example and word and live the great commandment of "Love Your Neighbor As Yourself." If they lived this way, they would then be able to explain the endowment properly to their members and the Church's critics. Furthermore, their explanations would radiate and project the beautiful representation of the plan of our Creators that the Temple Endowment truly portrays. But since the "God" in whom they have chosen to believe is *ever-changing* to please the rest of the world, the current LDS faithful receive an endowment that has been changed from its purity and tangled in secrecy and mystery, which *none* of them understand. Thus has the prophet Alma's words been fulfilled in them: "And they that will harden their hearts, to them is given the lesser portion of the word until they know *nothing* concerning his mysteries."

Like the Jews of old, the LDS people have left the purity of the simple message of Christ delivered to them by a *true* prophet and openly reject any other *true messengers* sent to them to bring these things to their remembrance. In fact, the parallels between the modern LDS Church and the ancient Jewish Church near the time of Christ are uncanny. Not only are their geographical areas uniquely similar in appearance (both Salt Lake City, Utah and Jerusalem, Israel are situated in valleys near great inland bodies of salt water having an unmistakable stench), but both groups center(ed) their spiritual beliefs on a "sacred" temple, which took almost the exact same time to build (40 years). When their political and spiritual beliefs are analyzed and compared, the similarities become even more extraordinary. Both groups believe(d) their people are an elect and chosen people and their religion to be the *only* truth given of God to mortals, referring to all who do not accept their ways as "Gentiles." Also, both believe(d) their respective temple ordinances are/were essential to personal salvation. But just as the ancient Jewish temple sacrifices and ordinances changed over time until they became but a small remnant of their original presentation, the LDS temple endowment is likewise evolving and changing.

Certain lessons can only be learned through repetitive experience. Even more convincing than the above comparisons, is the timetable concerning the Jews and the LDS people. It is remarkably in sync with relevant historical events. An honest student of history can measure from the time when the Great Roman Empire became the dominant world power (circa 200 years BC) to the time when the "Jew" (by ancestry) Jesus, the Christ, began his earthly ministry. Unknown to the LDS people, a man was called to preach a simple message of truth at the exact same time period (circa 200 years) after the establishment of the most dominant worldwide power ever known in human history—the United States of America. This exact time frame will unfold and testify of the mission given to the "Bearer of Christ" who came from LDS ancestry.

The true explanation of the symbolic temple endowment revealed for the first time throughout the pages of this book will confound the wisdom of the learned and abase the superiority of the successful of the world who believe that God has chosen and blessed them over all other humans. Well are the words of the propehts fulfilled in saying, *"For ye see your calling, brethren, how that not many wise men after the flesh, not many mighty, not many noble, are called: But God hath chosen the foolish things of the world to confound the wise; and God hath chosen the weak things of the world to confound the things which are mighty."* (I Corinthians 1:26–7)

Those who receive the endowment and believe in its power and relevance in their lives will be left without an excuse as to why they did not fully comprehend the valuable lessons given therein. They will have no excuse for not understanding the mysteries of God in their fullness. Though many will reject this work because it did not come by way of the ecclesiastical order of their church, none will be exempt from the embarrassment and personal condemnation they will experience when the "sword of truth" comes out of the mouth of their Lord and God, who then in his glory will reveal to all humankind the truths once hidden and now explained in plainness. Reject it as they may, few will be able to deny the profound truths of reality this work provides to the world.

Thus have the words of the prophets been fulfilled as they now say to the LDS people:

> *But behold, the LDS members are a stiffnecked people; and they despise the words of plainness, and would kill the true prophets, and seek for things that they do not understand. Wherefore,*

*because of their blindness, which blindness comes from **looking beyond the mark**, they must needs fall; for God hath taken away His plainness from them, and delivered unto them many things which they cannot understand, because they desired it. And because they desired it God hath done it, that they might stumble.* (Compare Jacob 4:14)

So that the human race will not have the excuse that it did not get the chance to understand the explanation of our Creators' plan in its plainness as given through the Holy Endowment, this book was prepared and published to explain the endowment that is presented and received in *secret* in the LDS temples throughout the world. What is explained herein is the *same* plan of our Creators that was represented in the endowments of ancient times. Upon understanding the mysteries of godliness given in this powerful teaching tool, it will become obviously apparent that it should be held......**SACRED, not SECRET**.

—Christopher

1
THE CREATION OF HUMAN BEINGS

THE TEMPLE ENDOWMENT CEREMONY

(NOTE: The following presentation of the LDS temple endowment is given as the modern Church of Jesus Christ of Latter-day Saints has practiced it for many years. The endowment had major changes incorporated into it circa 1990, and initiatory changes took effect in 2005. The transcript used throughout this book reflects the major changes incorporated into it for comparison. The Endowment is presented in blue text. ~~Red strikeouts~~ are used to indicate passages that were deleted; **boldface green font** is used to indicate new added text since the major edits took place. If important to a key concept that needs to be understood, normal black text (within parenthesis) is inserted within the body of the blue endowment text in order to clarify Joseph Smith's original text. The same black text is used for all commentary. Although many of the words have been changed from the original endowment, unless they present a significant doctrinal change in some way, the text is not changed to reflect the original endowment, but remains as it is currently presented in the LDS temples throughout the world. *Words in blue italics within parenthesis ( )* are the nonverbal elements of the endowment.)

The endowment seems to proceed chronologically for a time-bound mortal brain. However, THE ENDOWMENT IS FIGURATIVE IN EACH AND EVERY WAY, AND TRYING TO CONVEY REALITY INTO IT WILL ONLY CONFUSE THE READER. The commentary is intended to head the reader in the right direction, or better, the direction of reality; then it is up to him or her how much *reality* (real truth) he or she is willing to accept.

Before an individual may attend the temple, he or she must be baptized, confirmed, and (for men only) receive the Melchizedek Priesthood and office of an Elder. In the case of a convert to the Church, or one who has previously been excommunicated and re-baptized, the common rule is generally not to let an individual attend the temple until he or she has been a full tithe-paying member for a year. Previous to entering the temple, one must obtain a Temple Recommend.

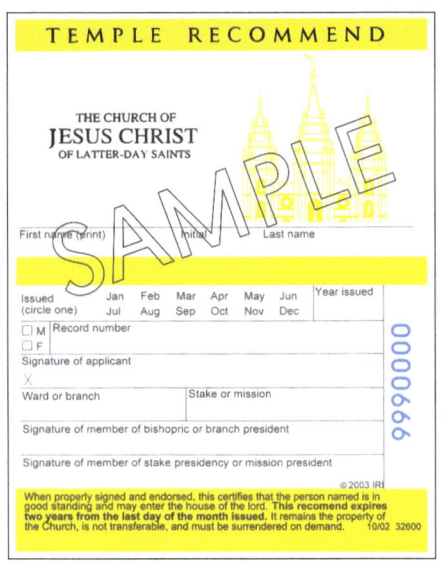

In order for a person to be found "worthy" of a Temple Recommend, one must undergo an interview process with their Bishop and also with the next higher authority above the Bishop (the Stake President). This is to make sure each member has been thoroughly screened for personal "worthiness" and "spiritual preparedness." During this interview, one must show his or her devotion to the LDS Church by supporting the appointed leaders and sustaining the First Presidency and Quorum of the Twelve Apostles as prophets, seers, and revelators of God. One must also attend all church meetings and pay a *full* tithe (10% of one's gross income) to the Church, among a long list of other requirements. According to the interview process, one must obey the "Gospel" in full. This list of requirements for the LDS faithful (indeed the Church itself as a whole) is looked upon by the LDS people as *actually being* the Gospel of Jesus Christ.

Ironically, as the Church labors under the weight of its own ignorance of the *true* gospel of Christ, no one is required or questioned to see if they obey the *actual gospel* Jesus taught to the Jews and to the Nephites. This pure and simple gospel is set forth in Matthew, chapters 5, 6, and 7 in the Bible and in 3 Nephi, chapters 12, 13, and 14 of the Book of Mormon, appropriately subtitled Another Testament of Jesus Christ. These identical passages of scripture support each other and give the reader a full foundation and premise of all of Christ's teachings and testify of what his message and intent actually were for the people to understand and obey. This simple oversight profoundly demonstrates that most LDS members seek to attend the temple to receive their endowment in order to please their leaders and the Church by complying with its requirements rather than following Christ's gentle and simple counsels. Most members have little or no regard for, or an accurate understanding of, the *true* gospel of Jesus Christ. As a result, the Holy Spirit is unable to help them understand the mysteries of God taught therein, as explained by Alma quoted in the Preface of this book. This is because they do not live according to the simple words of Christ sufficient to allow this *Holy Spirit* to aid them in their awareness and comprehension of what the *real truth is*. Later it will be revealed exactly what the "Holy Spirit" means and how essential it is to obtain a proper understanding of truth.

Moroni was very explicit and forthright in his first instructions to the young Joseph Smith at the time he appeared to him and informed him of an ancient record containing the history of the American people:

> *He said there was a book deposited, written upon gold plates, giving an account of the former inhabitants of this continent, and the source from whence they sprang. He also said that* **the**

fullness of the everlasting Gospel was contained in it, as delivered by the Savior to the ancient inhabitants. (Joseph Smith—History 1:34)

As explained before, and reiterated with specific purpose, nowhere in all the words of Christ, either in the Book of Mormon or the Bible, can there be found any instructions or commandments regarding the construction of temples or the performing of special ordinances therein. The **_fullness_** of the **_everlasting_** gospel delivered by Christ himself in the three parallel chapters of Matthew and 3rd Nephi mentioned above, is stipulated and coalesced in this one great commandment: Do unto others what you would have them do unto you, or better, Love thy neighbor as thyself—nothing more, nothing less.

In Joseph Smith's day, there were absolutely *no* requirements imposed upon those who were desirous to receive an endowment by entering into the early *school of the prophets* he established. The school was made available to *all* those who had a desire to learn more about the mysteries of God.

INITIATORY ORDINANCES
Preliminary to Receiving the Endowment

*(After entering the temple, the patron shows his or her Temple Recommend to a worker stationed near the entrance inside the building. The patron proceeds to the dressing area, where a private locker and dressing room is assigned (dividers and a door ensure privacy). After disrobing, he **puts on a garment and** covers himself with a "shield"— a white poncho-like linen covering with a hole in the top for his head and ~~open sides (held shut while walking)~~ **sides sewn shut. Wearing the garment, and** covered in the shield, he secures his "street clothes" in a locker, and ~~carries one pair of temple garments (one-piece style)~~ **goes** to the washing and anointing area, and waits on a bench until directed by a temple worker to enter one of the washing and anointing booths through a veiled partition. The booths are simply small cubicles made up of suspended lined curtains. When called for, the initiate enters the booth ~~and hands his garments to a worker, who places them on a towel rod~~. Throughout the initiatory, women officiate for women, and men for men. As the initiate stands upright in his garment and shield, the temple worker wets his fingers under a small faucet of running water in the booth, and places water on the initiate's head.)*

The initiatory procedure has recently been changed (2005) so that the patron does not have to stand essentially naked in front of the temple worker. Before the initiate enters the washing and anointing area, he or she is instructed to dress in garments that each is required to purchase from the authorized garment manufacturer/distributor (i.e., Beehive Clothing, an LDS-owned company) before coming to the temple to receive the endowment.

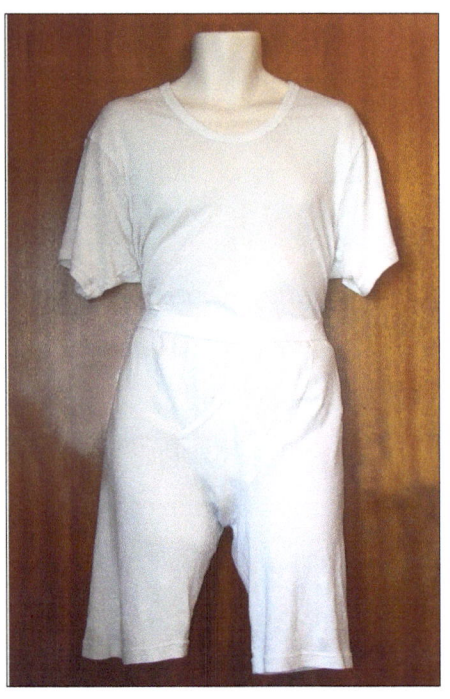 

What most members of the LDS Church call "garments" is believed to be the garment of the *Holy Priesthood*, received during the initiatory procedure. This assumption will later be shown as errant as the true meaning of the "Garment of the Holy Priesthood" is properly explained. Originally, the temple garment was a white, one-piece undergarment tied with strings that extended to the wrists and the ankles. Changes over time have now resulted in a two-piece garment resembling a T-shirt and knee-length boxer shorts—conforming to the changing fashion trends of the members. It is believed that by wearing this garment a person will be protected, both spiritually and physically, throughout his or her life. Only faithful LDS members wear the garment, believing that the privilege granted them sets them peculiarly and uniquely apart from their neighbor—a far stretch away from the premise of Christ's gospel of absolute equality. But as the true significance of the garment is revealed, one will soon learn to appreciate and come to understand that every human being upon the earth symbolically *wears the garment* all the days of their life during mortality.

While the other temple attire is used only *inside* the temple, the garment is regularly worn outside the temple as underclothing. LDS faithful use the wearing of the garment as an important sign of their identity as an endowed member of the Church, and as a demonstrative expression to others that they are keeping the covenants they made in the temple.

During the *washing ordinance* as well as the *anointing ordinance*, the temple worker (since the 2005 changes) no longer touches each area of the initiate's body through the shield, but places a small amount of water on the head for washing, and a small amount of oil on the head for anointing. In essence, the leaders of the LDS Church have done the same thing the Catholic Church did in turning "baptism by immersion" into "sprinkling" of Holy Water. This they have done so as not to be accused by concerned outsiders of any "inappropriate touching" by the workers inside of the temple; thus promoting and supporting the idea that the endowment is politically and morally correct, and creating a more positive image towards it among the general public. However, this unfortunately reveals the fact that the leaders who made the changes do not know why they are required to wash and anoint the entire body in the first place.

PREFACE TO THE WASHING ORDINANCE

Brother _____, the temple washing, anointing, and clothing ordinances were given anciently, as recorded in the book of Exodus: "And thou shalt bring Aaron and his sons unto the door of the tabernacle of the congregation, and wash them with water. And thou shalt put upon Aaron the holy garments, and anoint him, and sanctify him." (Exodus 40:12–13) **We likewise administer these ordinances in our day, but you are washed and anointed only symbolically, as follows.**

This initiatory explanation was put into the presentation of the endowment by the modern LDS Church in an attempt to demonstrate the comparison between the ordinances performed by the ancient Israelites and their modern-day counterparts, the Latter-day Saints. What is again interesting to point out is that both groups of people rejected the higher laws of God (i.e., the Law of Consecration, in which all are treated *equal*, with no leaders) and desired an organized church in which the hierarchy speaks for God and the rest listen to their words. This comparative symbolism further solidifies the fact that the modern Latter-day Saints are following in the exact same footsteps as the ancient Israelites.

In the Old Testament, the story is given of Moses preparing the people to speak with God face to face only to have them become afraid of the "fire, smoke, and thunder". Being afraid to approach God themselves, the people tell Moses to go speak *for* them and that they would then listen to him (Moses) and do what he tells them to do. This story is figurative of the natural tendency of a mortal to follow another instead of taking the responsibility for learning upon oneself. According to the story presented in the Bible, God gave the people what they desired and instituted lower laws of ordinances and sacrifices that were easy to follow in repetition, but hard for them to understand and make a meaningful correlation with their daily lives. He did this for a reason, which was eloquently taught by Jacob. (This scripture was mentioned previously in the Preface of this book, but is of such relevance to the nature of the modern Latter-day Saints that its repetition is profound. To liken the following scripture to these latter-day times, one needs only replace the word "Jews" with "Mormons/LDS" and the prophecy comes alive with relevant significance:)

> *But behold, the Jews were a stiffnecked people; and they despised the words of plainness, and killed the prophets, and sought for things that they could not understand. Wherefore, because of their blindness, which blindness came by looking beyond the mark, they must needs fall; for God hath taken away his plainness from them, and delivered unto them many things which they cannot understand, because they desired it. And because they desired it God hath done it, that they may stumble.* (Jacob 4:14)

THE WASHING ORDINANCE
The Creation of the Spirit

(NOTE: Only the male/brother variation of these ordinances is given for brevity and non-repetition of the same thing. The female/sister variation is very similar to that of the male/brother, but is not necessary for purposes of explaining what these ordinances mean.)

Brother _____, having authority, I wash you preparatory to you receiving your anointings [for and in behalf of _____ *(patron and then temple worker read name of deceased)*, who is dead], that you may become clean from the blood and sins of this generation.

(While pronouncing the blessings which follow, the officiator ~~lightly touches each part of the initiate's body as it is named through the open sides of the shield~~ **lays hands on the initiate's head.***)*

I wash your head, that your brain and your intellect may be clear and active; your ears, that you may hear the word of the Lord; your eyes, that you may see clearly and discern between truth and error; your nose, that you may smell; your lips, that you may never speak guile; your neck, that it may bear up your head properly; your shoulders, that they may bear the burdens that shall be placed thereon; your back, that there may be marrow in the bones and in the spine; your breast, that it may be the receptacle of pure and virtuous principles; your vitals and bowels, that they may be healthy and strong and perform their proper functions; your arms and hands, that they may be strong and wield the sword of justice in defense of truth and virtue; your loins, that you may be fruitful and multiply and replenish the earth, that you might have joy and rejoicing in your posterity; your legs and feet, that you might run and not be weary, and walk and not faint.

THIS IS SYMBOLIC OF OUR CREATION AS SPIRITS.

The first thing that occurred in the plan of our Creators was that we were all created as spirit entities in *the image* of our Eternal Parents. An "image" is not an actual person, but a likeness or reflection of something. We were given an entity of element (spirit) that when placed in a body, would work properly with a human head, brain, ears, eyes, nose, lips, neck, shoulders, back, bones, spine, breast, vitals, bowels, arms, hands, loins, legs, and feet. In other words, we were given all the necessary eternal elements that would allow us to come into existence and to have control over our bodies of flesh and bone, interacting with these tabernacles of flesh in order to fulfill the measure of our creation—the experience of happiness.

Water is used in this ordinance because it is an eternal element that is not "man-made," nor have humans had anything at all to do with the "life-giving" attributes afforded by natural water. As water exists and gives life to all of us, so in like manner, our Creators have given life to our spirits through no work or choice of our own.

(A second officiator enters, and both officiators then place their hands on the initiate's head. The second officiator seals the washing as follows:)

SEALING OF THE WASHING

Brother _____, having authority, we lay our hands upon your head [for and in behalf of _____ *(patron and then temple worker read name of deceased), who is dead]*, and seal upon you this washing, that you may become clean from the blood and sins of this generation through your faithfulness; in the name of Jesus Christ. Amen.

SOMETHING THAT IS "SEALED" CANNOT BE TAKEN AWAY.

For this reason, the "washing," or the creation of our spirits, has been "sealed" upon us, and none (except our Creators) has the power to take this away from us. We were brought into a "spirit" existence, being granted life and independence to act in the state in which we were created. Further, it is given metaphorically that we must live according to the commandments of Christ ("eat his body and drink his blood" / doing what he did while upon earth / or better, acting "in the *name* of Jesus Christ") in order for us to keep our spirits forever. If our Creators were to destroy our spirits after They created them, it would be an act contrary to Their perfect nature and the purpose of being a Creator. Since a "spiritual death penalty" (Second Death) is imposed *only* on those who refuse to follow the eternal laws that maintain peace and order in the Universe, our existence is thereby given (sealed) to us unconditionally upon our adherence to the gospel of Christ, or in other words, <u>living our lives</u> "in the name of Jesus Christ."

This "Second Death" comes upon those who, by their own choice, refuse to live in such a way that their free-willed actions do not impede upon the free agency of another, i.e., those who do not love their neighbors as themselves. These will not and cannot be allowed to live in any kingdom of God because they would cause misery and discord. This *spiritual death* only occurs if the individual, after eons of time of experiencing existence, freely decides that the eternal plan and balance of all things does not fit into that person's realm of happiness and desire. Because the eternal laws of heaven and earth have always been the same and will always be the same, if a free-willed creation chooses not to abide by them, there's only one option left—cease to exist at all. This is the most merciful option, as no Creator would allow one of Their creations to suffer eternally in what misled believers think of as "hell, fire, and damnation."

(The patron then steps through a veiled partition into another part of the booth where he sits upon a chair. He is anointed on his head with scented olive oil from a glass anointing horn.)

ANOINTING ORDINANCE
Our Independence And Free Agency Are Guaranteed

Brother _____, having authority, I pour this holy anointing oil upon your head [for and in behalf of _____ *(patron and then temple worker read name of deceased)*, who is dead], and anoint you preparatory to your (reigning in the kingdom of God forever) becoming a king and a priest unto the Most High God, hereafter to rule and reign in the House of Israel forever. *

(While pronouncing the blessings which follow, the officiator ~~lightly touches each part of the initiate's body as it is named through the open sides of the shield, as was done in the washing~~ **lays hands on the initiate's head**)*:*

I anoint your head, that your brain and your intellect may be clear and active; your ears, that you may hear the word of the Lord; your eyes, that you may see clearly and discern between truth and error; your nose, that you may smell; your lips, that you may never speak guile; your neck, that it may bear up your head properly; your shoulders, that they may bear the burdens that shall be placed thereon; your back, that there may be marrow in the bones and in the spine; your breast, that it may be the receptacle of pure and virtuous principles; your vitals and bowels, that they may be healthy and strong and perform their proper functions; your arms and hands, that they may be strong and wield the sword of justice in defense of truth and virtue; your loins, that you may be fruitful and multiply and replenish the earth, that you might have joy and rejoicing in your posterity; your legs and feet, that you might run and not be weary, and walk and not faint.

*In Brigham Young's thirst for absolute control (*anoint you preparatory to your becoming a king*) and to give more authority and efficacy to his erroneous belief that men who held the priesthood (*...and a priest unto the Most High God*) in fact "served" as they "ruled" (*hereafter to rule and reign in the House of Israel*) over others, he changed the words of the original endowment. This robbed many (particularly women and the weak) of their voice in Church and community affairs, and especially in their own families (*...forever*). "To reign" was meant to be a figurative expression of each person having power and authority over his or her own existence no matter where one chose to exist "*in the kingdom of God*" (which includes ALL of His creations).

Additionally, Brigham spread the erroneous perception that the Celestial glory was the *only* glory that would allow eternal happiness. There are three (3) main *figurative* degrees or measures of happiness/glory/salvation, and true happiness is certainly not limited to the Celestial sphere only. *Celestial* beings find their particular happiness in servitude. Those who are *Terrestrial* and *Telestial* in nature will be just as happy and glorious in each of their own individual eternal states as any *Celestial* being. All will be resurrected to that existence which makes them happy, thus fulfilling the measure, or purpose, of human creation.

Joseph taught concerning the mystery of the kingdoms of God in this solar system, and that one day all of the planets surrounding our sun would be prepared to become the eternal habitations of those assigned to this earth and its solar system. In publishing the Articles of Faith, Joseph revealed a great mystery concerning the future destiny of this planet earth to those with "eyes that see": *The earth will be renewed and receive its paradisiacal glory* (History of the Church, Vol. 4, pg. 541). Inasmuch as this earth is to be "renewed," it is logical to understand that there must also be a renewal of the adjacent *other planets* in order to create habitations for those who would choose the *other* degrees of happiness (glory) in the kingdom of God within this solar system.

Brigham Young, a youthful and inexperienced apostle at the time, confused the meaning of Joseph's teachings, and years later presented his own foolish doctrine:

> *Who can tell us of the inhabitants of this little planet that shines of an evening called the moon? ...when you inquire about the inhabitants of that sphere you find that the most learned are as ignorant in regard to them as the ignorant of their fellows. So it is with regard to the inhabitants of the sun. Do you think it is inhabited? I rather think it is. Do you think there is any life there? No question of it; it was not made in vain.* (Journal of Discourses, Vol. 13, pg. 271.)

Brigham was not the only one present at the time Joseph discussed some of the mysteries of God. There were also others present who did not understand. Oliver B. Huntington was one of many who misconstrued what had been taught and confused and distorted the true meaning of Joseph's discussions of the planets and the purpose of their creation with his own vain and foolish imagination. Jospeh Smith never mentioned anything concerning beings living on the moon. But in 1892, a very old Huntington (who had followed Brigham Young) wrote in the **Young Woman's Journal** (a Church publication):

> *Astronomers and philosophers have, from time almost immemorial until very recently, asserted that the moon was uninhabited, that it had no atmosphere, etc. But recent discoveries, through the means of powerful telescopes, have given scientists a doubt or two upon the old theory. Nearly all the great discoveries of men in the last half-century have, in one way or another, either directly or indirectly, contributed to prove Joseph Smith to be a Prophet. As far back as 1837, I know that he said the moon was inhabited by men and women the same as this earth, and that they lived to a greater age than we do—that they live generally to near the age of 1000 years. He described the*

men as averaging near six feet in height, and dressing quite uniformly in something near the Quaker style. In my Patriarchal blessing, given by the father of Joseph the Prophet, in Kirtland, 1837, I was told that I should preach the gospel before I was 21 years of age; that I should preach the gospel to the inhabitants upon the islands of the sea, and—to the inhabitants of the moon, even the planet you can now behold with your eyes. (Ibid., Vol. 3, pgs. 263–4.)

At this early point in the presentation of the endowment, we are taught that we have the potential ("anointed") to become like our Heavenly Parents—Celestial beings, who serve in eternity with exalted bodies of a Celestial nature that can perpetuate life, command element, and perform all the works of an omnipotent Creator. However, no matter what we choose for ourselves, we are promised that our existence will have the potential of happiness and personal prosperity. We were not created by sadistic supernatural Beings who want to be worshiped and adored and who enjoy inflicting pain and sorrow on Their creations if these do not do what They command. This is how mortal political and religious leaders act. We were created to experience eternal happiness, which will be the measure of our creation while existing forever in what is figuratively termed "the kingdom of God."

We are *anointed* with olive oil because this oil is not in its natural state, but must be refined and prepared through the works and hands of men; thus, it represents the works of mortal beings, not the natural work of our Creators, as the "water" that was "sealed" upon us represents. This oil is processed by using what nature has provided (natural olives) and by mortal works (the extraction and processing of the oil). The anointing of oil represents that *only by our <u>own</u> works* can we inherit any kingdom of God. These works must fall within the standard set by the *true* gospel of Christ (Do Unto Others), and are therefore figuratively represented as righteous, or "pure" works, by the use of pure olive oil.

(A second officiator enters. Both officiators place their hands on the initiate's head, and the second officiator "confirms" [does not "seal" as was done in the washing] *the anointing as follows.)*

CONFIRMATION OF THE ANOINTING

Brother _____, having authority, we lay our hands upon your head [for and in behalf of _____ *(patron and then temple worker read name of deceased),* who is dead], and confirm upon you this anointing, wherewith you have been anointed in the temple of our God, preparatory to becoming a king and a priest unto the Most High God, hereafter to rule and reign in the House of Israel forever **(see above*)**, and seal upon you all the blessings hereunto appertaining, through your faithfulness; in the name of Jesus Christ. Amen.

SOMETHING THAT IS "CONFIRMED" IS A PROMISE WITH RESTRICTIONS AND STIPULATIONS, AND IS ONLY GUARANTEED IF WE COMPLY WITH THE CONDITIONS.

For this same reason, the Holy Ghost is not "sealed" upon us, but rather "confirmed" upon us, as practiced in the LDS ordinance of Confirmation after Baptism. Our ability to learn and to understand depends on how well we comply with the commandments that Christ taught. He taught simple commandments that, if followed, would free our minds of the cares and worries of the world in such a way that the past experiences and lessons we learned in our pre-mortal existence would come back to our remembrance much easier. The concept of freeing up the mind of worldly stress and cares is similar to some of the techniques applied by mental health professionals who use hypnosis to free up their patients' minds so they are able to remember things in their distant past or overcome personal weaknesses. This is what is meant by obeying the commandments of God so that *His Spirit will be with you*. Jesus said it in this way to his disciples:

> *But the Comforter, which is the Holy Ghost, whom the Father will send in my name, he shall teach you all things, and bring all things to your remembrance, whatsoever I have said unto you.* (John 14:26)

Very few of those assigned to this earth will ever become Celestial people. This is because of their particular and individual desires for happiness, which are not those of Celestial beings. Celestial life is an existence of servitude. This type of life encompasses a sincere desire to bring happiness to others by serving their needs. It is *not* a life of glory or living as royalty as human piety would erroneously lead us to assume.

Those who are Terrestrial and Telestial individuals, who in some fashion are such because they would serve "self" or be served, are not permitted to have the same powers and knowledge as those of a Celestial state. If they had the powers of a God, they would use these powers for their own benefit and purpose and not in a capacity of service to others. But because we were all created equally in the beginning by our Creators and given equal opportunity to choose for ourselves (it is *confirmed* upon us), we each have the potential to become like Them, if we choose. However, our individual natures guide our individual courses towards our greatest happiness in the kingdom which is best suited for each of us. All kingdoms are *equal* and of the *same* importance to the plan of salvation incorporated by our Creators.

The LDS Church teaches that in the beginning, Lucifer tried to force everyone to become Celestial by taking away their free agency to choose for themselves which kingdom of glory would best suit their desires of happiness, thus guaranteeing that *all* of God's children would inherit the Celestial kingdom. Ironically, the LDS Church encourages the very same thing that its "Lucifer" promoted. It focuses solely on salvation in the <u>Celestial</u> kingdom and leads its members to believe that *no other* kingdom is acceptable to God. If a person does not live up to the requirements set by the Church to attain the Celestial kingdom, he or she is often shunned or excommunicated. The LDS people are indoctrinated into believing that the Celestial kingdom is the greatest of God's kingdoms, and the only one worth achieving. Upon learning the *true* meaning of their own temple endowment, they will come to understand that they themselves *are* the very *Lucifer* whom they believe tried to force them into only one kingdom according to the Mormon myth.

The LDS Church embraces many dogmas and myths evolved over time, and espouses many doctrines and beliefs with which Joseph Smith had nothing to do when he organized the early church. In fact (and this is of vital importance to keep constantly in mind as the truth is revealed throughout this commentary), Joseph told very few what he really believed, and hid the truths he understood of the mysteries with which he had been *endowed*, within the figurative presentation of the temple endowment.

(The patron now steps through a third veiled partition into another section of the booth. ~~A temple worker takes the garments off the towel rod and holds them open wide at the neck, for the patron to step into [right leg, left leg]. It is then pulled up the sides of his body and he slips his right arm and left arm through the sleeves.~~)

THE GARMENT OF THE HOLY PRIESTHOOD AND THE NEW NAME
Receiving Our Mortal Body of Flesh and Bone

Brother _____, ~~having authority, I place this garment upon you~~ **under proper authority, the garment placed upon you is now authorized** [for and in behalf of _____ *(patron and then temple worker read name of the deceased)*, who is dead], ~~which you must wear~~ **and is to be worn** throughout your life. It represents the garment given to Adam when he was found naked in the Garden of Eden, and is called the Garment of the Holy Priesthood. Inasmuch as you do not defile it, but are true and faithful to your covenants, it will be a shield and a protection to you against the power of the destroyer until you have finished your work here on earth.

THE GARMENT IS SYMBOLIC OF THE MORTAL BODY OF
FLESH AND BONE THAT WE ALL RECEIVE UPON BIRTH.

A human being is composed of a spirit combined with a physical body made from the elements of the planet on which it is created. We currently reside on the planet we call "earth"—a state of existence in which we can experience "sin," or rather, unhappiness, which is the *opposite* of happiness. In order to experience anything and have these experiences recorded in our spirit (which is, quite literally, an advanced memory database capable of recording and storing unlimited experiences), we must have bodies of flesh and bone. When our spirit enters a body, it has the ability to record our actions and thoughts, which experiences are recorded as memories. When we "die," our eternal spirit enters back into a spirit realm and remains there until it again enters into yet another body with which it can act and be acted upon to gain more experience. For this reason, the command is given by God to wear the garment throughout our entire life in order to accomplish the purposes for which the body exists. The garment will later be figuratively presented as a "coat of skin" of animals found upon the earth, symbolizing that our mortal bodies were created from the same earthly elements as all other animals.

IF we keep our covenants and live our lives in righteousness, we will not be under the power of *Lucifer* (the *enemy* of the spirit), or better, under the power and enticements of the body (the flesh). (It will soon be revealed that "Lucifer" is a symbolic figure that represents the part of our free will that fights the eternal laws established by our Creators to maintain order throughout the Universe. But for purposes of this commentary, the appropriate words will be used as accepted by tradition and religious concepts.) THE GARMENT (BODY) IS *ONLY* a shield and protection against the power of our flesh (Lucifer), IF we abide by the COVENANTS that we made with our Creators, which agreements were designed from the beginning to insure happiness in the human family by loving one's neighbor as one's self.

It is the conviction of many who wear "the Garment of the Holy Priesthood" that if one remains unspotted from the world that it will serve as a "literal" shield against bodily harm. However, these garments have absolutely *nothing* to do with a physical protection *of any kind*, aside from the peace that comes as a result of a love and acceptance of others as one follows the counsels of Christ. When we are at peace with our environment and those around us, our physical bodies react accordingly and we place ourselves in a peaceful situation that promotes physical and mental health and strength.

Lucifer (our fleshly lusts and desires) is not going to kill our body, especially when we are righteously following the plan of the Father. In other words, our body will protect us from ourselves if we are keeping our covenants (or doing unto others what we would want done unto ourselves). One is not going to commit suicide or consider it, if one is living the gospel. Once we understand who the "destroyer" is (ourselves) and what the "garment" is (our body), it is clearer what this part of the endowment actually means.

(In the case of a living endowment, the officiator continues as follows:)

With this garment I give you a New Name, which you should always remember, and which you must keep sacred and never reveal, except at a certain place that will be shown you hereafter. The name is _____.

THE NEW <u>NAME</u> IS SYMBOLIC OF <u>OUR WORKS</u> AND <u>EXPERIENCES</u> AS NEWLY–CREATED SPIRITS REARED IN INCORRUPTIBLE BODIES ON THE PLANET OF OUR CREATORS. WE CANNOT REMEMBER THESE EXPERIENCES (WORKS) IN OUR CURRENT MORTAL FLESH; THUS WE CANNOT REVEAL THE NAME (OR REMEMBER OUR WORKS BEFORE MORTALITY) WHILE WE REMAIN IN A <u>MORTAL</u> BODY.

The *New Name* is simply the name of an ubiquitously-accepted, righteous person whom we have been taught to believe is no longer on this earth, but exists as a spirit who has returned to the God who gave him or her life. At the beginning of our creation, all of us lived in incorruptible bodies made from the elements of our Creators' planet. Our actions and experiences were always righteous because of the consistent examples of our Creators and the way we were blessed with unconditional equality. Even the figurative being we recognize as *Lucifer*, whose personage and plan most do not understand, can be accepted as a *righteous* spirit in the beginning because it was his expressed desire that all of us be saved in the eternities. ...More on this will be revealed later in this official explanation of the endowment.

(The New Name is repeated by the patron, who has now completed the Initiatory Ordinances, and is ready to clothe for the endowment. On any particular day, each of the men and each of the women participating in an endowment session receive the same New Name. The New Name is changed daily and may be almost any personal name found in the Book of Mormon or the Bible [such as Ammon, Abraham, or Job, or Ruth, Martha, or Lucy for example]. An alternate New Name ["Adam" for men and "Eve" for women] is used when the patron's given name [or that of the deceased] is similar to the New Name in use for the day. When the patron has not undergone Initiatory Ordinances, but is simply going to do an "endowment for the dead," he receives the New Name in a booth, dressed in his white shirt, tie, pants, socks, and slippers. Holding a name slip of a deceased person, he obtains the New Name by the following rite:)

VICARIOUS PRESENTATION OF THE NEW NAME

Brother _____, having authority, I give you a New Name, [for and in behalf of _____, *(patron and the worker read name of deceased)*, who is dead], which you should always remember, and which you must keep sacred, and never reveal except at a certain place that will be shown you hereafter. The name is _____.

(Whether receiving their own endowment or doing an endowment for the dead, the patron next enters a chapel. Here the patrons all wait quietly on a bench until they are called by a temple worker to enter an endowment room. Each patron carries their own packet [or "envelope"], which contains temple clothing to be put on during the development of the endowment. Once in the endowment room, men sit on one side, women on the other.)

FIRST LECTURER: Brethren and sisters, we welcome you to the temple and hope you will find joy in serving in the house of the Lord this day. Those of you who are here to receive your own endowment should have been washed, anointed, and clothed in the Garment of the Holy Priesthood. **For those who are representing deceased persons,** the ordinances of washing, anointing, and clothing in the Garment of the Holy Priesthood, together with the ordaining on behalf of the deceased brethren, were preformed previously ~~for those deceased persons whom you are~~

~~representing~~. Each of you should have received a New Name in connection with this company. If any of you have forgotten the New Name, or have not received these ordinances as explained, please stand. *(Pause.)*

A person must be created as a spirit (washed), receive free agency to become what one wants to become (anointed), be raised in a pre-earth or pre-mortal state, and have progressed accordingly, until one is ready to enter into mortality. Being thus confined to the flesh, we do our works here without remembering (revealing) the works we did or the experiences we had (the *New Name*) in the pre-mortal life. Each human being is assured that all of these things have been carried out—whether they are alive upon this earth, dead and existing in the spirit realm awaiting another body, or residing as a resurrected immortal being on one of our Creators' planets. It should be plain to see that the true endowment is symbolically following the set and eternal course of existence of all mankind. However, the actual ordinances performed for the *dead* are strictly for the benefit and instruction of the *living* who perform them.

Our *New Name* represents what we became by exercising the free agency granted to us as *newly* created human beings. Just as we make a *name* for ourselves by what we do in mortality, our *New Name* is symbolic of who we became in our pre-mortal state.

Please be alert, attentive, and ~~refrain from whispering~~ **reverent** during the presentation of the endowment. As you are asked to proceed to the Veil, please do so in an orderly manner, row by row, as directed. After passing through the Veil into the Celestial room, and in other areas in the temple, if you need to communicate, please whisper; thus helping us maintain the quiet reverence that should prevail in the house of the Lord. We will now proceed with the presentation of the endowment.

SECOND LECTURER: Brethren, you have been washed and pronounced clean, or that through your faithfulness, you may become clean from the blood and sins of this generation. You have been anointed to become hereafter kings and priests unto the Most High God, to rule and reign in the House of Israel forever. (See * above.)
Sisters, you have been washed and anointed to become **hereafter** queens and priestesses (with) your husbands. Brethren and sisters, if you are true and faithful, the day will come when you will be chosen, called up, and anointed kings and queens, priests and priestesses, whereas you are now anointed only to become such. The realization of these blessings depends upon your faithfulness.

This is explained sufficiently by the notations above. It's important to keep in mind that Brigham Young interpolated much about becoming "rulers" in the kingdoms of God when no such idea was originally intended.

All human creations are destined to become like their Creators. These Celestial Beings are simply Advanced Human Beings who have found out through experience that They enjoy giving life to others and perpetuating human happiness. This does not mean that all of us will become like the Gods that serve us, but we are guaranteed that we *will* be happy in the state each of us has chosen. "*The realization of these blessings depends upon*" the ability of each free-willed being to accept the eternal laws which have always existed—which laws are established to promote and perpetuate happiness and maintain proper order in the Universe.

You have had a garment placed upon you, which you were informed represents the garment given to Adam **and Eve** when ~~he was~~ **they were** found naked in the garden of Eden, and which is called the "Garment of the Holy Priesthood." This you were instructed to wear throughout your life. You were informed that it will be a shield and a protection to you **inasmuch as you do not defile it and** if you are true and faithful to your covenants.

You have had a New Name given unto you, which you were told never to divulge, nor forget. This New Name is a key word, which you will be required to give at a certain place in the temple today. ~~The endowment is to prepare you for exaltation in the Celestial kingdom.~~ (prepare you for entrance into the kingdom of God.) **Your endowment is to receive all those ordinances in the House of the Lord which are necessary for you, to enable you to walk back to the presence of the Father, passing the angels who stand as sentinels, being enabled to give them the key words, the signs, and the tokens pertaining to the Holy Priesthood, and gain your eternal exaltation.**

    Just as Brigham Young did, the current LDS leaders have also interjected these arrogant and self-imposed words (**given in bold green text**), thereby once again revealing their folly as proclaimed "prophets, seers, and revelators," and imposing their lack of understanding on those who believe in them. These so-called "inspired leaders" have changed the beautiful figurative presentation of the *true* plan of the Father. They want the members to believe that the **signs** and **tokens** are literally necessary as some sort of "password" in order to gain entrance into the Celestial kingdom. Nothing could be further from the truth. For the faithful LDS member, the worth of knowing these passwords justifies any sacrifice or any price they have to pay to attend the temple (which includes at least ten percent of one's income). Not only is the literal knowledge of the actual signs and tokens NOT necessary to inherit a *mansion* of one's choosing in the *house* of the Father, but the true significance of the passwords and what they represent is now available to everyone by way of the commentary contained in this book, for free, as it has always been intended.

    Additionally, if "passwords" were truly necessary for entrance into the Celestial kingdom, then the **penalties**, which the current LDS leaders have *taken out* of the presentation of the endowment, would likewise be just as important to know and understand to gain passageway by the "sentinels." It should make a lot more sense to accept the fact that we have loving Creators who equally love Their *Terrestrial* and *Telestial* children just as much as They do those who are *Celestial*. They do not need any bodyguards protecting Them and keeping out any of Their children who only desire to come forth and give Them a hug, like any appreciative child would do to his or her parents. As the endowment proceeds and its *true* meaning is revealed, one will soon come to realize the importance of all of the **signs**, **tokens**, and **penalties** in gaining a complete understanding of what is actually going on in our Universe. Their symbolical meanings are consistent with the Eternal Plan of Salvation given freely and equally to us all.

If you proceed and receive your full endowment, you will be required to take upon yourselves sacred obligations, the violation of which will bring upon you the judgment of God; for God will not be mocked. If any of you desire to withdraw rather than accept these obligations of your own free will and choice, you may now make it known by raising your hand. *(Pause.)*

This part of the endowment demonstrates the importance of allowing all of us the right to exercise our free agency in deciding whether or not to follow the plan of our Creators. Those who choose not to follow this plan (figuratively presented as Lucifer and his angels) advocate otherwise, by proposing a different plan than that which has always existed. These claim that there is a better way to bring about happiness without meeting the requirements placed upon us through the established eternal plan, or better, things as they always have been—worlds without end. These are those who would make it known by raising their hand and being excused from proceeding with the presentation of the full endowment. As we proceed on our own, figuratively represented by following a course that is already known and proven by Celestial Beings *not* to produce happiness, we experience the "*judgment* of God," which is simply being left on our own without our Creators' influence to find this out for ourselves. Truly, our Creators' "judgment" is much better than our own.

The true meaning of "the Judgment of God" comes from the other definition of "judge" given in the English language: *The capacity to assess situations or circumstances and draw sound conclusions; good sense.* Expounding upon the correct meaning would include discernment or the ability to form sound opinions and make sensible decisions. It is an assessment made after observation and a consideration of the facts. This is what righteous judgment means. This is what the Judgment of God means as used by *true messengers*. It is a judgment made correctly by one who has assessed the situation or circumstance, has experienced the same situation or circumstance, and can draw a sound conclusion based on one's own experience. This should help us understand *why* our Christ had to come down and experience mortality in the flesh and go through the worst of what we as mortals have to go through. Thus, he is considered the *Supreme Judge*.

According to Joseph's figurative presentation of the eternal plan and mysteries of God incorporated in the temple endowment, the first person (besides our Creators—Elohim) to make a righteous judgment was Eve. Not Adam, but Eve. As "Adam" represents the part of us (left brain, if you will) that thinks linear, sequential, logical, verbal, and reality based, "Eve" represents the part (right brain) that thinks, holistic, random, intuitive, and non-verbal. The figurative "Lucifer" is the instigator that creates dissonance between the two. Because of our imperfect mortal brains, we struggle to combine the two sides of our brain activity in our thoughts. With a perfected brain however, we will be able to form thoughts that are influenced by both sides equally, thus eliminating the conflict (casting Satan out) and allowing us to experience a perfect conclusion that reflects the influence of our complete soul. These *righteous* conclusions are the judgments that will influence our eternal actions.

Everything our Creators do is influenced by a righteous judgment rendered by a perfect brain. Their capacity to assess situations and circumstances and draw sound conclusions comes from the ability of Their perfect Celestial brains to be utilized for this purpose. Keep in mind that there are physical differences between *Celestial*, *Terrestrial*, and *Telestial* brains. No brain is any better than another, but each is utilized for the purpose of allowing the individual to use their brain for the specific reason (serving others, serving oneself, or being served) associated with their individual desire of happiness.

It was the *Judgment of God* that created our bodies in such a way that would allow a free-willed spirit to enter therein and begin a new human life. It was this *judgment* that gave us a *New Name*. It was the *Judgment of God* that allowed us to be raised in the beginning in such a way as to foundationalize the very essence of who we would become as human beings versus other life forms without free agency. It was this *judgment* that created our conscience. It was the *Judgment of God* that "cursed us" or allowed us the opportunity to experience mortality (the opposite of all that is good) so that we would appreciate what we are given as eternal human beings. This *righteous judgment* planted the *Tree of Knowledge of Good and Evil* and gave us the choice to partake of it or not. It was the *Judgment of God* to create differing degrees of happiness (planets in a solar system) that would accommodate the free-willed desires of Their children. This *judgment* created the kingdom of God. It is the *Judgment of God* that decides when to intervene in the lives of mortal humans and when not to intervene. It is the *Judgment of God* that does all things for our good, whether we think it is a good thing at the time or not. This *judgment* brings about the immortality and eternal life of humankind.

The *Judgment of God* cannot be comprehended or compared to the judgments we make as mortal beings. We do not have the brain capacity to make these righteous judgments. Knowing we do not have the type of brain that will allow us to make the proper judgments, the logical thing for our Creators to command us to do is, "JUDGE NOT THAT YE BE NOT JUDGED."

Brethren and sisters, as you sit here, you will hear the voices of three persons who represent Elohim, Jehovah, and Michael. Elohim will command Jehovah and Michael to go down and organize a world. The work of the six creative periods will be represented. They will **also** organize man in their own likeness and image, male and female. This, however, is simply figurative so far as the man and the woman are concerned.

Deleting this last sentence was catastrophic to the symbolism needed to understand the mysteries of God. This is especially true for the state of creation being presented at this point in the endowment (our spiritual creation). We have not always existed as male or female. Here is one of the greatest of all the mysteries of God:

our spirits are *genderless*, and have been that way since their creation. Through our free agency and personal choice we enter mortality, where many of us experience different genders as we try to find what best suits our individual desires of happiness. It would neither be fair nor equal, and would negate our free agency, if our Creators created us as male and female, thereby choosing *for* us and forcing us to accept a certain gender whether we liked it or not.

Even more pertinent to us as mortals, and at the very root of *Lucifer's* rebellion, is the final disposition of all who will be resurrected. In knowing of the *Celestial* fruits of gender and sex in mortality, *Lucifer* desired that all should be permitted to retain a gender after the resurrection. In our Creators' Plan however, only those who are worthy of a *Celestial* nature and body will be able to produce offspring forever, which (contrary to some doctrines) is the ONLY purpose for which gender exists. A dirty trick would be played on us if our spirits were given gender upon creation for a purpose that most of us, in the end, would never be able to fulfill. Our Creators do not complete Their work this way. We are guaranteed our choices so that we can discover for ourselves what brings us the most happiness.

Joseph Smith was inspired to include the explanation that the Gods (the word "Elohim" is the plural form of the word "God" and will be further explained below) organized man in "Their own image," male and female. "Their…image" (being plural) obviously also has reference to our Eternal Mothers; "Their" including the female gender as well as the male. He then goes on to explain that, "*so far as the man and woman* (or better said, male and female) *are concerned,*" the description given in the scriptures and in this endowment is "*simply figurative.*" The "washing and anointing" is *figurative* of our spiritual creation and the "placing of the garment" is *figurative* of our transition into a body, first upon the planet where our Creators reside and created us, and second upon this earth; each being a progressive stage in our eternal progression.

2
THE CREATION OF THE EARTH

THE CREATION

FIRST DAY
The Organization of Matter

ELOHIM: Jehovah, Michael, see—yonder is matter unorganized. Go ye down and organize it into (worlds) like unto the **other** worlds that we have heretofore formed. Call your labors the First Day, and bring me word.

The corrupted endowment says "*into a world*" instead of the proper "*worlds*" as has been interpolated correctly above. When Brigham Young tinkered with the endowment, he was not aware that the other planets that exist in this solar system would one day become the habitable kingdoms that are presented as the Celestial, Terrestrial, and Telestial glories. Though this was taught privately to a few select friends, Joseph's words were later twisted and misunderstood, as demonstrated in Brigham Young's teachings to the LDS people years later. (Refer to quotations above concerning "*inhabitants of the moon*.")

Until The Sealed Portion, The Final Testament of Jesus Christ (the sealed portion of the gold plates of Mormon) was first translated and published in 2004, the Mormon people had no idea where the other "degrees of glory" would be established in the eternities. The LDS Church teaches that this earth will one day become one of the degrees in the Celestial Kingdom, based on the 10th Article of Faith as mentioned earlier.

If the endowment had not been corrupted, it would have given every indication that this solar system, with Divine purpose, included many more "worlds" upon which life will someday be placed rather than just upon the earth on which we presently exist. The same knowledge and power that created this solar system will one day transform its other planets into habitable environments in which humans can exist. Furthermore, the text of the endowment below presents the creation as matter being "formed" and not "created" into planets or worlds; thus relating the truth that something cannot be made from nothing. This negates the concept of a "Big Bang," or some other means of bringing something into existence in void and matterless space. Thus, the eternal truth that all matter has *always* existed is figuratively presented in the endowment. This lays the foundation for understanding that life has *always* existed, and that there have *always* been humans, Gods, flora and fauna, and everything else in the Universe in some form—worlds without end.

This profound revelation (that all matter has always existed) answers the age-old philosophical conundrum, "Which came first, the chicken or the egg?" The *real truth* has answered the question and leaves no other questions to be asked. There have *always* been chickens laying eggs and there have *always* been eggs hatching into chickens.

This, however, does not negate the fact that the Universe, in relation to new planets, solar systems, and galaxies, is continually expanding due to the workings of Celestial Creators, as the universe is an infinite space. Life is brought into existence from matter that is already present, which is then "formed" by processes that have *always* been used by Creators. These "processes" can best be described as the super-advanced "technology of the Gods."

JEHOVAH: It shall be done, Elohim. Come, Michael; let us go down.
MICHAEL: We will go down, Jehovah.

Here is presented for the first time with that which the Christian world has accepted as the Holy Trinity in its entirety—the Father, the Son, and yes, the Holy Ghost, *Michael*, who later in the endowment will become the man Adam and the woman Eve. This is the first indication that "all of us" are connected to this figurative Godhead. <u>Our</u> representation in this Holy Trinity is expressed as the "Holy Ghost." (This extraordinary insight and understanding will be expounded upon later.)

These things are explained very well by Moroni in <u>The Sealed Portion</u>, but Joseph Smith taught the doctrine unofficially. In many private conversations he had with others, Joseph expounded on the Eternal Plan of our Creators and some of the mysteries that he was not allowed to discuss in public. From Joseph's articulations on this simple doctrine, Brigham Young and others began to establish their own understanding and doctrines. From this simple doctrine came the much talked-about but generally confused "Adam/God Doctrine."

Nothing that Brigham Young taught or supposed can be taken as truth. He did not have the "keys" or the ability to understand the mysteries of God properly. He led a lifestyle that was disobedient and not in accordance with the gospel of Jesus Christ; thus, he was unable to receive true revelation as explained previously. From his mouth many deceptions and misunderstandings came forth that have filled the world of Mormonism with the plague of ignorance and false doctrine. Fortunately, hidden in the true meaning of the temple endowment is found a healing panacea for all of Young's false teachings.

"Elohim" is the name given figuratively to represent our Eternal Parents. "Elohim," translated to its most original form, literally means "Gods," not one, but a plural number. It is the plural version of the Hebrew word "Eloah," which means "one God."

"Jehovah" follows as a derivation of the word "Adonai," which means "My Lord." For this reason, Jehovah is often described as the Father, or He who created all things, even our spirits. Abinadi states:

I would that ye should understand that God Himself shall come down among the children of men, and shall redeem his people. And because he dwelleth in the flesh he shall be called the Son of God, and having subjected the flesh to the will of the Father, being the Father and the Son—The Father, because he was conceived by the power of God; and the Son, because of the flesh; thus becoming the Father and Son. (Mosiah 15:1–3)

Jehovah is the one that was chosen by our Creators and *sustained* by all of us as pre-mortal beings to direct the work of *Elohim* in this part of the Universe—the solar system that pertains to us. There is a significant difference between Jehovah and the rest of us. Perhaps it is easiest to understand Jehovah by describing his spirit as an exact "clone" of the Father. A clone is an exact copy. Therefore, Christ's spirit is an exact copy of his Father's spirit. In contrast, our spirits are as individual and different from our Creators' as they are from each other (in that we were created without the process of cloning). "The Father" is the title given to the Celestial Being who is responsible for and initiates the preperation and perpetuation of life in parts of the Universe where there exists no human life. Christ's mortal DNA patterns as the man Jesus were not a clone of his Father but were comprised of half of those he received from the Father and half from his earthly mother. His spirit entity, however, is an *exact* clone of the Father's. Thus said Christ:

And he said unto them, Ye are from beneath; I am from above: ye are of this world; I am not of this world. I said therefore unto you, that ye shall die in your sins: for if ye believe not that I am he, ye shall die in your sins. Then said they unto him, Who art thou? And Jesus saith unto them, Even the same that I said unto you from the beginning. I have many things to say and to judge of you: but he that sent me is true; and I speak to the world those things which I have heard of him. They understood not that he spake to them of the Father. Then said Jesus unto them, When ye have lifted up the Son of man, then shall ye know that I am he, and that I do nothing of myself; but as my Father hath taught me, I speak these things. And he that sent me is with me: the Father hath not left me alone; for I do always those things that please him. ...Jesus saith unto him, I am the way, the truth, and the life: no man cometh unto the Father, but by me. If ye had known me, ye should have known my Father also: and from henceforth ye know him, and have seen him. Philip saith unto him, Lord, shew us the Father, and it sufficeth us. Jesus saith unto him, Have I been so long time with you, and yet hast thou not known me, Philip? he that hath seen me hath seen the Father; and how sayest thou then, Shew us the Father? Believest thou not that I am in the Father, and the Father in me? the words that I speak unto you I speak not of myself: but the Father that dwelleth in me, he doeth the works. Believe me that I am in the Father, and the Father in me: or else believe me for the very works' sake. (John 8:23–9; 14:6–11)

No true prophet of God has ever, nor ever will, make the same claims as Jesus did in mortality. None of them is in any way a spirit clone of the Father. But like the Father, each is uniquely individual, having no pre-programmed instructions that would instinctually guide him in his actions. Christ is the *only* one who knows what the Father knows and acts as the Father would act in all situations. Why? Because his spirit (the very essence of what makes him think and act) is the Father's clone exactly. Our Creators have many other children and worlds that pertain to other solar systems. Of all the spirit entities created for this solar system, only one (a Christ) was prepared to oversee our Creators' work in this solar system. This process of life is the same that has been and is being done in all other parts of the vast Universe. Jehovah (Christ) alone acts in the *name* of the Father, and does exactly what the Father would do if He were present.

The system of government that mandates and oversees our existence is a righteous dictatorship of sorts, with only ONE person in charge. This type of government creates the best solution for us due to our desire to use our free agency according to each of our individual desires of happiness. A perfect, righteous dictatorship has no bureaucracy, which creates many (if not all) of the problems of democratic governments. Throughout human mortal history, these types of governments have failed to bring about the peace and equality that lead to happiness.

Jehovah is a perfect and righteous dictator, and is referred to by the prophets as the "King of kings, Lord of lords, the mighty God, the everlasting Father, and the Prince of Peace." He has been given the power of the Father, and serves the Father in righteousness—doing for us exactly as the Father would do in all situations. He has the authority to command the angels as well as the elements that comprise everything that is, which is something only a Celestial body can control. Thus, Abinadi's words given above start to make sense as we begin to understand the *real truth*.

Our Eternal Mothers were intimately and overwhelmingly involved in our existence as newly created human beings in our *first estate* (our pre-mortal life upon Their Celestial planet.) Except for tending to the creation of the first human bodies placed on planet earth at the beginning of human existence here, our Eternal Mothers have little to do with our *second estate* (mortality) and stay on Their eternal world creating other children for other solar systems in other parts of the Universe. These Wonderful Women find their joy and happiness in having children and raising them to adulthood, at which time these mature spirits are turned over to the Father to go through the trials, temptations, and vicissitudes of mortality. Eternal Mothers have the same desires and happiness as mortal women, who also love to raise their children—until they reach that stage as independent young adults when they seem to become more of a burden than a blessing of happiness as they pursue their own individuality and uniqueness. In consequence of being away from their Mothers, the children begin to realize from their own experience just how important their Mothers are to them. This same natural bonding takes place between mortal loving mothers and their offspring. But more importantly, being "away from home" gives a child the experience to understand that the rules enforced at home were necessary, and having their eyes opened, now make perfect sense.

Eternal Mothers receive the glory (happiness) of their children in the *first estate* (the world on which all spirits were created); the Father receives all the glory (happiness) for His work in the *second estate* (mortality). This is why few prophets make reference to Eternal Mothers during our mortal lives. The proper direction and dedication is given to the Father, who oversees the second estate. However, both of these Creators receive the glory of Their children in our *third estate* (our eternal kingdoms of glory/happiness).

Just as the name "Elohim" represents male and female Gods, the name "Michael" represents all of us, male and female, in mortality. (This will begin to make more sense as the endowment progresses and we see the figurative expression given in which Eve was taken from Adam—thus signifying that the female part of "Michael" is introduced as the woman, Eve.)

"Michael" represents the *holy* part of all of us. This part of us is eternally connected to our Creators (Elohim) and our anointed God (Jehovah). Being connected to Them means we work *with Them* in achieving salvation and Eternal Life for ourselves. We literally become part of the *Holy Trinity*, our part being referred to as the "Holy Ghost." In essence, the "Holy Ghost" is simply our human conscience which separates us, or should separate us, from all other animal species. It is the *foundation of experience* we have embedded in our spiritual makeup (which in mortality we cannot fully remember), established in us from our interaction with our Eternal Parents on Their planet before we were placed upon this earth where we could gain experiences *opposed* to those we had with Them.

It is important that each of us agrees to live and support ALL parts of our Creators' plan, because we cannot be forced to do *anything* against our will. This law of free agency is as eternal as any law in nature. For this reason, Michael *always repeats everything* that Jehovah is told to do by the Gods. We (Michael/Adam and Eve) *sustain* everything that is done on our behalf, and are never forced to do anything against our free will and choice. In the presentation of the endowment, the importance of Michael repeating everything that Jehovah tells him is of the utmost relevance to the nature of our creation as free-willed individuals, who act on our own accord in all situations. We are not puppets; we are not compelled to obey our Creator. Rather, the ability to exercise free will exists within each of us independently of all other beings. We are fully conscious of our existence and free agency, which makes us unique from all other life forms in the Universe.

JEHOVAH: Michael, see—here is matter unorganized. We will organize it into (worlds) like unto ~~the~~ other worlds that have heretofore (been) formed. We will call our labors the First Day, and return and report.

MICHAEL: (We will organize it into worlds like unto the worlds that have heretofore been formed and) We will return and report our labors of the First Day, Jehovah.

JEHOVAH: Elohim, we have ~~been down~~ done as thou hast commanded, and ~~have organized a world~~ (worlds) ~~like unto the worlds that have heretofore~~ (been) ~~formed, and we~~ have called our labors the First Day.

The words that have been deleted by the modern LDS Church are imperative to our understanding that Jehovah does *exactly* what the Father instructs him to do, and reports only to Him. Those who want to make the endowment less repetitive and shorter, make similar deletions many times throughout the endowment. However, *repetition* is the proper way that one learns imperative points of doctrine. Those who change these things do so because they have no understanding of the true intent of the endowment.

Herein, it is also important to note the changes in how Jehovah and Michael respond to Elohim's command. The correct presentation clarifies that neither Jehovah nor Michael had <u>anything</u> to do with the "worlds that we have heretofore formed" as Elohim had first commanded. Rather, the correct wording insinuates that the "Gods" (the Celestial Father and Mothers/Creators) had made and populated many worlds before this one, which "one" pertains only to the world created by Jehovah and Michael. Thus, the corrupted endowment erroneously leads one to believe that Jehovah and Michael played a role in the formation of other worlds by virtue of their words being changed to read, "…*organize it into a world like unto the other worlds that **we** have heretofore formed.*"

(NOTE: One of the many errors in the presentation of the endowment is the chronological order of the "days of creation." First, the appropriate "matter" was organized in an area of the Universe where no "organized matter" had previously existed. This "matter" was organized to create a sun, which entailed the appropriate elements being brought together to perform the specific function of causing a "nuclear-type" perpetual reaction. This is the figurative *First Day* of creation. Thereafter, this matter was further organized from the sun to create its associated planets and their moons; thus a solar system was formed and subsequently placed so the stars would appear in the heavens to those who would inhabit the newly-created planets. One of these planets was purposefully prepared and properly placed in relation to the sun so that it could eventually support life. This is the figurative *Second Day* of creation. Thus, the sun's creation effectuated the creation and placement of the rest of the planets that belong to this solar system. Understanding this establishes the fact that the earth could not have been created before the sun. The uninspired editors of the endowment did not understand these concepts of eternal truth and reality, and therefore, followed the flawed creation as it is given in the book of Genesis in the Bible. [Joseph Smith had it right in the original endowment and this proper sequence of events is given below.] It is also imperative to understand that the "days" of creation are just as figurative as everything else presented in the endowment. There are no "days" in eternity. Time, space, and the measurement thereof are purely inventions of mortal minds that cannot comprehend (or better, cannot remember) what eternity is like; and therefore, have no eternal perspective.)

ELOHIM: It is well.

SECOND DAY

The Creation of the Sun and Solar System

ELOHIM: Jehovah, Michael, return again to the earth (**matter**) that you have organized (**and**) divide the light from the darkness. Call the light "day," and the darkness "night." Cause the lights in the firmament to appear—the greater light to rule the day, and the lesser light to rule the night. Cause the stars also to appear and give light to the earth (**worlds**), the same as with (**the**) **other** worlds heretofore created. Call your labors the (**Second**) Day, and bring me word.
JEHOVAH: It shall be done, Elohim. Come, Michael; let us return again to the earth (**matter**) that we have organized.
MICHAEL: We will return ~~again~~, Jehovah.

Jehovah and Michael are reporting to the Father on His planet, far, far away from our solar system in another galaxy. Each time they perform the "will" of the Father, they return to the planet of the Father and report their "labors." This is figurative, because only Celestial beings can command element and create suns, planets, and solar systems. The idea of Jehovah and Michael being involved in the work of creation without yet arriving to the position of a Celestial Creator is a figurative representation of our own involvement in the progress of our own eternal experience. As our solar system was created, we watched and participated in much the same manner that a child would watch his or her father put together a bicycle so that it could be ridden for the first time. The placement of the decals, horn, basket, and other accessories would be up to the child, but performed by the father who has the tools and knowledge to do it right. Can you imagine the child's anticipation, thoughts, and expressions of joy as the bicycle was being put together?

LDS dogma erroneously states that the earth was created "spiritually" before it was created "temporally," and that the earth "fell" when it entered its state of "probation," where it was to be "baptized" with water first (alluding to the flood of Noah) and then by fire. This belief is as false as any other of the misconceptions invented in the minds of the early leaders of the Church (who misunderstood the prophet Joseph). These misguided leaders established their own "doctrines and precepts of men." Because these charismatic leaders presented themselves as prophets, seers, and revelators after Joseph's death, the faithful were led to accept many things that

Joseph never taught. This planet is made of element, not of spirit. Spirit is also made of element, but different types of element than those that make up the earth and all the temporal things that belong to it. (These spirit elements have not yet been discovered and understood by mortals, nor will they ever, but to those who choose an eternity of Celestial servitude as their personal desire of happiness.)

The earth was created and developed naturally to the state in which we find it presently. This is after going through millions of years of preparation, refinement, and "evolution" to reach its present state. It did not "fall," nor is it in need of baptism by water or by fire. "Baptism by fire" symbolically represents the cleansing of a corrupt and polluted heart and mind of a mortal being through the presentation of the truth. Presenting and understanding truth is figuratively given as the ministrations of the *Holy Ghost*, or remembering those things which we were once taught by our Eternal Parents. How can this "Holy Ghost" purify rock, dirt, and the rest of the elements that make up our earth? From what do these need to be purified, or further, in what way did the elements that make up the earth sin?

JEHOVAH: Michael, we will divide the light from the darkness, and ~~we will~~ call the light "day," and the darkness "night." We will cause the lights in the firmament to appear—the greater light to rule the day, and the lesser light to rule the night. We will cause the stars also to appear and give light to the world (worlds); the same as with other worlds heretofore created. We will call our labors the (Second) Day, and return and report.

MICHAEL: (We will divide the light from the darkness, and we will call the light "day," and the darkness "night." We will cause the lights in the firmament to appear—the greater light to rule the day, and the lesser light to rule the night. We will cause the stars also to appear and give light to the worlds; the same as with other worlds heretofore created and) We will return and report our labors of the (Second) Day, Jehovah.

JEHOVAH: Elohim, we have ~~been down~~ **done** as thou hast commanded, and have ~~divided the light from the darkness, and have called the light "day" and the darkness "night." We have caused the lights in the firmament to appear: the greater light to rule the day, and the lesser light to rule the night. We have caused the stars also to appear and give light to the earth~~ (worlds) ~~the same as with worlds heretofore created. We have~~ called our labors the (Second) Day.

ELOHIM: It is well.

THIRD DAY
The Creation of the Earth

ELOHIM: Jehovah, Michael, go down again. Gather the waters together and cause the dry land to appear. The great waters call ye "seas," and the dry land call ye "earth." Form mountains and hills, great rivers and small streams to beautify and give variety to the face of the earth. ~~When you have done this,~~ call your labors the (Third) Day, and bring me word.

JEHOVAH: It shall be done, Elohim. Come, Michael; let us go down.

MICHAEL: We will go down, Jehovah.

JEHOVAH: Michael, we will gather the waters together and cause the dry land to appear. The great waters we will call "seas," and the dry land we will call "earth." We will form mountains and hills, great rivers and small streams to beautify and give variety to the face of the earth. We will call our labors the (Third) Day, and return and report.

MICHAEL: (We will gather the waters together and cause the dry land to appear. The great waters we will call "seas," and the dry land we will call "earth." We will form mountains and hills, great rivers and small streams to beautify and give variety to the face of the earth and) We will return and report our labors of the (Third) Day, Jehovah.

JEHOVAH: Elohim, we have ~~been down~~ done as thou hast commanded, and ~~have gathered the waters together, and have caused the dry land to appear. The great waters we have called "seas," and the dry land we have called "earth." We have formed mountains and hills, great rivers and small streams to beautify and give variety to the face of the earth; and we~~ have called our labors the (Third) Day.

ELOHIM: It is well.

FOURTH DAY

The Creation of the Plant Kingdom

ELOHIM: Jehovah, Michael, return ~~again.~~ and Place seeds of all kinds in the earth that they may spring forth as grass, flowers, shrubbery, trees, and all manner of vegetation, each bearing seed in itself after its own kind, ~~as on~~ (this world and) ~~the worlds we have heretofore created.~~ Call your labors the Fourth Day, and bring me word.

All the seeds that were planted upon this earth were either brought from the Father's planet or created after the likeness of those plants that were created and planted on other worlds. The plants needed light to grow according to the established laws of nature, thus the sun was created first. In order for oxygen to exist, which is a prerequisite for the type of mortal bodies that our Creators intended to put Their spirit children into, there needed to be plants, and lots of them!

JEHOVAH: It shall be done, Elohim. Come, Michael; let us go down.

MICHAEL: We will go down, Jehovah.

JEHOVAH: Michael, we will place seeds of all kinds in the earth that they may spring forth as grass, flowers, shrubbery, trees, and all manner of vegetation ~~each bearing seed in itself after its own kind, as on the~~ (world from whence we came and on those) ~~worlds~~ (that) ~~have heretofore~~ (been) ~~created~~. We will call our labors the Fourth Day, and return and report.

MICHAEL: (We will place seeds of all kinds in the earth that they may spring forth as grass, flowers, shrubbery, trees, and all manner of vegetation, each bearing seed in itself after its own kind, as on the world from whence we came and on those worlds that have heretofore been created.) We will return and report our labors of the Fourth Day, Jehovah.

JEHOVAH: Elohim, we have ~~been down~~ **done** as thou hast commanded, and ~~have placed seeds of all kinds in the earth that they may spring forth as grass, flowers, shrubbery, trees, and all manner of vegetation, each bearing seed in itself after its own kind, as on~~ (this world and on those) ~~worlds~~ (that) ~~have heretofore~~ (been) ~~created; and we~~ have called our labors the Fourth Day.

ELOHIM: It is well.

FIFTH DAY
The Creation of the Animal Kingdom

Logically, to keep the plants in balance so that they did not overrun the earth and block out the sunlight for smaller vegetation (flowers and bushes), the next stage of creation was the placement of very large plant-eating animals (dinosaurs), some of which had very long necks that could reach the tops of the trees. In this eternally-balanced way, the smaller plants were guaranteed the sunlight that they needed to grow. Smaller animals were also created to keep the smaller plants in check, thereby keeping the symbiotic and perfect balance of natural law.

ELOHIM: Jehovah, Michael, now that the earth is formed, divided and beautified, and vegetation is growing thereon, return and place ~~beasts upon the land: the elephant, the lion, the tiger, the bear, the horse, and all other kinds of animals—fowls in the air in all their varieties, fishes of all kinds in the waters, and insects and~~ all manner of ~~animal~~ life upon the earth. Command the beasts, the fowls, the fishes, the insects, all creeping things, and other forms of animal life to multiply in their respective elements, each after its kind, and every kind of vegetation to multiply it its sphere; that every form of life may fill the measure of its creation and have joy therein. Call your labors the Fifth Day, and bring me word.

JEHOVAH: It shall be done, Elohim. Come, Michael; let us go down.

MICHAEL: We will go down, Jehovah.

JEHOVAH: Michael, now that the earth is formed, divided and beautified, and vegetation is growing thereon, we will place beasts upon the land: the elephant, the lion, the tiger, the bear, the horse, and all other kinds of animals—fowls in the air in all their varieties, fishes of all kinds in the waters, and insects and all manner of animal life upon the earth. We will command the beasts, the fowls, the fishes, the insects, all creeping things, and other forms of animal life to multiply in their respective elements, each after its kind, and every kind of vegetation to multiply in its sphere; that every form of life may fill the measure of its creation and have joy therein. We will call our labors the Fifth Day, and return and report.

"Evolution" is the only way that those who do not believe in the existence of more intelligent life, other than what is found on this planet, can justify who they are in comparison to the rest of the animal kingdom. They realize they are much more intelligent than other animals, but are pressed to believe that they became that way through an evolutionary process.

These free-willed minds have progressed enough now to have already presented the answer to their own question of evolution. These "wise ones" (the literal meaning of Homo sapiens) have invented the process of hybrid breeding, selective breeding, crossbreeding, and genetic engineering in both the plant and animal kingdoms. With their current knowledge, they can now command nature to a certain degree and create species that serve specific needs in order to satisfy their wants.

Indeed, the Neanderthal-like brains of modern humans (in comparison to human beings who have advanced millions of years beyond us) can not only do these things, but can cause them to occur relatively overnight. So, why is it hard to believe that when there came a need in the history of this earth for a bird to have a stronger beak in order to break a certain type of nut, which would aid in the promulgation of a specific tree, that Highly Advanced Humans (the Gods) could not use the same type (yet much more advanced form) of bio-science to create the bird with the hard beak?

The fact is, our Neanderthal-like modern scientists of today can develop a strain of plants that is resistant to all manner of disease and pests. If it so happened that there was no written history of the relatively brief process, or any other explanations given in the annals of human education, future generations on earth could look at these plants and say, "Oh, those plants evolved that way over millions of years!" Indeed, if there was no written history, they *could* justifiably believe this way. Did any plant or animal life evolve to its present state of existence? No, they did not—any more than the modern hybrids of plants and animals came into existence through the concept of millions of years of evolution. Advanced Human Beings who knew what They were doing created them as the need arose.

Ironically, as explained above, modern science has proven the Theory of Evolution to be false, and has unknowingly supported the idea that Advanced Human Beings (Gods/angels) can create any type of plant, insect, animal, or bacteria that They desire in order to aid in the stability of nature upon this earth. If it only takes a few years for modern humans to create an entirely different and more "evolved" species of flora or fauna, then wouldn't it be reasonable to expect that much more Advanced Human Beings could do the same in a matter of seconds?

MICHAEL: It is well, Jehovah. Now that the earth is formed, ~~divided, and beautified,~~ with vegetation growing thereon, (we will place beasts upon the land: the elephant, the lion, the tiger, the bear, the horse, and all other kinds of animals—fowls in the air in all their varieties, fishes of all kinds in the waters, and insects and all manner of animal life upon the earth. We will command the beasts, the fowls, the fishes, the insects, all creeping things, and other forms of animal life to multiply in their respective elements, each after its kind, and every kind of vegetation to multiply in its sphere; that every form of life may fill the measure of its creation and have joy therein.) and provided with ~~animal~~ **all manner of** life, it is glorious and beautiful.

JEHOVAH: It is, Michael.

MICHAEL: Let us return and report our labors of the Fifth Day, Jehovah.

JEHOVAH: Elohim, we have ~~been down~~ **done** as thou hast commanded. ~~We have placed beasts upon the land: the elephant, the lion, the tiger, the bear, the horse, and all other kinds of animals—fowls in the air in all their varieties, fishes of all kinds in the waters, and insects and all manner of animal life upon the earth. We have commanded the beasts, the fowls, the fishes, the insects, all creeping things, and other forms of animal life to multiply in their respective elements, each after its kind, and every kind of vegetation to multiply in its sphere, that every form of life may fill the measure of its creation and have joy therein.~~ ~~We~~ **and** have called our labors the Fifth Day.

ELOHIM: It is well.

SIXTH DAY
The Creation of the Human Kingdom

ELOHIM: Jehovah, Michael, is man found upon the earth?

JEHOVAH: Man is not found on the earth, Elohim.

ELOHIM: Jehovah, Michael, then let us go down and form man in our own likeness and in our own image, male and female, and put into ~~him his spirit,~~ **them their spirits,** and let us give ~~him~~ **them** dominion ~~over the beasts, the fishes, and the birds, and make him lord over the earth, and~~ over all things on the face of the earth. We will plant for ~~him~~ **them** a garden, eastward in Eden, and place ~~him~~ **them** in it to tend and cultivate it, that ~~he~~ **they** may be happy and have joy therein. We will command ~~him~~ **them** to multiply and replenish the earth, that ~~he~~ **they** may have joy ~~and rejoicing~~ in ~~his~~ **their** posterity. We will place before ~~him~~ **them** the Tree of Knowledge of Good and Evil, and we will allow Lucifer, our common enemy, whom we (shall also place upon the earth and whom we) have thrust out, to tempt ~~him~~ **them**, and to try ~~him~~ **them**, that ~~he~~ **they** may know by ~~his~~ **their** own experience the good from the evil. If ~~he yields~~ **they yield** to temptation, we will give unto ~~him~~ **them** The Law of Sacrifice, and we will provide a Savior for ~~him~~ **them**, as we counseled in the beginning, that ~~man~~ **they** may be brought forth by the power of the redemption and the resurrection, and come again into our presence, and with us partake of Eternal Life and exaltation. We will call this the Sixth Day, and we will rest from our labors for a season. Come; let us go down.

JEHOVAH: We will go down, Elohim.

At this point in our progression through the endowment, it is imperative to note that, except for the initial placement of human beings upon this earth, the Gods (our Eternal Parents) are not omnipresent, nor are They directly involved in the work that *other* free-willed Celestial Beings desire to do. These "other Celestial Beings" are often referred to as the angels of God. The Gods are directing the work being done in this solar system, but are leaving the details to the *One* chosen to oversee this work: Jehovah, **and** to Michael; in other words, to all of US! Though the Gods, through advanced technology, can see any part of the Universe, it is clearly reiterated just how *uninvolved* They are in the affairs of this earth and those things that we are allowed to do for ourselves and our own happiness. These things are accomplished by the angels of God who serve us. These angels come from the same galaxy our Father lives in, having chosen to serve in a different capacity than a "Father," but having all the same creative powers any God possesses. If God was truly omniscient, why would *Elohim* ask if man is found upon the earth? Wouldn't He have known?

This gives reference to John's explanation in the New Testament's book of Revelation that *only* Christ was found worthy to open the seals of the book that was seen in the right hand of God. The seals represent the different stages of human development that are as eternal as the Universe itself. What is said to be *The Book of Life* is a figurative representation of the course of creation and human development that has followed the same course of repetitive transitions and "evolution" throughout the eternities—worlds without end.

Our Creators have obtained such a vast amount of experience in observing human nature from all the worlds that have existed, that They well understand exactly what is going to take place when free-willed beings are created and allowed to work out their own salvation, i.e., their own happiness. *The Book of Life* is presented in John's book of Revelation as being "written within and on the backside, sealed with seven seals," figuratively representing that nothing is going to transpire differently on this earth or in this solar system than has happened previously in all other parts of the Universe; therefore, there is no room for further additions to be made. The Creators have seen it all and understand all aspects of creation and the eventual outcome of life. They always follow the same "recipe" for life that has *always* been and will *always* be followed—worlds without end.

While the changes that were made to this part of the presentation of the endowment by making the male pronoun plural are more consistent with the original intent of the endowment, they needed not to have been made, as it has already been established that the male and female are figurative expressions of pre-mortal beings (and pre-mortal beings are genderless). However, with respect to mortality, there always exists some kind of gender, whether male, female, or both (hermaphrodite); each of which are derived from the figurative name "Michael," who then became, figuratively speaking, the man Adam, and from whom was created Eve, also speaking figuratively.

From this point forward in the presentation, one will note that Michael no longer indicates his agreement with Jehovah in the functions of complying with the commands of the Gods. For it was the Gods, our Father and Eternal Mothers, who came down to this planet in the beginning to create the mortal bodies necessary for us. These Celestial Beings have the ability to create according to Their will and pleasure; and in this pleasure, they created bodies of flesh and bone patterned after the DNA of their eternal bodies. This time, however, it was according to the composition of the elements that pertain to this *Telestial* earth versus the incorruptible composition of the bodies They had created for us in Their *Celestial* world. We came from Their Celestial sphere, where we possessed our first bodies in which were placed our newly-created spirits; and where we lived for eons of time in (what is known in mortality as) our pre-mortal state.

One will note that the presentation of the endowment does not include any mention of a "Seventh Day." It only mentions that Elohim tells both Jehovah and Michael, "*we will rest from our labors for a season*." From this, the corrupted understanding of uninspired men created a Seventh Day that they sanctified and called holy. There is no mention in the gospel of Christ of the necessity to keep the Sabbath Day holy. Though mentioned in the Ten Commandments given to the Jews by Moses, one should keep in mind that these commandments were a lower law that replaced the higher law of God. Jesus' teachings on the meaning and significance, or better, the lack of significance, of the Seventh, or Sabbath Day, greatly offended the pious people of the earth who had been misled by this false doctrine all of their lives. The *true* and undefiled endowment does not, in any way, mislead by false doctrine. Thus, the "Seventh Day" is not mentioned.

"Resting from our labors for a season" means that neither God nor His *real truth* will interact with human beings on earth. The only "labor" of the Father is to bring His creations happiness. Putting them in a position to experience unhappiness (which the choice of partaking of the fruit in the *Garden of Eden* does) is not a part of the *work of the Father* when this "labor/work" is understood as ONLY those things which bring His creations happiness. Therefore, exposing innocent and naive newly-created human beings to the opposite of happiness is the *figurative* equivalent of "resting from His labors for a season."

3
THE CREATION OF HUMAN MORTALS

THE CREATION OF ADAM AND EVE
Our First Bodies of Flesh and Bone on Earth

(The scene now changes to a lush, tropical area. A thick mist rises from the earth.)

ELOHIM: Jehovah, see the earth that we have formed. There is no man to till and take care of it. We are here to form man in our own likeness and in our own image.

JEHOVAH: We will do so, Elohim.

(The youthful body of Adam, who lies in a comatose state, is shown from the shoulders up.)

ELOHIM: Jehovah, man is now organized, and we will put into him his spirit, the breath of life, that he may become a living soul.

(Light shines on Adam's face, and his chest expands as he begins to breathe. He stirs, as if awakening.)

Here is given the first indication that the spirit does *not* enter the mortal body until the first breath is taken. After that first breath, the spirit becomes encapsulated in the flesh, where it is not able to leave until (what has erroneously been termed as) "death." The spirit cannot *die* out of the body. It exists exactly as it did before it entered. The argument that the spirit is alive and well inside the womb is an untrue doctrine of imaginative persons.

Only flesh and bone is growing inside of the woman, where natural reflexes of the newly-formed cells that make up the baby's body cause the movement that the mother experiences.

The truth that the spirit does not enter the body until the first mortal breath is profoundly supported by the communication Nephi had with Jehovah the day before he was born into this world as Jesus, son of Mary:

> *And it came to pass that he cried mightily unto the Lord, all that day; and behold, the voice of the Lord came unto him, saying: Lift up your head and be of good cheer; for behold, the time is at hand, and on this night shall the sign be given, and on the morrow come I into the world, to show unto the world that I will fulfill all that which I have caused to be spoken by the mouth of my holy prophets.*
> (3 Nephi 1:12–13)

If the spirit of the unborn Jesus was inside the body of Mary in the Eastern Hemisphere the day before his birth, then how did it communicate with Nephi in the Western at the same time? When one comes to understand that spirit matter is consistent with the elements that exist in our atmosphere (oxygen, nitrogen, etc.), but composed of somewhat different elements yet to be discovered and understood, then one is in a much better position to comprehend *how* the spirit enters the body when an infant takes its first breath. However, since a physical body is needed to communicate, Christ's spirit was still in the body he received on the planet where he was first created. And just as our modern communication technology allows us to be in contact with any individual of our choosing anywhere on earth, the more advanced technology of our Creators allows Them to communicate with whomever They choose anywhere in the Universe from Their own planet. Therefore, the day before he was born in Bethlehem, Christ spoke to Nephi from the planet upon which he was created.

ELOHIM: Jehovah, is it good for man to be alone?
JEHOVAH: It is not good for man to be alone, Elohim.
ELOHIM: We will cause a deep sleep to come upon this man whom we have formed, and we will take from his side a rib, from which we will form a woman to be a companion and helpmeet for him.

(Adam lays his head upon the ground as he loses consciousness.)

NARRATOR (Jehovah): Brethren and sisters, this is Michael, who helped form the earth. When he awakens from the sleep, which (we) Elohim and Jehovah have caused to come upon him, he will be known as Adam (and Eve), and having forgotten all, will have become ~~like~~ **as** a little child. Brethren (and sisters), close your eyes as if you were asleep.

(All male patrons in the room close their eyes.)

Chapter 3 - *The Creation of Human Mortals*

The earth is now prepared to receive mortals. It is explained here that the first bodies of flesh and bone on earth were created and prepared by the Gods to receive our spirits. These bodies were made male and female, patterned after the makeup of the eternal bodies of our Eternal Parents, or in other words, "Elohim." The wording is somewhat misleading and should have been given in concert with the creation of the body given above, having the man *remain* asleep until after the Gods "took the rib." The rib is merely a figurative representation of the structure of a human body (a bone from the skeletal system) into which spirit matter may enter. The "rib" was chosen as a symbolic representation of how the female holds up and supports the male, even as the skeletal system is the main framework that holds up and supports the flesh. In the original endowment, *both* Adam and Eve take their first breath (thus drawing their spirits into their bodies) and awake *together*, and are then commanded to arise. Standing together, side by side, the presentation of the endowment should then proceed.

"Michael" represents both genders, male and female, as it has been explained previously. The human species is androgynous as far as our spirits are concerned, where each person has both male and female potential according to our free will to choose which gender brings the most happiness to us as individuals. The desire of a human male to become female, or to act as a natural female according to the flesh, or for a female to do likewise to become and act as a male, is consistent with the eternal plan of fairness and equality granted by the free agency given us of our Creators. Had Joseph Smith revealed this eternal principle during his day, surely he would have been killed by his friends. Homosexuality is as natural and appropriate in the human race as the righteousness of the symbolic creation of both male and female bodies from the "sleeping Michael."

This part of the endowment refers to the creation of our mortal bodies which consist of the elements from the earth upon which we now reside. On the other hand, the initiatory ordinances explained above are symbolic of our very first experience of life when our newly-created spirit was placed in a body consisting of flesh and bone made from the elements of the exalted planet upon which our Eternal Parents reside.

ELOHIM: Adam (and Eve), awake and arise.

(Adam obeys the command, and is shown with foliage in front of him, which conceals his body from view. The youthful Adam appears to be in his 20's, is in good physical condition, and is clean shaven.)

NARRATOR (Jehovah)**:** All the brethren (and sisters) will please arise.

(The male patrons open their eyes and rise from their seats. An attractive, youthful Eve enters the scene and stands beside Adam. They are both shown from the shoulders up.)

ELOHIM: Adam, here is a woman whom we have formed and whom we given unto you to be a companion and helpmeet for you. What will you call her? (The *Original Endowment* said: Adam and Eve, here is a world that we have formed for you and have given you to be companions. Adam, what will you call your companion?)

ADAM: Eve.

(For the first time, the Gods, Elohim and Jehovah, are shown. They are two bearded, luminescent, glorious personages, clothed in flowing white robes. They appear standing in mid-air above and in front of Adam and Eve, and are surrounded by a radiant aura of silvery-white light.)

ELOHIM: Why will you call her Eve?
ADAM: Because she is the mother of all living.
ELOHIM: That is right, Adam; because she is the mother of all living. ~~Adam,~~ we have organized for you this earth and have planted a garden, eastward in Eden. We will place you in the garden and **we** will there command you ~~and Eve~~ to multiply and replenish the earth, that you may have joy and rejoicing in your posterity. Jehovah, introduce Adam **and Eve** into the garden which we have prepared for ~~him~~ **them**.
JEHOVAH: It shall be done, Elohim.

Many changes were made to the original endowment that place the man *over* the woman and make him appear as though a male has more authority and privilege from God than a female. This was not the case in the beginning of our existence, but was part of the "curse" placed upon the woman later on in the presentation.

NARRATOR: We now go with Adam and Eve into the garden. The brethren **(and sisters)** will now be seated.

The *Garden of Eden* is a symbolic representation of the original location on this earth that was prepared for the first human beings who were not affected by the long process of natural evolution as was the rest of the world. This "garden" was patterned after the world where our Creators live on their eternal planet. There were no animals in this part of the mortal world that ate human flesh, and there were few noxious weeds and plants that would irritate a human being. The *Garden of Eden* was located in the middle of North America near the present-day state of Missouri, in the United States. Here, the Gods allowed the modern human race to begin. It is important to understand that the human race that was started by Elohim was NOT the race of beings that evolved naturally over many, many years and which is recognized as the *Homo sapiens* species of the animal kingdom. This understanding is given and clarified more fully in <u>The Sealed Portion, The Final Testament of Jesus Christ</u>.

It is necessary here to explain more about the *Theory of Evolution* than what was given above. Ironically, as stated before, modern science is proving this long-believed theory to be false. The domesticated chicken, for example, is not a product of a natural evolutionary process, but became as it is from the ingenuity and knowledge of mortal humans and their attempts at crossbreeding certain species of wild fowl to obtain the desired result. Furthermore, modern science has developed many other new species of animals that fulfill desired, premeditated purposes. The long-stemmed rose and insect- and disease-resistant plants, etc. have all been produced by the knowledge of science in these modern times. These human-made plants and animals *did not evolve* to become what they are today—they were created.

It is unreasonable to the honest and wise mind, that a plant (again, for just one of many examples—a rose) can develop thorns through the process of evolution so that the plant-eating animals would not consume it as easily. Evolution would suggest that as the stems of the rose plants were irritated by being constantly devoured that they would eventually develop a defense mechanism to protect them. Another theory speculates that some fluke or abnormal growth in a rose stem, which at one time did not have thorns, miraculously produced thorns and somehow prospered while the unprotected rose stems did not. This makes no sense, because the plant-eaters would have devoured all the tasty rose bushes before they had a chance to evolve a defense mechanism.

Modern science is actually helping to prove the truth—which is, that Advanced Human Beings (angels of God) from other planets and solar systems watch over this earth and use Their advanced means of hybrid breeding and cross-pollination to develop the perfect animals and plants necessary for the purposes of keeping a natural order and control upon this planet. From the smallest bacteria to the largest plant-eating dinosaurs, all creatures are completely under the control of Advanced Scientists, *per se*. The only purpose of these Advanced Humans is to sustain and protect order upon planet earth, so that we (whom They were once like) might learn and experience life in a way that will allow us to become as They are. It was once expressed, and properly so: "As man is, God once was. As God is, man may become." It's really that simple.

Concerning our mortal state, human bodies were created in an Advanced Scientific Laboratory, if you will, into which were placed the spiritual essences that record all of our experiences. These mortal bodies started out as infants and were raised in the "Garden of Eden" by Celestial Mothers who came to this planet for that purpose. Thus, it is easy to comprehend how "Adam and Eve" walked and talked with "Elohim" in this place. To properly understand the figurative expressions of the prophets who gave allegories instead of plain truths, the "Garden of Eden" *always* represents a place where we lived among the Eternal Celestial Beings who created us. Whether that "place" is upon this earth, or upon a planet in another galaxy, the figurative reference stands.

The natural effects of this earth supported by the Theory of Evolution, in that the strongest survive, is indeed the very purpose why the Gods *only* intervene when necessary to maintain order and balance. In order for us to understand the necessity of maintaining complete control over nature (which absolute control is contrary to the free will granted us), the Gods allowed this earth to develop *naturally* without using Their advanced science and technology to create the perfect situation for human mortals in the beginning. If, for example, we had had the perfect washing machine at first and never had to wear dirty clothes that we were forced to laboriously wash at the river's edge, then how would we ever learn to appreciate what a *perfect* washing machine can do? Likewise, had the Gods intervened and not allowed the creation of animals that kill and eat each other, how would we ever be able to appreciate the gentleness of the animals created for our pleasure and joy? For a comparative value, this earth and its environment were allowed to act in and of themselves through natural evolution and selection. "Angels of God" only intercede to keep the earth from destroying itself before human beings have the chance to experience living upon it. For this very reason, technology was purposefully withheld from the human race through the intervention of the "angels of God" until near the end of the period of Divine (or "Advanced," depending on how you see it) *non*-intervention. Had humankind been allowed to understand even the very basic components and production of electricity a few hundred years before it was *allowed* to be discovered, the human race would have already destroyed itself and the world.

The idea that only the "strongest survive" is diametrically opposed to the equality promised to all of us in the beginning. The "least among us" are just as important and worthy of happiness and life as the greatest and strongest. In order to assure this equality, the Greatest must assure that the "least" survive just like the "strong." We are learning that without our Creators' intervention and control, when we are left to ourselves, the concept of "the strongest survive" is the only way we can survive. But when we submit to the rule of a righteous Christ, *"Whosoever shall exalt himself shall be abased; and he that shall humble himself shall be exalted."* (Matthew 23:12)

(As the male patrons sit down, Adam and Eve are shown turning to follow Jehovah into the garden. The scene quickly changes to the garden.)

ELOHIM: Adam (and) **Eve**, we have created ~~for you~~ this earth, and have placed upon it all kinds of vegetation and animal life. We have commanded all these to multiply in their own sphere and element. We give you dominion over all these things, and make you **Adam**, lord over the whole earth and all things on the face thereof. We now command you ~~and Eve~~ to multiply and replenish the earth, that you may have joy and rejoicing in your posterity. We have also planted for you this garden, wherein we have placed all manner of fruits, flowers, and vegetation. Of every tree of the garden thou mayest freely eat, but of the Tree of Knowledge of Good and Evil thou shalt not eat; nevertheless, thou mayest choose for thyself, for it is given unto thee. But remember that I forbid it; for in the day thou eatest thereof, thou shalt surely die.

The "slight" change to this paragraph by LDS Church leaders (which was perceived by them to clarify the individual roles of the male and female) results in a gross misstatement of an incredible truth. The original endowment referred to **both** the male Adam and the female Eve when the pronoun "you" was used above. The endowment actually intended to reveal this truth concerning the true equality shared by the genders, which is the same equality they shared as genderless spirits. That a spirit is born into mortality as a male or female is inconsequential to the nature of individual equality. The corrupted bias held by these leaders and shared by most religions of the world overcame the model that was set up by Creators who are Themselves unconditionally equal and are no respecter of persons. The *real truth* presents an understanding about a free-willed spirit's individual right to choose which gender is desired in mortality as was explained previously.

In the original statement by Elohim, He would have faced both Adam and Eve and referred to *them* as "Adam," even as the masculine pronoun (i.e., he, him, etc.) is commonly used to reflect both genders to avoid excessive wordiness. This incorrect understanding currently held by LDS leaders emboldens them to elevate the male Priesthood over all members, and to imply that males, in particular, were given control and "dominion over all these things, and…lord over the whole earth." The Gods who created humankind in *"Their own image,"* both male and female, did not place one gender in any greater authority or respect over another. The corruption of LDS doctrine and worldly beliefs becomes obvious in the changes that crept into the endowment as compared to its original text.

In order to arrive at a complete understanding of what mysteries of God have been unfolded up to this point in the presentation of the endowment, it is necessary to revisit some of what has been explained in this commentary. Its repetition is important to help the reader who has more than likely become confused because of the false doctrines and principles taught since birth and reinforced by religious dogma. The indoctrinated thinking patterns of a human being are not easily overridden. This is what Jesus meant when he said:

And he spake also a parable unto them; No man putteth a piece of a new garment upon an old; if otherwise, then both the new maketh a rent, and the piece that was taken out of the new agreeth not with the old. And no man putteth new wine into old bottles; else the new wine will burst the bottles, and be spilled, and the bottles shall perish. But new wine must be put into new bottles; and both are preserved. No man also having drunk old wine straightway desireth new: for he saith, The old is better. (Luke 5:36–9)

By now in the chronology and presentation of the endowment, it has been figuratively shown that the Gods (Elohim) have come to this *"new world patterned after the one where we used to live"* and formed bodies from the elements of this earth for the spirits which were transported here from Their home planet. Though answered appropriately above by explaining that the creation of Adam and Eve *"is simply figurative as far as the man and the woman are concerned,"* the question still remains: Who were Adam and Eve, really? Were they actual people? Were they really the first and only ones in the beginning? How did they get here? How were they formed? Did they and their children commit incest in producing offspring? These questions are rational and important to consider, and are answered in the correct transcript, presentation, and understanding of the endowment.

In the presentation of the endowment, Adam and Eve figuratively represent every human being created on this earth. The Being, "Michael," presented earlier in the endowment as a member of the Godhead, represents all human spirits destined to live forever in this solar system. In mortality, "Michael" became Adam, and it was figuratively expressed that Eve was taken from one of his ribs. This fits correctly with the idea that <u>all of us</u> belong to the Godhead, having the ability to be ONE with the Father and the Son, as Christ taught. We have this ability because we have the exact same spiritual makeup as our Creators. We have the shared ability with Them to become *one* in the happiness we each receive based upon our individual desires and personalities. Put another way: For the large body of spirits (represented in the Godhead as "Michael/Holy Ghost") destined to this solar system, mortal tabernacles of flesh and bone were prepared. That *re*-birth here upon this earth was the beginning sojourn and first experience our spirits had as gendered bodies. When placed upon this planet, our physical bodies were originally patterned after the "image" of the Gods who created us (not as other primate bodies or the fantasized caricature of a green alien, but in the form of human beings). These natural bodies were created through Advanced scientific technologies using the elements of this earth. These mortal bodies are capable of housing free-willed (human) spirit entities throughout their existence upon the earth in mortality. This is the origin and source of the white-skinned among the human race.

The human race was indeed created upon this earth by "Alien Beings"—only referred to as such because They are alien to this planet. These "aliens," or Advanced Human Beings, came to this earth to create bodies for Their children in a place of peace patterned after the planet from which They came. This *place* is known symbolically as the *Garden of Eden* (as mentioned earlier, in the United States in the approximate location of Missouri). Here, They could rear Their children without the effects of the pain and turmoil of the natural world impeding Their ability to do so. Though not recognized as any special place by our first ancestors, the *Garden of Eden* was a location upon the earth that was affected differently in its evolving state than the rest of the world. Its environs did not include any animals that would harm human beings, and there were few noxious weeds and plants that would bother us. It was the perfect place to begin the civilized human race and teach us how to live with each other in peace and harmony.

These Celestial Mothers (Advanced Human Beings) do not conceive Their children as mortals do. By means of Their advanced technology, They create bodies outside rather than within Their own bodies, using the elements of the surrounding world. This is easy enough to understand in light of *in vitro* fertilization which we are capable of today. Given this current technology, coupled with genetic engineering and techniques advanced millennia into the future, it is possible to conceptualize how these Celestial Mothers created the first human inhabitants upon this planet without causing pain to or sacrificing Their own bodies. This pain and sacrifice will later be introduced as the *curse* given to females upon this earth as they experience mortality. This *curse* is simply the opportunity for us to experience life *without* the superior technologies that Advanced Human societies enjoy, purposefully, so that we can learn to appreciate what these advancements can do for us.

There were many newly-created mortals (male and female) raised on this earth by these Immortal Beings from another galaxy. However, these children now functioned as if "veiled" from their former memories because of the type of body created for them. In other words, the brain they now possess as mortals does not allow full access to memories beyond their mortal birth. After they were raised properly in the *Garden of Eden* and shown how to relate to and get along with each other in their new environment (having lost all recollection of any past existence), the Gods left them alone. It is the mortal brain that is the figurative Veil that prevents us from remembering anything but the present lifetime. This is why Adam (in this "new world") is described as being innocent ("having forgotten all"). Every time we get a new body, we get a new brain (a Veil). Upon the spirit entering a non-perfect body in this world, all recollection of its former lives is inaccessible because of its limited brain capacity. The Celestial Parents reared the infants to maturity and then left and returned to Their own home planet from whence They came.

"Adam" and "Eve" were not the *only first* individuals upon this earth, but instead, *figuratively* represent those mortals given bodies patterned after their Creators and placed on the earth at the premier of human history. Again, their story is simply figurative "*so far as the man and woman are concerned.*" (See the text of the endowment [pg. 18], which unfortunately, is crossed out of the modern-day presentation.) Therefore, Adam and Eve's children procreated with children of other first human beings in order to propagate the human race.

The story that Cain and Abel were their first children is negated appropriately, but hidden in other purposeful symbolism by Joseph Smith:

And Adam knew his wife, and she bare unto him sons and daughters, and they began to multiply and to replenish the earth. And from that time forth, the sons and daughters of Adam began to divide two and two in the land, and to till the land, and to tend flocks, and they also begat sons and daughters. ...And Adam and Eve blessed the name of God, and they made all things known unto their sons and their daughters. And Satan came among them (their children), ...and they (their children) loved Satan more than God. And men began from that time forth to be carnal, sensual, and devilish. ...And Adam and Eve, his wife, ceased not to call upon God. And Adam knew Eve his wife, and she conceived and bare Cain, and said: I have gotten a man from the Lord; wherefore he may not reject his words. (Moses 5:2–3, 12–13, 16)

The above LDS scripture should have revealed to those of the Church the fact that the biblical version of the Adam and Eve story (beginning with the Garden of Eden and continuing to the introduction of their supposed firstborn son, who was said to be Cain) is not correct. During the presentation of the endowment, "Adam and Eve" represent the mortal state of *all* humans, male and female, placed upon this earth. Adam is a figurative moniker attached to *all males* raised as the first human inhabitants of this earth. Eve is the moniker for *all females*. However, there was a male who stood out and was appointed to be a teacher and servant of the people after the Gods had left. The name of this particular man is not important, but "Adam" has been used figuratively by the prophets, and also literally by Moroni in the context of his abridgment of the words of the brother of Jared in <u>The Sealed</u>

Portion. He was the very first *true* prophet, and his job was to reinforce the standards set by the Gods in how we should treat each other. He simply taught the gospel of Jesus Christ. Regardless, the eternal truth of the matter is that God is no respecter of persons, and has always treated everyone the same in all situations on this earth as upon every other planet that has been prepared to support and perpetuate human life.

To help the reader retain an understanding and "pour out the old wine" previously learned and believed, it is important to reiterate that "Michael" represents *all* of the spirits of the free-willed beings destined to inhabit this solar system, and for these spirits, bodies of flesh, both male and female, were created. Michael became the man Adam, from whom came the woman, Eve. This completes the *Holy Trinity*, which consists of our Creators, our Christ, and us—worlds without end.

ELOHIM: ~~Adam~~ **(and Eve)**, remember ~~this commandment~~ **these commandments,** which we have given unto you. Now go to, dress this garden, take good care of it, be happy and have joy therein. We shall go away, but we shall visit you again and give you further instructions.

This latter part of the instructions to Adam and Eve from Elohim leads us to one of the most misunderstood parts of our Creators' plan. Why would God command Adam and Eve, on the one hand, to multiply and replenish the earth by having mortal children, yet on the other hand, command them to not partake of the *Tree of Knowledge of Good and Evil*—the very partaking of which was the only way to comply with the first commandment that they might have joy and rejoicing in their posterity?

Foremost, it should be noted that the nature of a God will not allow Them to give a commandment that would bring heartache and pain upon Their creations. In other words, no commandment given to us by our Creators has any chance of ending in misery and pain. All commandments are given to bring us happiness and joy—this is a God's true nature, and cannot be changed or amended in any way.

This being said, it would be prudent to inquire as to what the *Tree of Knowledge of Good and Evil* truly is.

THE TREE OF KNOWLEDGE OF GOOD AND EVIL IS A SYMBOLIC REPRESENTATION OF THE ENTICEMENTS OF THE MORTAL FLESH.

The sensory capabilities of flesh, coupled with a veil of forgetfulness over all previous memories, make us like kids in a candy store; left unrestrained, it is not long until the enticement of pleasure (Lucifer) turns on us and we discover pain and suffering as a result. Our God Parents had no capacity for teaching or demonstrating evil to us, thus it became necessary in our temporary bodies of mortal flesh to experience every possible kind of pain and suffering so that we could comprehend the goodness of our Creators and Their plan of happiness for us. In the presentation of the endowment, Elohim's commandment to Adam and Eve was simply that we exercise proper control over the enticements of the flesh so as not to be led by them, but that we might be led by our true nature, which is what is recorded in our spirit.

One of the most enticing "fruits" of this symbolic tree is the sexual desire that we naturally possess because of the mortal flesh that has been provided for us. This flesh naturally entices us to partake of this "fruit" so that we might reproduce and create other fleshly mortal bodies for the children of God. The power of sexual attraction has become one of, if not *the most*, powerful and uncontrollable forces in all of humanity, especially since humans have discovered new ways and provided means of their own (through modern technology) to circumvent it's only true purpose.

In the beginning, Adam and Eve were given these mortal bodies, but perceived each other only as "brother" and "sister," having similar feelings towards each other as mortal brothers *should* have towards their sisters, and as mortal sisters *should* have towards their brothers. It is not natural for a human sibling to lust sexually after another sibling, and this natural restriction remains unbreached *unless* either of them begins to act against it. Incest does not occur naturally in the human species until the lust overcomes the natural desire of restraint. When brothers and sisters breach this natural boundary, the lust overcomes them and the flesh becomes numbed to, and then finally unaware of, the fact that the natural restriction has been breached.

During the rest of the presentation of the endowment, "Adam and Eve" represent the mortal state of all humans, male and female, regardless of color or origin, placed upon this earth for probationary purposes without an intimate knowledge of their Creators, who left them alone to "*go to, dress this garden, take good care of it, be happy and have joy therein.*"

(The scene changes, and it is understood that the Gods have again ascended. The following scene occurs in the garden, and no indication is given as to how much time has passed since the Gods' departure. Adam and Eve explore the garden, examining the plant and animal life. Adam peers over a hedge of bushes and smiles as he watches a lion lazily stretching on the ground. Lucifer, the devil, is shown standing nonchalantly observing Adam, and is clad in red robes and a black cloak and is also wearing a square black apron tied to his waist. Though youthful, Lucifer appears perhaps a few years older than Adam. His speech is fluid, persuasive, and without hesitation. He stands in the shadows as he begins to speak, and then steps forward into the light. He wears a beard and mustache.)

LUCIFER: Well, Adam, you have a new world here.

ADAM: A new world?

LUCIFER: Yes, a new world, patterned after the old one where we used to live.

ADAM: I know nothing about any other world.

LUCIFER: Oh, I see; your eyes are not yet opened. You have forgotten everything. You must eat some of the fruit of ~~this~~ that tree.

At this point, we have been given an understanding that Adam has been restricted in his ability to remember much of his previous life on the planet where he came from. This restriction occurs because of our natural brain's inability to be utilized to its full extent by our spirit matter. The mortal human brain records only those experiences that have occurred in its lifetime, whereas the spirit retains a record of *all* its intelligence and experiences from the beginning and all throughout its existence, completely independent of the human brain. The mortal brain cannot remember what has never been recorded by way of an immediate experience stored in in the constructs of its cells. However, there are instances of abnormal brain development in which autistic, savant, child prodigy, or other extraordinary abilities are manifested. These abilities associated with what we have determined are "abnormalities" are evidence that our brains have capabilities beyond their normal functions. But for all intents and purposes, our Creators expect us to experience an existence *without* a perfect brain that works like Their's does.

The conversation with *Lucifer* is meant to be innocent and comfortable, as if Adam and Lucifer communicate on a regular basis. This allegorically teaches the easiness of our being influenced by Lucifer. Lucifer is enticing Adam through the ministrations of the spirit world; or better, in our own minds and hearts where our ideas and desires are formed. In other words, Adam is beginning to be enticed by the flesh, as indicated by Lucifer offering him some of the fruit.

(Lucifer plucks two pieces of fruit from the Tree of Knowledge of Good and Evil, and presents it to Adam.)
LUCIFER: Adam, here is some of the fruit of ~~that~~ **this** tree. It will make you wise.
ADAM: I will not partake of that fruit. Father told me that in the day I should partake of it I should surely die.
LUCIFER: You shall not surely die but shall be as the Gods, knowing good and evil.
ADAM: I will not partake of it.
LUCIFER: Oh, you will not? Well, we shall see.

Here it is important to understand that *Lucifer* is an allegorical representation of the thinking patterns and emotional reactions of the mortal flesh. Adam refuses to give in to the enticements of the flesh offered him because he is not comfortable acting contrary to what his spiritual roots tell him, or in other words, what brings peace and comfort to his mind. Adam's subconscious feelings of dissonance (conflict) come from the enticements of his flesh contradicting that which he was taught and experienced with the Celestial Mothers who reared him on Their perfected planet. This follows the mindset of those who, in their ego to remain steadfast and immovable in keeping the "letter" of the law, do not have enough spiritual insight to understand the "spirit" of *why* the law was given in the first place. Women, on the other hand, are much more prone to understand the "spirit" in spite of the "letter." That's why most churches are started by men—they need the "letter" to teach them, whereas women learn much easier from their spiritual roots, as will be shown symbolically next in the endowment.

In this figurative representation of our conscience, *Lucifer* realizes that he is not going to get anywhere through his spiritual enticements. In other words, Adam does not give in to the temptations of the flesh to have sex with his sister, Eve. Therefore, Lucifer (remember, allegorically representing the flesh) does what he knows will ultimately entice Adam and Eve. It's important to note that in the above conversation, Adam does not recognize Lucifer, because he is being inspired in his mind by communications of his own spirit. However, one will quickly note that Eve *will* see an actual person whom she questions as to who he is; thus signifying that she is communicating with an actual person. She is told that he is her "brother" because he has a body that is similar to Adam's.

(Adam leaves, and Lucifer finds Eve, who is tending flowers [in other versions of the endowment, Eve is carrying a small lamb].)

LUCIFER: Eve, here is some of the fruit of that tree. It will make you wise. It is delicious to the taste, and very desirable.

EVE: Who are you?

LUCIFER: I am your brother.

EVE: You, my brother, and come here to persuade me to disobey Father?

LUCIFER: I have said nothing about Father. I want you to eat of the fruit of the Tree of Knowledge of Good and Evil, that your eyes may be opened; for that is the way Father gained His knowledge. You must eat of this fruit so as to comprehend that everything has its opposite: good and evil, virtue and vice, light and darkness, health and sickness, pleasure and pain; and thus your eyes will be opened and you will have knowledge.

EVE: Is there no other way?

LUCIFER: There is no other way.

EVE: Then I will partake.

(Eve takes the fruit from Lucifer, and takes a bite. Lucifer approves and places the other piece in her hand, which he closes around it and pats gently.)

Eve reacts differently to the enticement than Adam did above, because she is confronted with an actual *male* species of flesh. A woman's mortal body naturally craves to have children, thus necessitating the desire for sex and the support of a male. Figuratively, the "fruit of that tree" is the experience of being a mother. In the endowment presentation storyline, Eve recognizes Adam as her brother, but does not recognize Lucifer. The scenario is set up to represent the idea that in order to gain the experience of mortal life, we have to procreate and mix our bodies with naturally spawned bodies (of the Homo sapiens species), who are not our "brother," so that we can experience all that is necessary to have our "eyes opened." "Partaking of the fruit" is a symbolic representation of the female submitting to the sexual advancements of the male so that she can have children.

Eve is enticed by a man who was inspired and directed spiritually by Lucifer (the flesh, i.e., sex—the natural and strongest appetite of men). <u>The Sealed Portion</u> reveals that this is when Eve had sex with a man of the Homo sapiens race, represented allegorically by her "brother" Lucifer. (This is also presented figuratively in some aspects by Moroni.) It reveals that the *Homo sapiens* race was created over a long period of time by means different than those by which the bodies of Adam and Eve were created. This is the source for the black-skinned among the human race. Ultimately, all the different skin colors upon earth have arisen through the blending and interbreeding of various combinations of the first two races (black and white). Subsequent to the occasion of mixing with Eve, this new species became the primary means by which some of the first spirits that were brought to this planet could be housed in mortal bodies. Today, this *Homo sapiens* race consists of all us, as we have each been a part of every race and have all participated as black, white, and every shade in between at one time or another during our mortal sojourn. More will be said about the *Homo sapiens* later in the endowment. When Eve gave in to the desires of the flesh, she enjoyed the feeling, and realized the great joy that came from acting upon these desires. Now she could begin to see her "brother" Adam in a completely different light.

Notice also that both "Lucifer" and the "forbidden fruit" were two entirely different things to the man Adam and the woman Eve. Adam had his temptation that he fought in his mind with respect to Eve, which temptation was his "Lucifer," or his enticement of the flesh. Alternately, Eve was tempted by what she saw (a prospective male provider who could impregnate her) and emotionally felt (the natural yearning to mate). It becomes very apparent from this presentation that *Lucifer* is not a single person or even the same thing to different people, but only the representation of those particular desires of the flesh to which we each, individually, are tempted.

When we perform an action, we make the decision to do so from either being enticed by our natural appetites or by our sub-conscience. Our actions make a "name" for us. Figuratively speaking, when we follow the natural enticements of our flesh, we are "following Satan" or the "arm of the flesh." But when we follow the gentle enticings of peace emanating from our subconscious, which always tells us to do the right thing, we follow the "Holy Ghost" and act in the "name of Christ." (This will be expounded upon later.)

When we do something in the "name of Christ," it is not that we do anything in the actual word of "Christ," but rather follow his *works*. In this way, the prophets force us to break the paradigm of our own language barrier in order to teach the things of God. Similarly, as taught in <u>The Sealed Portion</u>, *our* works constitute the "name" by which *we* are known. Either way, *acting* on the name of "Lucifer" or on the name of "Christ," indicates the works of which one we follow, either the *flesh* or the *spirit*.

LUCIFER: There. Now go and get Adam to partake.

(Eve seeks Adam, fruit in hand. She finds him kneeling by a brook dipping his hand into the water. As Eve speaks to Adam, he stands and smiles as he sees her. Eve presents the fruit to him with a persuasive tone of voice.)

EVE: Adam, here is some of the fruit of that tree. It is delicious to the taste and very desirable.

ADAM: Eve, do you know what fruit that is?

EVE: Yes, it is the fruit of the Tree of Knowledge of Good and Evil.

ADAM: I cannot partake of it. Do you not know that Father commanded us not to partake of the fruit of that tree?

EVE: Do you intend to obey all of Father's commandments?

ADAM: Yes, all of them.

EVE: Do you not ~~recollect~~ **remember** that Father commanded us to multiply and replenish the earth? I have partaken of this fruit and by so doing shall be cast out, and you will be left a lone man in the Garden of Eden.

Eve proves the great spiritual insight that most women have over men. Women in general tend to be more apt to sacrifice than men. Most men, if forced by nature to go through the pains of childbirth, would never have another. The nurturing nature of a woman allows her to more likely follow the course set by her subconscious rather than her immediate fleshly urges.

ADAM: Eve, I see that this must be ~~so~~. I will partake that man may be.

(Adam takes a bite, and Lucifer walks to their side with a look of approval.)

It should be obvious why Joseph Smith was inspired to give this part of the plan of the Creators in this way. Can one imagine what would have happened if he had taught the people that Adam and Eve's fall was because of sexual intercourse? The religious world would have fainted! Yet, what kind of fruit could a person possibly eat that would make one disobey a commandment of a just God? The Gods knew that the enticements of the flesh would bring great unhappiness upon Their children; and for this reason, They were forced by Their divine nature to command against it—though They fully expected us to partake (or to succumb to these enticements), so that we could have children and perpetuate the course of nature upon this earth.

LUCIFER: That is right.

EVE: It is better for us to pass through sorrow that we may know the good from the evil.

EVE: *(speaking to Lucifer)*: I know thee now. Thou art Lucifer, he who was cast out of Father's presence for rebellion.

LUCIFER: Yes, you are beginning to see already.

How is it that at the moment Eve partakes of the fruit and then persuades Adam to follow her, that she now recognizes *Lucifer* for who he really is; whereas just moments before, she did not recognize him? "Lucifer" represents the lusts and enticements of the mortal flesh, which are largely concentrated in the natural sex drive of the human species. In the presence of Celestial Beings (Father's presence) there is no lust, no jealousy, no lasciviousness, no vanity, and no intrinsic yearning to mate. These things were, figuratively speaking, "cast out" of a perfect human environment. By the end of this book, the reader will come to realize that the means that motivates natural human responsiveness (i.e., the sex drive) has also caused us the most problems. It is this motivating force that will be taken from all free-willed beings without them using their free agency to give it up voluntarily (for none would).

It is hard for the person participating in the endowment ceremony to categorize those things that are literal and those things that are symbolic. Even as this commentary is given as plain as it can be, there will still be those who forget the caveat given at the beginning of Chapter One (see page 1): **THE ENDOWMENT IS FIGURATIVE IN EACH AND EVERY WAY, AND TRYING TO CONVEY REALITY INTO IT WILL ONLY CONFUSE THE READER.** With this in mind, a brief description of the characters must again be reviewed:

"Adam," "Eve," and "Lucifer" each represent a different part of every one of us. (For this very reason, the original endowment *only* mentions "Adam" as the one to whom Elohim and Jehovah are referring in most instances. The modern LDS changes include Eve, because the leaders of the Church do not understand the true symbolism of the endowment [refer to all **bold green** additions of "Eve"].) Remember, Adam and Eve came from Michael, a member of the Godhead. Lucifer appears out of nowhere *after* Michael is put to sleep and caused to forget all that he once knew. Adam wants to live by the "letter of the law," while Eve follows her feelings. Lucifer creates the conflict between the two. The best way to properly describe these three characters as they refer to each of us would be to borrow some ubiquitously accepted psychological terms used in society. Adam represents our **SUPEREGO**, Eve represents our **EGO**, and Lucifer represents our **ID**. When we are born (as Michael awakens and becomes the mortal man Adam in a *fallen* state), our **ID** (Lucifer) first appears. The **ID** is associated with our natural instincts, our sense of pleasure, and our fleshly needs and desires. It's goal is to satiate these feelings any way possible, regardless of what the means to accomplish this end does to anyone else. In essence, the **ID** is diametrically opposed to the concept of "Do Unto Others." As we grow, we become more aware of our **SUPEREGO** (Adam) due to the moral and ethical restraints placed on us, and also due to the example given by our caregivers (Creators). It is the moral part of us and was developed in our pre-mortal state. The **SUPEREGO** is our conscience. It is that part of us that recognizes good and evil, right and wrong, and establishes a subconscious foundation of everything that is good, happy, beautiful, peaceful, fair, and secure. It was established in our first estate, or during our interactions and experiences with Celestial Beings in a perfected (non-fallen) world. The **EGO** (Eve) is based on the reality of what is happening around us, regardless of what the **SUPEREGO** and the **ID** motivate us to do. The **EGO** takes a look at the "big picture" and determines the best action to take that will satisfy both our conscience and our natural desires. It is the part of us that attempts to control our basic instincts and impulses; in other words, it is in a constant battle to mediate among the **ID**, the **SUPEREGO**, and the external world, attempting to find a balance between them. The **EGO** (Eve) understands that other people have needs and desires and that sometimes being impulsive or selfish can hurt us in the long run. Its the **EGO**'s job to meet the needs of the **ID** by taking into consideration the needs of the **SUPEREGO** and the reality of the situation (Eve does a fine job at this). In mortality, we find ourselves (**EGO**) surrounded by our natural, fallen state (**ID**), longing for what we experienced before but cannot remember (**SUPEREGO**).

A Celestial being does not have any of the problems associated with the **ID** ("he who was cast out of Father's presence for rebellion," i.e., Lucifer) because it conflicts with a Celestial nature. Once we give in to our fleshly desires (partake of the fruit) we experience its benefits and try to convince our conscience (**SUPEREGO**) that there is much wisdom in these benefits. But as soon as we start to experience the pitfalls of giving in to the flesh, we *recognize* why these things cause us misery ("I know thee now") and why they can never be a part of eternal felicity.

The blessings associated with the power and drive associated with procreation are reserved *only* for those who will go on to become Creators throughout the Universe. In this profoundly symbolic expression presented in this part of the endowment, Eve has now recognized what was "cast out of Father's presence" because it is diametrically opposed (rebellion) to the ability of a human being to experience peace and lasting happiness in one's associations with others. Eve had been taught by her Celestial Mother about this drive and its blessings, but was also warned of its problems. In other words, all of us were taught about the power of procreation, its blessings, and its downfalls in human nature; and the effects of these teachings are part of our conscience.

This is what was figuratively presented as Eve saying to Adam, "Do you not recollect (remember what we were taught) that Father commanded us to multiply and replenish the earth?" In essence, our Eternal Parents made us aware of Their abilities to procreate, but explained why most of us would never be allowed to possess the same abilities forever. After Eve partook of the fruit (experienced sex) her eyes were opened, and she began to see that she now possessed the propensity to experience lust, jealousy, lasciviousness, and vanity caused by her desire to have children.

ADAM: What is that apron you have on?

A close look at the apron worn by the actor that is portraying Lucifer reveals the Masonic signs of secular intelligence and industry—the honors and glories of the world—the square and the compass, which ironically, (and this is important), are the same marks sewn into the LDS temple garments worn by the patrons who receive their endowments. Joseph Smith specifically instructed that these things be placed in Lucifer's apron (being a representation of his works) and also in the garments of the participants, worn throughout their lives as a representation of their works done while in the mortal body.

The garments represent the mortal flesh, and the marks thereon (being identical to the symbols found on Lucifer's apron) represent that our flesh entices us to desire the things of the world and the honors and glories thereof. Unbeknownst to the unenlightened LDS members, who faithfully wear their garments, they are wearing the exact same symbols as Lucifer wears upon his apron.

(Lucifer draws his cloak back to reveal a black apron.)

LUCIFER: It is an emblem of my power and Priesthoods.
ADAM: Priesthoods?
LUCIFER: Yes, Priesthoods.

  LDS leaders here deleted a very important part that would explain the *true* doctrine that Joseph Smith tried to teach in this part of the endowment. Lucifer's work and glory comes from the works, achievements, and honors of men, which are further amplified by our own delusion and vain imaginations. These are presented as "Priesthoods." Only when men set themselves up as a "light to others" do they introduce Priesthoods. There is no Priesthood in a kingdom of God where equality is the general rule. Males do not have any special authority or honor over any other *anywhere* in the Universe—that is why no one else in the presentation of the endowment wears an apron of "priesthoods" except for Lucifer. His plan (the enticement of fleshly honors and glory) provides for "Priesthoods," by which he can extend exclusionary titles, privileges, and glory to those who are his leaders and ministers. In our Creators' plan there are NO leaders—only servants. "Priesthoods" (like "priestcrafts" mentioned in canonized scripture) are the culmination of the glory that men lust after, and that which Lucifer uses to reward those who follow him and his plan. For this reason, Adam was confused.

  Adam simply did not understand what "Priesthoods" meant, neither by ego nor by word, because he did not receive these things from the *Holy Spirit* as it has been explained as being *common sense*. If the "Priesthood" is everlasting, as many LDS Priesthood Holders would like to believe their's is, then why is it that Joseph put this part in the endowment, even as those holding "Priesthood" positions of authority sat in the endowment listening? It should be noted that the Reorganized Church of Jesus Christ (now known as the Community of Christ)—which was founded by those who were more intimate with Joseph Smith and had a deeper insight into his teachings than Brigham Young—gives the "Priesthood" to women as well as to men, seeing it differently from the mainstream LDS Church. Though the leaders of the Community of Christ are also considerably misled in understanding the true mysteries of God, it is not they, but the modern LDS leaders, who have stricken out this part of the endowment. These LDS leaders have everything to lose if their supposed "Priesthood" authority is jeopardized or threatened by any possible misunderstanding of the original text and its true meaning.

  Religious priesthood would not be necessary if people would look inside themselves for the guidance and inspiration they seek. Most people look outside of themselves to others for such "revelation." It was the *figurative* Moses who first incorporated "priesthood" into a religion of strict ordinances and specific sacrifices that replaced the simplicity of the Higher Law he received from God. When the people refused to face God themselves, they were given leadership and priesthood to guide them. Likewise in his own day, Joseph Smith first attempted to get his followers to live the **Law of Consecration** and abide simply by the words of Christ as given to the Nephite and Lamanite people as described in the <u>Book of Mormon</u>. When the people could not live these simple laws, Joseph organized a religion and then introduced the "priesthood authority" that would eventually destroy the simplicity of the Royal Commandment: Love your neighbor as yourself.

ADAM: I am looking for Father to come down to give us further instructions.
LUCIFER: Oh, you are looking for Father to come down, are you?

Adam is confused by Lucifer's "Priesthoods" and is waiting to be instructed in all things by the Father, signifying his reliance on what feels "right" to his spirit, or in other words, what makes sense. Mortals are easily led by powerful or charismatic leaders when they fail to rely on their own spirit within. Our desire to act on beliefs that are taught to us by other mortals, who cannot remember anymore than we can, frequently leads us to overlook the obvious, the rational, and what speaks to our common sense.

(The Gods' voices are suddenly heard in the garden, reverberating through the air.)

ELOHIM: Jehovah, we promised Adam **and Eve** that we would visit ~~him~~ **them** and give ~~him~~ **them** further instructions. Come; let us go down.
JEHOVAH: We will go down, Elohim.
ADAM: I hear Their voices. They are coming.
LUCIFER: See, you are naked. Take some fig leaves and make you aprons. Father will see your nakedness. Quick! Hide!
ADAM: Come; let us hide.
NARRATOR: Brethren and sisters, put on your aprons.

The apron that is worn as part of the endowment is a dark color—usually green, which is a representation of our natural world. The apron is a dark contrast to the purity and whiteness of the rest of the temple clothes. It represents "our works" in the mortal flesh, which are usually *dark* in comparison to the *true* nature of our beings (represented by the white temple clothes worn), which is spiritual. On each apron are nine (9) leaves of a tree. The leaves come from the *Tree of Knowledge of Good and Evil* (the enticements of our flesh), and are the representations of our works, which manifest the way we react to the enticements of our flesh. Just as leaves are the natural product of a tree full of life, the leaves on the apron represent the *product* of our works, or the kingdoms of glory that we will inherit according to our individual works, or according to our individual desires of happiness. The Gods created this earth and the other planets in this solar system for us. The glory or happiness that we chose for ourselves places us within one of those kingdoms (one of the nine [9] planets in this solar system), depending on the way that our spirit reacts with the flesh—this reaction being our works.

Guilt is introduced as being the product of living contrary to our *natural order* of creation, which is in the similitude of our Heavenly Parents. We feel a sense of guilt when we act contrary to our spiritual natures, which is literally our *common sense*. Adam's mind experiences guilt, and he conspires with Eve to hide from God, as these feelings alter their rational view of God's love for them. Figuratively speaking, Adam and Eve are literal brother and sister because they share the same Eternal Parents. They sinned against the command of the Gods by having intercourse, and were further convinced of their guilt by Lucifer (their flesh).

The dogma thrown around that Adam and Eve were married by God in the Garden of Eden is speculative and untrue, owing to the fact that "Adam and Eve" are symbolic representations of each gender of the human race. Even if they were real people, there would never be a "marriage" performed by the command of God. Marriage is an earthly contract that can easily come to dissolution by divorce. During the time of ancient Israel, marriage, as a contract, was introduced *after* the Jews rejected the *higher* laws of the Gods, and had to settle for what they received through the *lower* laws of Moses. "Wife" was a distinguished title given to a special woman who depended upon a man for her sustenance. The union of a man and woman, or marriage, is derived from the Latin word "*maritare*," which means "*to own*." It should be interesting to note that the title of "Master" is a derivative from the same root. In the *true* kingdom of a righteous God, nobody owns another, but all act equally with the same power of free agency.

Promises made between a man and a woman are often symbolized by the giving of a ring, which is a symbol of eternity, or the promise that each makes to the other for eternity. No man can assure this promise will be fulfilled; thus no man of pretended authority has any power from God to marry a man to a woman and "seal" them forthwith in a guarantee that the marriage will last forever. Only the two individuals responsible for the promise have any power to bring about its realization. Christ referred to this when he said:

For in the resurrection they neither marry, nor are given in marriage, but are the angels of God in heaven. (Matthew 22:30)

There is no sealing power that can assure the continuation of a relationship between two spirit children of God when each one possesses equal free agency. Only the "Holy Spirit of Promise" can assure such a union. This is simply an *eternal promise* made between two Celestial-destined spirits. If two free-willed human beings desire to make a commitment to each other as man and woman, it is done *only* by the *spirit of this promise*. They do this by exercising their free agency and desiring to remain together as eternal partners throughout the eternities, serving the plan of our Creators as a male and female so that they can bring other souls into existence. This is the symbolic meaning of the *Holy Spirit of Promise* by which all things are eternally sealed.

Because of Joseph Smith's understanding of the "true" doctrine of marriage, there were no temple sealings of husband and wife during his lifetime. Temple marriage ceremonies began many years later, after the "keys" that open a *correct* understanding were taken from the earth with Joseph's death. These "keys" are simply the knowledge of truth—which *only* Joseph possessed. The ability to perform 'sealings,' or any ordinance, is made possible only through an understanding of the things of God (keys), not magic, motions, ceremony, or titles received from the "priesthoods" of Lucifer. Brigham Young and those who followed in his footsteps introduced this misleading doctrine to maintain further control over the hearts and desires of their followers. This should come as a relif to some to know that the *only* power binding you to your eternal companion is locked safely within your own heart, which means that you will not be bound to anyone you were allegedly "sealed to for time and all eternity," if you no longer desire it.

In the endowment, Joseph Smith specifically used the word "nakedness" allegorically as it is used throughout the Old Testament to represent "sexual intercourse" (see Leviticus 18:6-19, and the many other references to "nakedness" being "sexual intercourse"; also see Ezekiel 23:29 and other such references to the term "nakedness" referencing actions contrary to the commandments of God). In the figurative sense, Adam and Eve had sexual intercourse (partaking of the fruit), and they were convinced by Lucifer (fleshly guilt) that they were "naked." The symbolism of this term is constant throughout the words of the prophets and the law given to the Jews, they having corrupted forms of the *true* Holy Endowment given to them by ancient *true* prophets.

Adam and Eve truly were "naked," resulting from their works, and thus needed something to cover themselves and hide from God. That which "hides us from God" is the guilt that we feel when we act contrary to our *common sense* (Holy Spirit), or our inability to remember what we were once taught by Celestial Parents and the fact that we follow what *others* tell us is right. It was *Lucifer* wearing his apron (works) of "priesthoods" that pointed out the guilt. Likewise, it is only invented religions and philosophies of mortals that cause us to *feel guilty* about being who *we really are* (our naked state), and acting according to our *true* individual conscience and desires.

(The film pauses temporarily while the patrons remove their fig-leaf aprons from the packets that have been resting on their laps. Each patron has his or her own packet, which contains additional temple clothing to be put on later

in the endowment. All patrons tie the aprons on around their waists. When the film resumes, the Gods have once again descended, represented as before. Adam hides behind foliage.)

ELOHIM: Adam. ...Adam! ...Adam!! Where art thou?
ADAM: I heard thy voice and hid myself, because I was naked.

Here we are introduced to the *first* general reaction of those who have a sense of guilt and hide themselves from the inspiration that comes from our Creators through the Holy Ghost. Figuratively speaking, the Father is continually calling out to us through the Spirit, but we hide ourselves from hearing Him because of our guilty consciences. These actions of the "Father" and "Holy Ghost" are figurative of what a person feels after doing something that he or she knows deep down inside is not correct. This feeling comes from subconscious memories of our past pre-earth life, in which we experienced a constant state of <u>righteousness</u>, which our flesh recognizes as happiness. (This will be expounded upon more fully later.)

ELOHIM: Who told thee that thou wast naked? Hast thou partaken of the fruit of the Tree of Knowledge of Good and Evil, of which we commanded thee not to partake?
ADAM: The woman thou gavest me, and commanded that she should remain with me—she gave me of the fruit of the tree, and I did eat.

Now we learn the *second* general reaction of those who have a sense of guilt. When a feeling of guilt arises, we want to escape personal responsibility and find someone else on whom to blame our actions. This is a typical human emotion that is consistent with the nature of a child who hides from a parent or blames it on someone else (usually another sibling or an imaginary friend) to avoid getting into trouble.

ELOHIM: Eve! What is this that thou hast done?

(Eve enters, standing behind the foliage.)

EVE: The serpent beguiled me, and I did eat.
ELOHIM: Lucifer! What hast thou been doing here?

(Lucifer enters.)

LUCIFER: I have been doing that which has been done in other worlds.

ELOHIM: What is that?

LUCIFER: I have been giving some of the fruit of the Tree of the Knowledge of Good and Evil to them.

Eve displays the same reaction as Adam, but steps up to the plate and admits her guilt—very indicative of the general difference in nature of a mortal male and female. But she still makes an excuse for her actions by blaming it on Lucifer. Likewise, most of us either blame the devil for enticing the actions we do that are bad, or the Lord for the actions we do that are good. Either way, we seldom take responsibility for using our free agency.

The term "Lucifer" is interchangeable with the "flesh." The "*War in Heaven*" led by Lucifer is simply figurative of our rebellious and impatient desire to possess perfected bodies and be like our Creators without paying the necessary price. There are many free-willed humans who lived with our Creators in our pre-mortal state, and in exercising their free agency, decided that there might be a better plan for the human race than the Eternal Plan that has always been followed by Celestial Creators. These free-thinkers did not agree that we should have to comply with the eternal **Law of Sacrifice**, which necessitated our giving up a perfect life for a mortal (far less-than-perfect) one in order to learn. We were well aware of what had happened and what was happening on planets where other human beings were going through, or who had gone through, what was to be required of us. Our free will and *common sense* told us that there must be a better way than *natural mortal* development and suffering to learn what we needed to know.

The natural development of the earth over millions of years was allowed to occur to give us the opportunity to experience a corrupt body of flesh and bone. It took many, many years to allow for the arrangement and production of the *Homo sapiens* species without the intervention of advanced scientific technology that could have enhanced or improved the result. This process of "natural evolution" is what we were taught as the best way for us to learn to appreciate who we are and why we exist. It became quite apparent to us that our Creators were much smarter than we were and that They had the ability to continue to give us everything we needed to be happy. But had They continued to, we could have never experienced the opposite, therefore negating the positive aspects of humanity and happiness. In other words that might make things a little clearer, the process of producing a perfect body that is fit for a human spirit to reside in can only be done properly by those Gods who know how to do it; but when left to nature (incomplete understanding) without the supervision and experience of an Advanced Scientist, imperfect bodies of flesh and bone result. We are living with this natural, uninhibited result.

Moroni explains this with some figurative prose in <u>The Sealed Portion</u>:

And it came to pass that the creatures that had been possessed by Satan and his followers found their way into the land in which lived the children of Adam and Eve. And the sons and daughters of Adam and Eve, who did not hearken to the words of their father, or to the words of their brothers who had been called by the Lord as prophets to preach repentance unto them; yea, even these began to breed with those creatures who were not created by the Father to house the spirits of His children. And from these unions there came to be many different peoples upon the earth. And the bodies that were created by these unions began to be the vessels in which the Father was required by the eternal laws of heaven to put the spirits of His children. And thus had Satan corrupted the natural bodies that God had created for Adam and Eve. Nevertheless, all this was done according to that which the Father had already known and that which He had expected. For in this same manner did the other worlds in which life was created bring about the mortal bodies for the spirits of the children of God. And all these things were necessary so that the children of God might partake of that which is imperfect, so that they might know that which is perfect. And the bodies that the Father created for Adam and Eve were perfect according to the laws of the nature in which they were formed. And their bodies were also like unto the bodies that He and their Eternal Mothers possess. And how is it that we might know that these bodies are perfect, unless it so be that we experience the effects of a body that is imperfect, and therefore, have some type of comparison that we might know these things? And Satan continued to do that which had been done before in the worlds that were created for the salvation and happiness of the children of God. Therefore, in the beginning, the children of men were given a body like unto that of the Father, and they were also given commandments pertaining to this body that it might not be defiled. But in the space of not many generations, all of the children of men began to possess bodies that were imperfect and unlike the perfect bodies that had been created for Adam and Eve. (TSP 16:18–24)

ELOHIM: Lucifer, because thou hast done this, thou shalt be cursed above all the beasts of the field. Upon thy belly thou shalt go, and dust ~~shalt thou~~ **thou shalt** eat all the days of thy life.

This is a symbolic representation of what happens to a person who follows Lucifer's plan (the enticements of the flesh) in mortality. "*Upon thy belly thou shalt go*" means that a person will be led by their *appetites* and the desires of the flesh. However, the appetite of these people will never be satisfied following this plan, because the "food" that they eat will be the "dust" of the earth, or that which remains after a person acts in the flesh. (When we walk along a path, we raise up dust.) This "dust" has no nutritional value whatsoever. This person will continually be "eating" in an attempt to satisfy the "belly" upon which they proceed through life, but will never feel satisfied or fulfilled. In order to feel satiated, or better, completely happy, a human must act according to his or her own conscience, which has been explained above. As we "eat the dust of the earth" we never become who we *really* are and find lasting happiness. We fail because we often follow a *dusty* path carved in the earth by those who have the same limited brain capacity as we do and who likewise fail to live righteously in equality according to their innate human conscience.

(As Lucifer speaks, he becomes angry and a storm begins to well up and the winds blow.)

LUCIFER: If thou cursest me for doing the same thing which has been done in other worlds, I will take the spirits that follow me, and they shall possess the bodies thou createst for Adam and Eve!

A natural, free-willed human tendency is to assert our independence and value as an individual apart from all others. This trait is formed and embellished when we see that others possess certain attributes or qualities that we think we do not have. In experiencing life and nurturing from Celestial Beings who possessed powers and attributes that we had not yet obtained, it naturally became our desire to have them as well. But the way to obtain them was not within our present state of being at the time. We began to conceive of shortcuts or other ways to obtain these powers and abilities within the realm of our free agency. Thus, shown figuratively here, *Lucifer* thought that he did not need any part of the Father's plan to bring happiness to himself and those who agreed to follow him.

Lucifer knew (i.e., we knew) that in all the other worlds that had been created, independent and free-willed spirits were given the right to create their own systems of laws and government that serve them. He was (we were) only doing what he (we) knew had been done throughout the Universe (in allowing the exercise of free agency) by instituting his (our) *own* plan; and which he (we) had convinced many that there was a better plan than our Creators'. It's easy to envision this way of thinking when we consider the independent and rebellious nature of teenagers. When rules of the house are established, it is natural to challenge those rules and rebel. In this way, teenagers develop self-esteem and individuality apart from their parents, who have established rules that they know are for the teenagers' own good. The only way teenagers will ever understand the significance and relevance of the established rules is to experience the consequences of *not* following them. In experiencing the consequences, only then will they be convinced that their parents were right all along.

According to the command of God just given him concerning those who follow his plan, Lucifer assumed that it would be impossible for the spirits who followed him to find a way to satisfy their fleshly "appetites" in the bodies that he caused to be created through *mortal nature*. Realizing this, Lucifer threatened to take over the bodies that were created for Adam and Eve. This again can be understood by comparison to the actions of a normal teenager. Even though (through experience) teenagers come to the conclusion that their ways do not bring them happiness, they do not want to admit defeat to their parents—this would take away the individuality established by their actions of rebellion, which actions they do not want to admit have failed to bring the expected result. Therefore, to maintain the integrity that comes through the continuity and justification of their actions, teenagers will take what their parents have established as the right thing in the first place and change it to conform to their own plan and agenda for their life.

ELOHIM: I will place enmity between thee and the seed of the woman. Thou mayest have power to bruise his heel, but he shall have power to crush thy head.

This "enmity" is our conscience, or better, the "Spirit of Christ" as spoken of by Moroni:

*Wherefore, all things which are good cometh of God; and that which is evil cometh of the devil; for the devil is an enemy unto God, and fighteth against him continually, and inviteth and enticeth to sin, and to do that which is evil continually. But behold, that which is of God inviteth and enticeth to do good continually; wherefore, everything which inviteth and enticeth to do good, and to love God, and to serve him, is inspired of God. Wherefore, take heed, my beloved brethren, that ye do not judge that which is evil to be of God, or that which is good and of God to be of the devil. For behold, my brethren, it is given unto you to judge, that ye may know good from evil; and the way to judge is as plain, that ye may know with a perfect knowledge, as the daylight is from the dark night. For behold, <u>the Spirit of Christ is given to **every** man,</u> that he may know good from evil; wherefore, I show unto you the way to judge; for every thing which inviteth to do good, and to persuade to believe in Christ, is sent forth by the power and gift of Christ; wherefore ye may know with a perfect knowledge it is of God. But whatsoever thing persuadeth men to do evil, and believe not in Christ, and deny him, and serve not God, then ye may know with a perfect knowledge it is of the devil; for after this manner doth the devil work, for he persuadeth no man to do good, no, not one; neither do his angels; neither do they who subject themselves unto him.* (Moroni 7:12–17)

Our conscience is the capability each of us has been given so that we can tell the difference between good (following the plan of our Creators, i.e., that which creates a lasting happiness) and evil (following the plan of Lucifer—or the appetites of our flesh, i.e., that which creates unhappiness).

As we "*walk*" throughout our lives and do things contrary to the prompting of our consciences (the enmity), our "*heels*" are bruised by the suffering we experience when we succumb to enticements of the flesh. However, in the end, we will *all* have power to "crush" the head (the part that controls our actions) of Lucifer by recognizing the enticements of the flesh and controlling his power over us. In the end, before we are allowed to resurrect, we will be required to bring our actions under control to such a degree that we will never be a problem to another free-willed being. The plan of our Creators in providing us with the opportunities for experience up until that time, prepares us to become this manner of person in conjunction with experiencing those things that bring each of us our individual eternal happiness.

LUCIFER: Then with that enmity I will take the treasures of the earth, and with gold and silver I will buy up armies and navies, ~~popes and~~ **false** priests **who oppress, and tyrants who destroy,** and reign with blood and horror on the earth!

Here we are given an explanation of how our flesh (Lucifer) fights our conscience (enmity) to entice us with money and worldly possessions to follow our fleshly desires (i.e., Lucifer's plan.) The way he will deceive us is further described as setting up religions and governments to impose his plan upon us. When a government or religion entices our fleshly desires of pride, glory, material prosperity and individual value apart from and above others (i.e., patriotic feelings, holding the priesthood or titles, or religious feelings of belonging to the "only true church"), it is our nature (Lucifer) which leads us to endorse and to support these institutions. Yet these human institutions (armies, navies, and organized religions) are the main causes of all the *"blood and horror on the earth!"* By changing the above words, the LDS leaders hoped to steer any significant questions away from themselves—surely *they* could not be the corruptible priests who could ever be *bought* by Lucifer. They also did not want to make any enemies of the other *Popes and Priests* with whom they share control over the hearts of humankind.

ELOHIM: Depart!

(Thunder cracks and the storm ceases as Lucifer looks defiantly at Elohim; he then turns and walks away.)

ELOHIM: Jehovah, let cherubim and a flaming sword be placed to guard the way of the Tree of Life, lest Adam **and Eve** put forth ~~his hand~~ **their hands**, and partake of the fruit thereof, and live forever in ~~his~~ **their** sins.
JEHOVAH: It shall be done, Elohim.

(Jehovah commands, and stretches his arm toward the tree. Light is shown shining through.)

JEHOVAH: Let cherubim and a flaming sword be placed to guard the way of the Tree of Life, lest Adam **and Eve** put forth ~~his hand~~ **their hands** and partake of the fruit thereof, and live forever in ~~his~~ **their** sins. It is done, Elohim.

This "*cherubim and a flaming sword*" is the veil of forgetfulness, or our inability to know more concerning the planets, solar systems, and other kingdoms of our Creators throughout the Universe. In fine, it is the symbolic representation of our inability to understand the mysteries of godliness as purposefully intended for our mortal probationary state of existence. This Veil is nothing more than the inability of the human brain to be utilized to its capacity by the spirit entity that controls it. If we are able to free up sufficient energy and brain cells through the sacrifice of worldly cares and desires, the Veil is then capable of becoming more transparent.

A "sword" has often been compared to the "word" that comes forth from the mouth of God. *Cherubim* have always been given as protectors of something sacred. The "*flaming sword*" symbolizes the refining fire of the word of God (the *real truth*, or reality) that is given by prophets and others who preach repentance to us without revealing the mysteries of God, which mysteries can only be known by the power and ministrations of the

Holy Ghost (through common sense and logic). The mysteries of God are protected from mortals who would "*put forth [their] hand and partake of the fruit thereof*" (or gain the knowledge of them), as they continue to be led by false leaders, nonsense, and irrational beliefs.

IF we really understood the true nature of our Creators, Their mercy, Their love, and Their dedication in serving us and bringing us happiness, many of us as mortals would not even try to do good, and would probably kill our mortal bodies (suicide) so as not to have to go through the problems of this life. Others would accept the state of their mortal natures and justify living contrary to what they know will bring them happiness, continually searching for that which they will never find outside themselves, accepting without reservation the promise of our Creators that our end will always be eternal peace and happiness in the kingdoms of God.

This was taught symbolically by Jesus through the parable of *The Prodigal Son*:

Likewise, I say unto you, there is joy in the presence of the angels of God over one sinner that repenteth. And he said, A certain man had two sons: And the younger of them said to his father, Father, give me the portion of goods that falleth to me. And he divided unto them his living. And not many days after the younger son gathered all together, and took his journey into a far country, and there wasted his substance with riotous living. And when he had spent all, there arose a mighty famine in that land; and he began to be in want. And he went and joined himself to a citizen of that country; and he sent him into his fields to feed swine. And he would fain have filled his belly with the husks that the swine did eat: and no man gave unto him. And when he came to himself, he said, How many hired servants of my father's have bread enough and to spare, and I perish with hunger! I will arise and go to my father, and will say unto him, Father, I have sinned against heaven, and before thee, And am no more worthy to be called thy son: make me as one of thy hired servants. And he arose, and came to his father. But when he was yet a great way off, his father saw him, and had compassion, and ran, and fell on his neck, and kissed him. And the son said unto him, Father, I have sinned against heaven, and in thy sight, and am no more worthy to be called thy son. But the father said to his servants, Bring forth the best robe, and put it on him; and put a ring on his hand, and shoes on his feet: And bring hither the fatted calf, and kill it; and let us eat, and be merry: For this my son was dead, and is alive again; he was lost, and is found. And they began to be merry. (Luke 15:10–24)

Knowing all the mysteries of God without the struggle required to understand them, would negate the purpose of our existence. We are here to experience life *outside* of the guidance, direction, and knowledge of God so that we can be enabled to conclude that the eternal plan and laws that support it is the <u>only</u> way to happiness.

The prophets, under the direction and command of Jehovah (therefore Jehovah and NOT Elohim, gives the command) are the *Cherubim* who wield the *flaming sword* and preach in parable to all mortals on the earth. It is

Jehovah who commands *true prophets* saying: *"Go, and tell this people, Hear ye indeed, but understand not; and see ye indeed, but perceive not. Make the heart of this people fat, and make their ears heavy, and shut their eyes; lest they see with their eyes, and hear with their ears, and understand with their hearts, and convert, and be healed."* (Refer to Isaiah 6:9–10.)

Ancient prophets spoke with allegories and metaphors. They did this so that subsequent editors and publishers of their writings would be limited in the ability to arrange the prophets' words in the way these editors and publishers wanted, and not necessarily how they were originally written. Furthermore, when these words were translated into various languages, the integrity of the message was again thwarted by the ineptness of translators or their own uninspired way of reading a language that was not their native tongue. It is almost impossible to translate an allegory or metaphor from its original language into another language. The original meaning is usually lost completely in the translation.

Needless to say, the scriptures are hard to understand at times because of the corrupt hand of well-intentioned mortals and the way in which the true prophets hid the real truth in parables. Presented for the first time and repeated for profundity, are the "plain and precious," correctly-translated words of Isaiah referring to how and why he was to teach the people: (The ***bold-italic*** indicates the difference from the King James Bible.)

> Go, and tell this people, Ye hear indeed, but ***ye do not*** understand; and ye see indeed, but perceive not ***that which ye see. Therefore thou shalt give unto them that for which they seek, and those things which they do not understand, for they seek to hear heavy things, and their hearts are full of excess because they desire that which maketh their ears heavy, even that which they do not understand. Preach unto them much*** and make their ears heavy ***with your preaching; yea,*** make the heart of this people fat ***in that which they desire, but*** shut their eyes ***to the truth that would heal them; For they are a fallen people who seek not the Lord to establish his righteousness so that*** they see with their eyes, and hear with their ears, and understand with their heart, and convert, and be healed. (Isaiah 6:9–10)

What Isaiah said above is the same thing as saying, "*God placed at the east of the garden of Eden cherubim, and a flaming sword which turned every way, to keep the way of the tree of life lest Adam put forth his hand and partake and live for ever in his sins.*" (Compare Genesis 3:24.) "Sin" means the "absence of happiness" in <u>every</u> instance it is used throughout the written word. It means nothing more. "The Tree of Life" means the *real truth* in every instance. It means nothing more. To experience happiness, we have to understand the absence thereof, and we cannot understand something we have not experienced. Therefore, if we were to be able to remember all truth (or partake of *the Tree of Life* as Adam was doing all along in the Garden of Eden before his fall), we would not experience an existence where this truth does *not* exist, and would thus live forever in the "absence of happiness."

The Temple Endowment was established by Joseph, that in seeing, those receiving it would not perceive, and in hearing, they would not understand. Millions participate in the temple endowment each week, yet none of these understand what they are doing and what the symbolism of the endowment actually means.

ELOHIM: ~~Eve, because thou hast hearkened to the voice of Satan, and hast partaken of the forbidden fruit and given unto Adam, I will greatly multiply thy sorrow and thy conception. In sorrow shalt thou bring forth children; nevertheless, thou mayest be preserved in childbearing. Thy desire shall be to thy husband, and he shall rule over thee in righteousness.~~ Adam, because thou ~~hast hearkened unto the voice of thy wife and~~ hast partaken of the forbidden fruit, the earth shall be cursed for thy sake. Instead of producing fruits and flowers spontaneously, it shall bring forth thorns, thistles, briars, and noxious weeds to afflict and torment man. And by the sweat of thy face shalt thou eat thy bread all the days of thy life; for dust thou art, and unto dust shalt thou return.

Once again, in order to appease the misunderstandings that most have regarding the symbolic nature of the endowment, the LDS leaders changed this part because of their own inability to understand the purpose for which it was included in the presentation in the first place.

Elohim was simply explaining the natural course of the environments that our Creators have designed for our existence. These circumstances are necessary so that we experience an opposition in all things in order that we might come to recognize and know eternal happiness. The human race (carnal man/Lucifer) has always existed in direct opposition (an enemy) to the plan of God. Everything given in this part of the endowment is given as something diametrically opposed to the happiness that God has promised to all of us.

Eve being subjected to her husband is very much in opposition to the true nature of the relationship between a Celestial Man and a Celestial Woman. A man will *never* rule over a woman, except in the fallen state in which the human race finds itself because of the mortal flesh. The Father symbolically "punishes" Eve for partaking of the fruit by changing her eternal status of absolute equality to that of being subject to the will of her husband. Similarly, referring to the curse given to Adam, the way that God provides for our necessities was changed in contrast to the wonderful blessing it truly would be to have everything provided for us without work, stress, and anxiety.

In the kingdoms of God, all things are provided for us without toil or worry, and women are very much equal to, if not more exalted in their natures, than men. These are the blessings of God that Adam and Eve (who represent all of us) gave up when they entered into mortality to experience a state of existence without the laws of God and the blessings that come from abiding by perfect eternal laws.

We should now understand the great symbolism of the *Garden of Eden*. Though there *was* a place where the very first bodies were created from the elements of this earth by Advanced Human Beings, the prophets could not reveal this mystery of God to the people for their own sake. Therefore, they used the symbolism of the *Garden of Eden* as the time when we dwelt in the presence of our Creators and were taught by Them. The "Garden of Eden" represents both instances when we existed in Their presence: The first instance was before we entered into mortality. This is also known in Mormon dogma as our "preexistence." However, this is not actually correct because we did not *exist* before our existence. We existed in the state of newly-created spirits encased in perfected bodies long before we became mortal. Therefore, a more correct term would be "pre-mortal" state. Mortality is generally described as an existence where we are left to ourselves without Divine intervention and where we experience "death" juxtaposed to Eternal Life. The second instance in which the term "Garden of Eden" is used, is when the first human beings upon this earth lived for a relatively short period of time with Celestial Beings as they were raised to adulthood and taught the proper way to live and associate with each other.

Throughout the commentary of this book, the term "Garden of Eden" will be used to mean the time we lived with and were instructed by Celestial Beings. In essence, it is the return to this "Garden of Eden," this paradise, which we seek all the days of our lives. We hope for, imagine, and desire a time when we will once again live in a state of peace and everlasting happiness where equality and love reign supreme. We are looking to return home. This desire comes from deep inside our hearts, or better, embedded in the secret but real realm of our subconscious mind, where our memories of these experiences will remain with us forever.

As the reader continues with this commentary, it will make sense if whenever the "Garden of Eden" is mentioned, one makes a mental reference to the time period we lived with our Creators. Whether that time was on Their Celestialized planet or upon this earth in the figurative *Garden of Eden* where Adam and Eve are introduced, the most important thing to keep in mind is that we once dwelt with Them and were taught and received the proper foundation required of a free-willed human being. Living among Them in the *Garden of Eden* (in either instance) we established our human conscience.

4
THE FIRST SACRIFICE

THE LAW OF OBEDIENCE
To Our Creators' Eternal Plan

ELOHIM: Inasmuch as Eve was the first to eat of the forbidden fruit, if she will covenant that from this time forth she will obey ~~your law in the Lord~~ **the law of the Lord** and will hearken unto your counsel as you hearken unto mine, and if you will covenant that from this time forth you will obey the Law of Elohim, we will give unto you the Law of Obedience and Sacrifice, and we will provide a Savior for you, whereby you may come back into our presence, and with us partake of Eternal Life and exaltation.

EVE: Adam, I now covenant to obey ~~your law as you obey our Father~~ **the law of the Lord and to hearken to your counsel as you hearken unto Father.**

ADAM: Elohim, I now covenant with thee that from this time forth I will obey thy law and keep thy commandments.

This part of the endowment symbolizes our acceptance of the plan of our Creators (Elohim) when we lived with Them in the "Garden of Eden," the symbolism of this garden having been explained previously as our existence in the presence of our Creators. It was there that most of us used our free agency and concurred with and supported the eternal plan that incorporates the laws which govern this Universe. We entered into this covenant by our own choice after having the plan presented to us. This covenant, often referred to as the "Covenant of the Father," promised us eternal joy if we followed the plan. As previously indicated in the figurative presentation, *Lucifer* and those who would not covenant to follow the plan, used their own free agency to devise a compromise to the universal and eternal laws. These were figuratively "cast out." This term is grossly misunderstood and misapplied by those unaccustomed to the manner in which true prophets communicate. Being "cast out" merely means that "Lucifer and his followers" (i.e., those who follow the natural course of the appetites of the flesh and choose to act contrary to the laws that create peace, equality, and happiness) would not be allowed to exist in any part of the kingdom of God. In other words, they refuse to submit to the eternal laws that maintain consistent order and have existed forever in every part of the Universe—worlds without end.

This part of the presentation of the endowment symbolizes a free-willed being's acceptance of the eternal plan, which mandates leaving the planet on which we were created and experienced the perfection of following these eternal laws. The plan requires us to come to a new solar system where the Gods would not be around to enforce the rules for a time ("resting from their labors") in order to allow us to experience what life is like without these laws. We knew from being taught by our Eternal Parents that this part of the plan would bring us misery, pain, and sorrow. We also knew that we would have to leave the security of our first home and come to this one in order to adequately prove to ourselves who we truly are and what makes us happy. By exercising our free agency and being allowed to see the progression of other worlds and the free-willed choices made by their inhabitants, it became quite clear to most of us that we would *not* end up like our Celestial parents, but would discover that other degrees of happiness suited our individual needs.

As free-willed beings, we had the choice. No one forced us to accept the plan as outlined, nor can it ever be forced upon us. Those who choose not to follow the plan will be "cut off from the kingdom of God" forever and cannot progress eternally; or in other words, because of their choice, they cannot be trusted to exist among other free-willed beings without causing problems that impede continued peace and happiness forever.

The term "cut off" has reference to the *first penalty* described in the endowment, which is indicated by being "cut off at the head." The head symbolizes the entire kingdom of God and all of its glory, powers, and the desires of happiness for those who exist there. This is represented in giving the first **penalty** (the consequences of the works) associated with the **name** (the works), the **token** (the capacity in which these works are performed), and the **sign** (the demonstration of these works) of the first great covenant made between Celestial Creators and those whom They created in Their own image.

A covenant is a binding promise wherein each party receives a desired result in consideration for fulfilling their part of an agreement. The words "covenant" and "law" are sometimes used interchangeably in the English language, in which language the presentation of the endowment was given by Joseph Smith. A covenant can also be described as "the common-law action to recover damages for breach of such a contract." Therefore, the covenants we make with God assure us that we will receive the blessing (that which was promised) or the punishment (as a result of the breach of the contract) stipulated in the law or covenant. If we keep the law, we will be led to the *land of promise* and prosper therein (always symbolically representing the enjoyment of eternal happiness in the kingdom of God).

As the endowment progresses, we will learn that each covenant made is symbolic of the conditions set forth by our Creators in order to inherit a degree of glory in the kingdom of God, or better, a planet in this solar system. The eternal promise will always be fulfilled as long as we fulfill our part.

Our Creators do not force Their will on anyone, nor can They force any of us to obey the laws that we accepted and became a party to upon covenanting to obey them (the covenants). According to the terms of the covenant that we enter into, we receive one thing, and They receive something else. In return for Their promise, the Gods receive nothing more than the same joy (increased 100-fold) that all mortal parents feel when they watch their children open Christmas presents and receive the gift that they asked for and expected. In other words, what our Creators receive when we keep our covenants with Them is the mere joy of knowing that we are receiving what we were promised. We were promised eternal joy.

NO PART of our Merciful Creators' purposes or plans in our creation and existence includes punishment for any form of life that is created. How can we be punished for using the very agency afforded us to seek our individual happiness? By nature of our creation, we have the ability to choose (reflected symbolically by giving Adam and Even the choice to partake or not to partake of the *Tree* that the Gods planted), and we were taught the consequences of our choices ("nevertheless, thou mayest choose for thyself, for it is given unto thee. But remember that I forbid it; for in the day thou eatest thereof, thou shalt surely die"). The Gods knew that the environment in which we were allowed to exist without Their intervention would allow the freedom and opportunity for us to disobey the laws instituted for our sake. Therefore, it would not seem right and proper that the Gods would create us so that They could punish us for doing that which They *expected* us to do.

We were created so that we might have joy, not punishment. Nevertheless, before we covenanted to obey the eternal laws, it was explained to us that there were varying degrees of happiness (the state of joy for which we were created) that would be provided for us, and that certain restrictions were associated with all but one of these states or degrees of happiness. These restrictions would be *penalties*, or the sum to be forfeited, to which each of us willingly agreed to be subjected. These penalties did not really seem like a negative thing to us when the restrictions were described to us in our pre-mortal state by our Creators. We accepted that we were all different individuals with completely unique ways of experiencing happiness. As we learned the differences in our general dispositions in our first estate, we could see that the different degrees in the kingdom of God would each have its own equally immeasurable happiness pertaining to it. For example, those whose desire for happiness is to be served by others forever (Telestial) could not imagine what kind of joy a Celestial life of endless servitude could possibly afford those who made that particular kingdom their choice, and vice-versa. In our pre-mortal state, each of us arrived at an exact determination of who we are *not;* and therefore, what others had, which we would then have to forfeit, did not seem like a bad thing at all. When we made the determination in which degree of glory our happiness was found, we were given the choice to proceed towards that end, being completely aware of the scope and limitations of the restrictions or forfeitures surrounding our choice. The covenant we made with our Creators was to do what would be necessary to find happiness for ourselves, while They provided the means to accomplish this.

Unlike modern LDS understanding, there is no inequality in the *kingdoms of God*. There is no "higher" or more glorified degree. The *Celestial* kingdom provides the exact same joy to its inhabitants as do the *Telestial* and

Terrestrial kingdoms. They are simply degrees of responsibility, happiness, and chosen desires granted to free-willed beings according to their free agency to choose—nothing more, nothing less. The guilt and pressure placed on the LDS member to attain what they refer to as the "Highest Kingdom; i.e., the Celestial Kingdom, has caused continued misery and sorrow among them. It has adversely affected the way they treat other people. They believe that unless a person is "Celestial," he or she is not counted worthy or equal with those who are. Many non-LDS mothers and fathers are kept from attending LDS marriages performed inside the walls of the temples because they are not "worthy" (of worth). How a son or daughter can exclude his or her parents from witnessing this traditionally family-oriented union is evidence of the hypocrisy and inequality promoted by this false LDS doctrine and perception. Joseph Smith never taught this, and most certainly, neither did Jesus Christ. Brigham Young incorporated this inequality and perversion of eternal truth into his own doctrines, which, upon close examination, were largely set up to take away the free agency of his followers; ironically, much like the LDS member believes that a beguiling Lucifer tried to do in the pre-mortal existence.

Upon "agreement" to the stipulations of the covenant that we made with our Creators, we also "agreed" that if we failed to meet those stipulations, we would "suffer the penalty" associated with not having certain powers and abilities that are restricted to other degrees of happiness. As mentioned above, this is NOT a punishment, because we have *chosen for ourselves* which place we accept for our individual desires of happiness, which **include** any stipulations and restrictions placed on the happiness that we desire. The truth is, we would not be happy with, nor would we need or be able to handle, anything associated to another place of happiness that we have not chosen for ourselves.

The kingdoms of glory, or rather, the degrees of happiness, are provided for us to fulfill the purpose for our creation (that we might have joy). They are figuratively divided into nine (9) basic degrees. As part of the temple clothing, the apron (as mentioned before) is an expression of the varying degrees of happiness given to each of us according to our works. For this reason, the apron always has nine (9) leaves embroidered thereon.

The degrees of glory all have penalties affixed to them, except for one—the Celestial glory, in which no penalty is given. As the presentation of the endowment progresses, one will begin to understand how important the *names*, *signs*, *tokens*, and *penalties* are to understanding the message of the endowment. Again, it is important to keep in mind exactly what these things represent:

The **penalty** (the consequences of our works) is associated with the **name** (our works), the **token** (the capacity in which we perform works), and the **sign** (the demonstration of these works). Always remember that there is no penalty given by a God who cannot do anything that would curtail our individual happiness. *Our choices* determine our works (our **name**), which determine the consequences (**penalty**) thereof.

When the LDS Church took out the penalties, they nullified the covenants and should have removed all of the associated covenants from the endowment. The covenants with their **names**, **tokens**, **signs,** and **penalites** are inseparably and symbolically tied together and cannot be dissected according to the doctrines and precepts of men.

Had the leaders of the LDS Church properly understood the true meaning of their symbolism beyond the temporal and literal sense of their appearance, they would have realized their great importance to a proper presentation of the endowment.

As we experience the sources of joy that we receive with a body of flesh (*Lucifer*), they are in direct contrast to the stipulations of our Creators' plan and lead many of us to "rebel." We begin to think that this eternal plan of "degrees of glory" is not fair. Our flesh (Lucifer) encourages us to think that ALL of us, being created by no choice of our own, should be given all of the blessings, powers, and glory of our Creators. In other words, that we should ALL be inheritors of the Celestial kingdom and benefit from the blessings one receives in this kingdom *without* any *penalties*. Lucifer makes a good case, which will not be discussed herein, as the endowment is a presentation of the Father's plan, and not Lucifer's. However, eventually upon understanding Lucifer's plan, the Father's plan will make that much more sense. Nevertheless, to teach the eternal plan of our Creators as intended by the endowment and to not distract from its beauty and glory, *Lucifer's plan* will only be touched upon incidentally in the course of this commentary. If one desires to know and understand Lucifer's plan, one simply has to give in completely to the desires of the flesh in every way and the fruits of *his* plan will abundantly manifest themselves. There will be great amounts of temporary joy in following *his* plan, but no lasting and constant happiness will be possible. It's like the difference between eating an apple and a candy bar: one will bring you immense temporary pleasure that in the long run will produce misery, and the other will bring you lasting health and happiness.

ELOHIM: It is well, ~~Adam~~. Jehovah, inasmuch as Adam and Eve have discovered their nakedness, make coats of skins as a covering for them.

JEHOVAH: It shall be done, Elohim.

(At this point the film pauses and the lights come on.)

NARRATOR (Jehovah): Brethren and sisters, the garment ~~which~~ **that** was placed upon you in the washing room is to cover your nakedness and represents the coat of skins spoken of. ~~Anciently it was made of skins. You have received the garment, also your New Name. The officiator will represent Elohim at the altar.~~

It is well to take note that Elohim instructs Adam and Eve to be clothed in a "coat of skins" to cover their *nakedness*, whereas Lucifer told them to make themselves aprons from the leaves grown in the *Garden of Eden* (in order to "hide" the same nakedness from Elohim and Jehovah). This is symbolic of what was described above as Lucifer attempting to persuade us to *not* follow the eternal plan that all free-willed beings must follow (i.e., the *War in Heaven*). The leaves taken from the *Garden of Eden* represent our effort to provide a way to escape the *penalties* of not being a Celestial human. The greatest penalty being that we will never be able to experience sex, the strongest of our fleshly (Lucifer) desires. The leaves of the tree figuratively represent our knowledge of the eternal plan, or rather, an understanding of all things that happened in our pre-mortal life; as partaking of the fruit of the trees is the nourishment (knowledge and experience) that constituted our experience there. With this knowledge, we make an attempt to beat the consequences affixed to the eternal laws by which our Creators live and operate.

The purpose of the eternal laws is to help us experience the most profound sense of joy possible. This can never be done by wearing an "apron" made of the leaves provided by the trees of the *Garden of Eden*. The only way it can be done is to provide us with an imperfect body. This will help us appreciate and recognize the grand design and immortality of the type of body we had in our pre-mortal state. This imperfect body is the mortal flesh and bone in which we reside presently upon the earth.

The *garment* spoken of here represents the body of flesh and bone that we received upon our entrance into mortality in this world as it has been explained. In a figurative sense, Lucifer and his followers chose not to follow the plan of the Father; therefore, they chose not to take a body that God originally created for Adam and Eve, meaning that by use of their free agency, they desired to exist contrary to our Creators' eternal plan. *Lucifer*, or better, those who thought they knew a better way to experience happiness than that outlined in the plan of the Father, was allowed to inhabit other bodies of flesh and bone. These are the *Homo sapiens* bodies, which are the only other bodies in the animal kingdom that can support the elements that make up our spirits. The symbolism of a "coat of skins" indicates that our mortal bodies are made up of the exact same elements of which other animals' bodies are made. Throughout our mortal existence, each of us will experience the effects of a "*Homo sapiens*" body. Yes, all of us will live as black, white, and every race and color in between; this to assure our equality and perfect our understanding of what it is like to live in an imperfect body.

It is vital to a perfect understanding of how things really are (the truth) to know *why* the Gods allowed nature to run its own course upon this earth without intervening with Their advanced technology and controlling every aspect of creation, the natural environs, and the effects of nature. The earth could very well have been created in a matter of days and provided with the advanced technology and lifestyle of the Gods. Yet, how would we ever experience an understanding of what nature would do if it was left to its own discretion, if we had the "Technology and Understanding of the Gods" from the beginning to circumvent it?

Part of the ego of all human beings is that we do not like to be controlled or told what we have to do. We choose democracy over a dictatorship and are wont to believe that *our* way is the *right* way. However, wherever free-willed beings exist in the Universe, there are no democracies, except on those planets experiencing their probative *second estate* (mortality). And on these planets where there are democracies, there are always wars and chaos. The Universe is controlled and order is maintained through a righteous dictatorship of Gods, who know what They are doing and control all aspects of creation and progression. This is how it has always been. This is how it will always be. Can you imagine what our Universe would be like if its government was put up for reelection each year? Not only would there be many free-willed beings who would think they could do a better job and become powerful government officials supporting their own plans, but those who *really* serve would be treated like those who serve in all democracies of the present world—the lower class, maids, servants, slaves, and underpaid employees. There is little joy in democracies for the servants. Yet it is the servants who become the Eternal Gods of this Universe. They deserve happiness too; therefore, all power and authority resides in Their dictatorship over others. The difference is, Their authority is a righteous, selfless dictatorship. Can one imagine the transformation current governments would go through if there were no more leaders, but instead servants of the people's needs?

Human experience has appropriately concluded that nature left to itself would be the author of its own demise. The end of nature would not occur if all aspects of it were precisely controlled. Nevertheless, nature in and of itself did pretty well alone until free-willed beings were introduced into it. Outside of human beings, all other parts of the natural world are strictly instinctual, having no awareness of themselves apart from their environs, and do not have the ability to reason. It wasn't until humans came along with their non-instinctual propensities that the course of nature was drastically changed. Since the time that these "wise ones" (which is the literal meaning of *Homo sapiens*) were allowed to understand and use some of the "Technology and Understanding of the Gods," they (we) have *really* messed up nature.

ELOHIM: A couple will now come to the altar.

(A pre-selected witness couple now comes forward and kneels at the altar, resting their hands upon it as they face the officiator. The officiator pantomimes all movements and gestures as a model for the patrons to follow when directed.)

NARRATOR (Elohim): Brethren and sisters, this couple ~~at the altar~~ represents all of you as if at the altar. You must consider yourselves as if you were, respectively, Adam and Eve.

While Adam and Eve represent each of us as males and females, respectively, more importantly, the figurative nature of the presentation of the endowment teaches us that the use of these terms extends beyond the specificity of the representation of gender. *Eve* represents the flesh ("the mother of all living"), as all things that are alive in mortality must have flesh. *Adam* represents our spirit, or our connection to our Creator, personifying the Being who was presented as Michael, a member of the Godhead. With intended purpose, Eve (the flesh) is put under commandment to obey Adam (the spirit); therefore, the terms bear a genderless relationship and are thereby used in association with everyone who comes into mortality on this earth. Part of our covenant with the Father, or better, the way that we go about experiencing happiness, is to bring the flesh under control of the spirit and not let it overpower us. Indeed, the spirit is willing, but the flesh is weak. Thus, to fulfill the covenant (to find happiness), we must learn to subject the flesh to the will of the spirit.

ELOHIM: We will put ~~the sisters~~ **each sister** under covenant to obey the law of ~~their husbands~~ the Lord, and to hearken to the counsel of her husband, as her husband hearkens unto the counsel of the Father. Sisters, arise.

(Female patrons stand as instructed.)

ELOHIM: Each of you bring your right arm to the square. You and each of you solemnly covenant and promise before God, angels, and these witnesses at this altar that you will each observe and keep the law of ~~your husband and abide by his counsel in righteousness,~~ the Lord, and hearken unto the counsel of your husband as he hearkens unto the counsel of the Father. Each of you bow your head and say, "Yes."
WOMEN: Yes.
ELOHIM: That will do.

(The female patrons now resume their seats.)

The modern LDS Church once again succumbed to outside pressure, not understanding the real purpose and symbolism of the endowment. All that was symbolized by the woman covenanting to obey her husband was that this was the "punishment" of entering mortality (as explained above), where the female (the flesh) is weaker by nature than the male (the spirit). This also was meant to symbolize the dependence the woman has on the male for her sustenance, protection, and ability to have children; just as the flesh is dependent on the spirit for sustaining our individuality and lifting us up in emotional times of need. This temporal order of mortal nature does not exist in the kingdom of God, wherein those Celestial Beings who are male and female are instead very *equal* in power, knowledge, and glory.

The analogy of Adam being to Eve as the spirit is to the body, respectively, is similar to what Abinadi said to express how the Father (the spirit) and the Son (the flesh) are the same Being:

> *And now Abinadi said unto them: I would that ye should understand that God himself shall come down among the children of men, and shall redeem his people. And because he dwelleth in flesh he shall be called the Son of God, and having subjected the flesh to the will of the Father, being the Father and the Son—The Father, because he was conceived by the power of God; and the Son, because of the flesh; thus becoming the Father and Son—And they are one God, yea, the very*

Eternal Father of heaven and of earth. **And thus the flesh becoming subject to the Spirit, or the Son to the Father, being one God** ("Eve" becoming subject to "Adam"), *suffereth temptation, and yieldeth not to the temptation, but suffereth himself to be mocked, and scourged, and cast out, and disowned by his people.* (Mosiah 15:1–5)

ELOHIM: Brethren, arise.

(Male patrons stand as instructed.)

ELOHIM: Each of you bring your right arm to the square. You and each of you solemnly covenant and promise before God, angels, and these witnesses at this altar that you will obey the law of God and keep his commandments. Each of you bow your head and say, "Yes."
MEN: Yes.
ELOHIM: That will do.

(Male patrons resume their seats.)

Thus has the **Law of Obedience** ("obey the law of God") been presented figuratively to all of us.

THE LAW OF SACRIFICE
Our First Sacrifice

Though relevant, in this instance "sacrifice" does not mean just giving up something of value, but also indicates an offering to do something *sacr*ed. The root word is from "*sacr*ificium," the same Latin word used for sacred and *sacr*ament, which means to "consecrate" or dedicate to a *sacr*ed purpose all of your thoughts and actions. The sacrifice we make is "in similitude" to the sacrifice that Christ made, him being an example of the perfect and *Ultimate Sacrifice*. The Law of Sacrifice means doing exactly as Christ did. It is what is presented to Nephi as "the condescension of God":

And it came to pass that I looked and beheld that great city of Jerusalem, and also other cities. And I beheld the city of Nazareth; and in the city of Nazareth I beheld a virgin, and she was exceedingly fair and white. And it came to pass that I saw the heavens open; and an angel came down and stood before me; and he said unto me: Nephi, what beholdest thou? And I said unto him: A virgin, most beautiful and fair above all other virgins. And he said unto me: Knowest thou the condescension of God? And I said unto him: I know that he loveth his children; nevertheless, I do not know the meaning of all things. And he said unto me: Behold, the virgin whom thou seest is the mother of the son of God, after the manner of the flesh. (1 Nephi 11:13–18)

We make "a condescension" by sacrificing the peaceful, perfect state of our pre-mortal existence with our Creators to come to this earth and be born "after the manner of the flesh," just as Christ did. The **Law of Sacrifice** is given in connection with the **Law of Obedience** (both are given in unison by Elohim above in the presentation of the endowment) because when we accept to enter into mortality, we are <u>obeying</u> the eternal laws. In the flesh, Jesus showed us how to sacrifice all that we are to will of the Father. He showed us how to live our lives so that we are ONE with the Father in all things. Simply stated: When we lived with our Eternal Parents in Their solar system, we were taught all that we needed to know and do to be happy. The purpose in obeying (*Law of Obedience*) the **Law of Sacrifice** is in giving up this *perfect* life to experience mortality. Christ's *ultimate sacrifice* is in doing the same thing, but he offers a greater sacrifice in that he gives up his status as a God (he having been created as a God; whereas we must prove ourselves worthy of the power) to reside in mortality. His life demonstrates how a God would act in the flesh. Not only did he go through every vicissitude, including murder, equated to misery in this life, but he forgave *all* things done against him, showing us an example of what we should do to each other in order to fulfill the eternal laws that create peace and harmony among us.

ELOHIM: Brethren and sisters, ~~you are about to be put~~ **we will now put you** under covenant to obey and keep the Law of Sacrifice, as contained in the ~~Old and New Testaments~~ **Holy Scriptures**. This Law of Sacrifice was given to Adam in the Garden of Eden, who, when he was driven out of the garden, built an altar on which he offered sacrifices. And after many days, an angel of the Lord appeared unto Adam, saying, "Why dost thou offer ~~sacrifice~~ **sacrifices** unto the Lord?" ~~And~~ Adam said ~~unto him~~, "I know not, save the Lord commanded me." And then the angel spake saying, "This ~~thing~~ is a similitude of the sacrifice of the Only Begotten of the Father, which is full of grace and truth. Wherefore, thou shalt do all that thou doest in the name of the Son, and thou shalt repent, and call upon God in the name of the Son forevermore."

Inasmuch as Adam did as he was commanded, this "similitude" is symbolic of submitting our own lives after the manner of the example of Christ (Jehovah), whom the Father has assigned to be the leader of this solar system. Christ is "full of grace and truth." This means that he knows all that we need to do that will bring us back to an eternal situation where we will live as our Creators live, or as exalted Beings who eternally experience happiness. As always, doing all that we do in the "name of the Son" is symbolic of us patterning our works after his; therefore, we are given to understand that we must obey (the *Law of Obedience and Sacrifice*) the words of

Christ and follow his example in all things. If he had to come to this earth and subject himself to the vicissitudes of mortality, then so do we. The example he would have us follow is that he loved both his neighbor, friend, and enemy as himself, and always did unto others as he would have them do unto him…in all things.

Those members of the LDS faith (though few they may be) who study the scriptures in the Old and New Testaments, are prone to find passages in them that contradict the modern doctrine and precepts of their leaders. They are taught to accept the scriptures as the "never-changing word of God," which leaves many Mormon students of scriptures confused by these contradictions. To avoid disuptation and to rectify and conform their "modern-day revelation" with the "word of God," the leaders changed the reference to the books of the Bible to include all the "Holy Scriptures," which the members are taught *include* all the words and teachings (modern-day revelation) of their current leaders.

ELOHIM: The posterity of Adam down to Moses, and from Moses to Jesus Christ, offered up the firstfruits of the field, and the firstlings of the flock, which continued until the death of Jesus Christ, which ended sacrifice by the shedding of blood. And as Jesus Christ has laid down his life for the redemption of mankind, so we should covenant to sacrifice all that we possess, even our own lives if necessary, in sustaining and defending the Kingdom of God.
ELOHIM: All arise.

(All patrons stand as instructed.)
ELOHIM: Each of you bring your right arm to the square. You and each of you solemnly covenant and promise before God, angels, and these witnesses at this altar that you will observe and keep the Law of Sacrifice, as contained in the ~~Old and New Testaments~~ Holy Scriptures, as it has been explained to you. Each of you bow your head and say, "Yes."
PATRONS: Yes.
ELOHIM: That will do.

(Patrons resume their seats.)

This is in reference to the atonement of Jesus Christ, which is the sacrifice that he made in giving us his perfect example by taking upon himself the *same* flesh that we did, and showing us that it is possible to be in the flesh (subject to Lucifer) and still obey the will of the Father (submit to the will of our *common sense*). This part of the endowment figuratively occurred in the kingdom of our Creators (the Garden of Eden), where we all lived as newly-created, free-willed beings before coming to this solar system and taking upon us mortal and corruptible flesh and bone (putting on our garments of skins as described above concerning Adam and Eve). This was all part of the plan that was presented to our newly-created spirits, and will become clearly evident as the **name**, **sign**, **token**, and **penalty** accompanying this **Law of Sacrifice** are explained below.

At that time, *all of us* who would eventually come to this planet to experience mortality followed the plan and supported the election of Christ to be our God and to direct all things in this solar system. Our agreement by covenant to this plan and to the conditions of mortality is symbolically represented in the endowment by each of us bowing our heads in submission and saying, "Yes."

THE FIRST TOKEN OF THE AARONIC PRIESTHOOD

ELOHIM: We will now give unto you the First Token of the Aaronic Priesthood with its accompanying name, **and** sign, ~~and penalty~~. Before doing this, however, we desire to impress upon your minds the sacred character of the First Token of the Aaronic Priesthood, with its accompanying name, **and** sign, ~~and penalty,~~ as well as that of all other tokens of the Holy Priesthood, with their names, **and** signs, ~~and penalties,~~ which you will receive in the temple this day. They are most sacred, and are guarded by solemn covenants and obligations ~~of secrecy to the effect that~~ **made in the presence of God, angels, and these witnesses, to hold them sacred;** and under no condition, ~~even at the peril of your life,~~ will you ever divulge them, except at a certain place **in the temple** that will be shown you ~~hereafter. The representation of the execution of the penalties indicates different ways in which life may be taken~~.

This part of the endowment was given to impress upon our minds the importance of keeping the covenants. "Even at the peril of your life" further emphasizes the **Law of Sacrifice** as it has just been explained (meaning we give up our perfect bodies and lives of peace and happiness and agree to come to mortality). As indicated by what the LDS Church in ignorance deleted, *"the representation of the execution of the penalties indicates different ways in which life may be taken."* This means that each penalty represents the limitations for each of us in the kingdom of glory that we choose for ourselves—this glory being the "life" that we each will experience (*the "different ways* [or paths] *in which life may be taken"*) for all eternity. Even as we go through mortality, each of us is choosing each day the "different ways in which (our) life (is being) taken."

ELOHIM: The First Token of the Aaronic Priesthood is given by clasping the right hands and placing the joint of the thumb upon the first nuckle **(between the first and second knuckles)** of the hand, in this manner.

(The officiator, representing Elohim, takes the right hand of the male witness (who represents Adam) at the altar, and demonstrates the token. The male witness, who remains kneeling, is obliged to raise his hand above his head while receiving the grip, thus enabling the patrons to view the manner in which the token is to be given.)

ELOHIM: Adam, we give unto you the First Token of the Aaronic Priesthood. We desire all to receive it. All arise.

(As the patrons stand, the witness couple returns to their seats. The officiator and several other temple workers circulate around the room and administer the token to the patrons as they stand at their seats. Male workers attend to the male patrons, female workers to the females. The witness couple also receives the token at this time. Each patron sits after receiving the token.)

ELOHIM: If any of you have not received this token, you will please raise your hand. *(Pause.)*

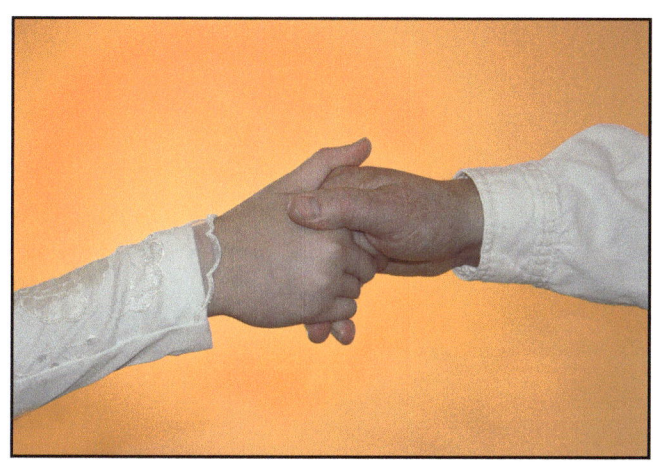

This is where a major error has crept into the presentation of the endowment: the *First* and *Second Tokens of the Aaronic Priesthood* have been switched. The *First Token* should be given by clasping the right hands and placing the joint of the thumb *between* the first and second knuckles of the hand. This token represents the creation of our *spirits*, which spirits (in composition) are devoid of flesh and bone. The placement of the thumb upon the bone (first knuckle) should not occur until that part of the endowment in which we symbolically receive a body of flesh *and bone* in conjunction with the *Second Token of the Aaronic Priesthood* in the Telestial World, which represents mortality.

The use of the thumb is also very important in receiving these tokens, because the human being is the only animal in the primate world that can use its thumb, representing symbolically that humans are the *only* animals that receive a different spirit entity than that which the laws of nature provide for all other animals upon earth. We are the offspring of Gods; all other animals are not. We have free agency, whereas animals are preprogrammed to act instinctually. This will be covered at greater length later as the order and purpose of nature is more fully explained.

This *First Token* is given to all those present in the endowment session, and it is further ascertained and confirmed that all patrons have received it, symbolic that all of us have received a *spirit*.

ELOHIM: The name of this token is the New Name that you received in the temple today. If any of you have forgotten the New Name, please stand. *(Pause.)*

The "New Name" of this token is symbolic of one's works or experience as a newly-created spirit; thus, it is always represented by the actual name of an honored person who is believed to be residing in the *spirit* world. The temple officiators have a list of names that they give on certain days. For example, all of those who went through a particular booth in the Salt Lake Temple where one received the "New Name" on December 2, 1961, were given the name, "Enoch." If one forgets his or her *New Name*, all they would have to remember is the exact date that they received their first endowment and the temple workers can look it up. The name "Adam" is given as a generic *New Name* if the patron already has the same earthly name as the one assigned for that particular day. This is because *Adam*, who was figuratively introduced in the beginning of the endowment as Michael, remains in the spirit world as the Holy Ghost, and represents all of us as members of the Godhead. (Always keep in mind that all these things are figurative and represent some greater understanding that will be unfolded as we proceed in the endowment.)

Unfortunately, each LDS member who receives a "New Name"—that they are threatened never to reveal to another—does not realize that there are literally tens of thousands of others who are alive, and many more who are dead, who have the exact same *New Name*. There is nothing sacred, secret, or necessary about it. It is simply a figurative representation.

(The officiator, again at the altar, demonstrates the sign ~~and penalty~~ as the descriptions below are given.)

ELOHIM: The sign is made by bringing the right arm to the square, the palm of the hand to the front, the fingers close together, and the thumb extended. This is the sign.

The right arm in the raised position is the eternal sign of agreement in righteousness. When one is chosen for ordination or for a calling to a position in the LDS church, the congregation is asked to acknowledge the ordination by uplifting the right arm to the square, thus sustaining the person who has been called. In our existence as newly created spirits, all of us who accepted the plan of the Father similarly sustained the ordination of Jehovah (thereby showing acceptance for the *Law of Obedience* and the *Law of Sacrifice*) as our God and our leader for mortality, the second estate of our existence. Those who did not accept the plan of the Father and sustain the chosen Jehovah as their leader, thus "reveal the *token*" by their refusal; which means they will receive the associated *penalty* as a consequence. In other words, they will have no part in the kingdom of God and are "cut off" as it has been explained previously.

It should be given here that all of the spirit beings created on the planet of our Eternal Parents came to this solar system. However, not all of them accepted the plan of the Father and agreed to support it. With great mercy, the Creator allowed those rebellious ones to come here and participate in mortality. After doing so, if they still reject the plan and believe there is a better way, even after experiencing mortality for themselves, they will be subjected to what is known as "the Second Death." This is when the Creator who gave them the ability to have and record experience as a spirit according to free will, disassembles the spirit. It is at this time that the realization of the "penalty" will be given. However, it is not really a *penalty* because these will no longer exist to experience anything; therefore, they are mercifully not punished at all.

Again, the **penalty** for not accepting the plan of the Father and His Son as our God (the *Law of Obedience* and the *Law of Sacrifice*) is that a person will be "cut off" from the kingdom of God forever. The kingdom of God is represented by the head, which is later covered by the temple hat for males and a veil for females. The temple hat has three (3) distinct ribbons on its side representing the Father (the *Celestial* kingdom), the Son (the *Terrestrial* kingdom), and the Holy Ghost (the *Telestial* kingdom). A string extends from the hat to a shoulder applet on the temple robe (or Robes of the Priesthood), which represents "revelation" and a line of authority from the kingdom of God given to those who are worthy and ordained to receive it. This is not limited *only* to those "ordained" in the LDS church, but the symbolic representation of "revelation" is available to all those who have been *washed* and *anointed* to become Priests and Priestesses, i.e., all of us. Joseph Smith did not introduce the term "priesthood" until much later after the organization of the Church. What eventually became known as the *Melchezedek Priesthood* was first called, "The Holy Order After The Son of God," and all who chose to follow Christ, male and female, belonged to this "order" of people. It wasn't until other early church leaders pestered and then persuaded Joseph to incorporate roles of leadership that the term "priesthood" was used.

The **penalty** received by those who do not keep their first estate is executed in such manner (indicated by the deleted words above) as to represent cutting the string and severing oneself from the kingdom of God, thereby signifying the end of one's ability to progress into the eternal kingdoms of God because they are cut off from the kingdom forever.

Of course, with the changes made by the modern LDS Church, this penalty is no longer given; therefore, they have done exactly what Lucifer desired in the first place: i.e., remove the penalties so that *all* might have a Celestial glory, which is the *only* glory of concern to the LDS Church. Along with the blessings that he falsely promises, Lucifer imposes arduous standards and responsibilities on his followers—to justify that they have properly *earned* his blessings and promise through giving service and glory to him, and to delude them into believing that they will ascend to the Celestial Kingdom. No other church upon the face of the earth presents Lucifer's plan in its fullness with such deceptive similarities to the plan of the Father as does the modern LDS Church.

~~**ELOHIM:** The execution of the penalty is represented by placing the thumb under the left ear, the palm of the hand down, and by drawing the thumb quickly across the throat to the right ear and dropping the hand to the side.~~

ELOHIM: I will now explain the covenant and obligation ~~of secrecy~~ which are associated with this token, its name, and sign, ~~and penalty,~~ which you will be required to take upon yourselves. If I were receiving my own endowment today, and had been given the name of "John" as my New Name, I would repeat in my mind these words after making the sign *(officiator makes the sign)*, ~~at the same time representing the execution of the penalty:~~

I, John, covenant **before God, angels, and these witnesses,** that I will never reveal the First Token of the Aaronic Priesthood, with its accompanying name, **and** sign, ~~and penalty. Rather than do so, I would suffer my life to be taken~~. ~~(The officiator demonstrates the execution of the penalty.)~~

ELOHIM: All arise.
(All patrons stand.)

ELOHIM: Each of you make the sign of the First Token of the Aaronic Priesthood, by bringing your right arm to the square, the palm of the hand to the front, the fingers together, and the thumb extended *(officiator makes the sign)*. This is the sign. Now, repeat in your mind after me the words of the covenant, ~~at the same time representing the execution of the penalty~~. I _____, think of the New Name, covenant **before God, angels, and these witnesses** that I will never reveal the First Token of the Aaronic Priesthood, with its accompanying name **and** sign, and penalty. Rather than do so, I would suffer my life to be taken.
That will do.

(Patrons sit down.)

  Very few of us will ever "reveal" (best defined here by its synonym, "betray") this *First Token*. Only those who pass through mortalities here on earth and experience the *plan of Lucifer* along with the *plan of the Father*, and who still honestly believe that the plan of the Father is unfair and not what they should follow for a fullness of happiness, will receive this penalty—the Second Death, or being cut off forever from the kingdoms of God.
(NOTE: When the endowment was given to the first mortals placed upon this earth, the explanations of the reason why the tokens are named after the "Priesthood" were given in clarity. The Sealed Portion reveals this in more depth than what will be given here. However, it should be noted that when the endowment was first given, it was not called the

"*First Token of the Aaronic Priesthood*," because no such person as Aaron had yet existed. The reason why they are called after the priesthood names now can be understood from reading the revelation of <u>The Sealed Portion, The Final Testament of Jesus Christ</u>.)

ELOHIM: Jehovah, see that Adam ~~is~~ **and Eve are** driven out of this beautiful garden into the lone and dreary world, where ~~he~~ **they** may learn from ~~his~~ **their** own experience to distinguish good from evil.
JEHOVAH: It shall be done, Elohim.

(As the lights are turned down, the film presentation continues.)

Again, it is important to recap the symbolism of the *Garden of Eden*. Though there *was* an actual place where the first human beings were placed upon this earth when their mortal bodies were created for them from the elements of this earth (as the land of Eden), many of the prophets were bound from revealing these mysteries of God to the people. Therefore, as they taught the people in parable, the prophets interchangeably used the symbolism of the *Garden of Eden* to represent the time and place when we all dwelt in the presence of our Creators and were taught by Them before we were left to ourselves in a "lone and dreary world."

To reiterate, though many use the term "preexistence," it is not actually correct in the way we might normally understand it, because we also *existed* in a state as newly-created spirits encased in perfected physical bodies long before we became mortal. "Mortality" is generally synonymous in meaning with "death," and so it should be, because we actually **leave our first, perfected bodies behind** (with reference to our original state as innocent spirits) and enter mortality, again where we face a mortal death as our only exit. We are thereby **buried** in mortality/death (our "fallen" state), and later are **reborn**, or raised up again (resurrected) through the death of the mortal body and the creation of an eternal one.

In this part of the endowment, Elohim instructs Jehovah to allow us to experience death (mortality), so that we can learn from our "*own*" experience" instead of relying on what we learned while residing with our Father and Eternal Mothers. Mortality will teach us that our Creators' plan is indeed the *only* plan that will truly bring us eternal peace and happiness.

As stated before, in rearing teenagers, we have the perfect example of why our Creators knew it was necessary for us to experience pain, sorrow, sickness, stress, and every other human condition. This is so we would "KNOW," without a doubt, that His plan is the ONLY plan that will bring us happiness. Teenagers are realistic examples of how we act as free-willed beings who cannot remember what it was like to be a little child. Our state of existence in mortal flesh (Lucifer) allows us the latitude to vary from the counsels of our Parents and to have an ego that thinks it knows what is best for itself. Teenagers lack the knowledge and experience of their parents. Parents have already experienced considerably more in life and know from their own experiences which paths lead to happiness and those that lead to disaster. Unfortunately though, mortal parents are generally more like Lucifer than they are like our Creators. They try desperately to restrict their children from experiencing life by setting strict rules with dire consequences. They incite fear and threaten reprisal if the children rebel, in hopes that this will motivate the children to keep *their* rules—this is Lucifer's way, as well as the way of most organized religions.

Our Creators, in love and patience, taught correct principles to Their children (us) from the beginning; They then allow us to govern ourselves. When we have messed up our lives entirely by shirking Their counsel, They continue to love us and throw a "party" for us when we figure out that They were right all along. (See the parable of the *Prodigal Son*.)

Since the *true* gospel of Christ has been taught the same throughout the earth by different messengers according to the culture and traditions of the different people, other inspired teachers (prophets of God) taught the *same* principles of truth. The Buddhist parable similiar to that given as the "Prodigal Son" by Jesus is profound. It has been passed down and interpreted from the teachings of the prophet, Siddhartha Gautama:

> A young man left his father and ran away. For a long time he dwelt in other countries: for ten, then twenty, then fifty years. The older he grew, the more needy he became. Wandering in all directions to seek clothing and food, he unexpectedly approached his native country. The father had searched for his son all those years in vain and meanwhile had settled in a certain city. His home became very rich; his goods and treasures were fabulous.
>
> At this time, the poor son, after wandering through village after village and passing through countries and cities, at last reached the city where his father had settled. The father had always been thinking of his son, yet, although he had been parted from him for over fifty years, he had never spoken of the matter to anyone. He only pondered over it within himself and cherished regret in his heart, saying, "Old and worn out I am. Although I own much wealth—gold, silver, and jewels, granaries and treasuries overflowing, I have no son. Someday my end will come and my wealth will be scattered and lost, for I have no heir. If only I could get back my son and commit my wealth to him, how contented and happy would I be, with no further anxiety!"
>
> Meanwhile, the poor son, hired for wages here and there, unexpectedly arrived at his father's house. Standing by the gate, he saw from a distance his father seated on a lion-couch, his feet on a jeweled footstool, and expensive strings of pearls adorning his body, revered and surrounded by priests, warriors, and citizens, attendants and young slaves waiting upon him left and right. The poor son, seeing his father having such great power, was seized with fear, regretting that he had come to this place. He reflected, "This must be a king, or someone of royal rank. It is impossible for me to be hired here. I had better go to some poor village in search of a job, where food and clothing are easier to get. If I stay here long, I may suffer oppression." Reflecting thus, he rushed away.
>
> In the meantime, the rich elder on his lion-seat had recognized his son at first glance, and with great joy in his heart had reflected, "Now I have someone to whom I may pass on my wealth. I have always been thinking of my son, with no means of seeing him, but suddenly he himself has come and

my longing is satisfied. Though worn with years, I yearn for him."

He instantly sent off his attendants to pursue the son quickly and fetch him back. The messengers immediately hastened forth to seize him. The poor son, surprised and scared, loudly cried his complaint, "I have committed no offense against you, why should I be arrested?" The messengers all the more hastened to lay hold of him and took him back. Following this, the poor son thought that although he was innocent he would be imprisoned, and that now he would surely die. He became all the more terrified, then fainted away and fell to the ground.

The father saw this from a distance, and sent word to the messengers, "I have no need for this man. Do not bring him by force. Sprinkle cold water on his face to restore him to consciousness and do not speak to him any further." Why did the father do this? He knew that his son's disposition was inferior, and that his own lordly position had caused distress to his son; yet, although convinced that he was his son, tactfully did not say to others, "This is my son."

A messenger said to the son, "I set you free. Go wherever you will." The poor son was delighted upon obtaining the unexpected release. He arose from the ground and went to a poor village in search of food and clothing. Then the elder, desiring to attract his son, set up a device. He secretly sent two men (sorrowful and poor in appearance) to his son, telling them, "Go and visit that place and gently say to the poor man, 'There is a place for you to work here. We will hire you for scavenging, and we both also will work along with you.'" Then the two messengers went in search of the poor son, and having found him, presented him the above proposal. The poor son, having received his wages in advance, joined them in removing a refuse heap.

The father, upon beholding the son work among the refuse heap, was struck with compassion for him. One day, while watching through the window, he saw his son's figure at a distance. He was haggard and drawn, lean and sorrowful, filthy with dirt and dust. The father took off his strings of jewels and his soft attire and put on a coarse, torn, and dirty garment. Then he smeared his body with dust, took a basket in his right hand, and with a fear-inspiring appearance said to the laborers, "Get on with your work; don't be lazy!" By such means he got near to his son, to whom he afterwards said, "Ay, my man, you stay and work here, do not leave again. I will increase your wages, give whatever you need: bowls, rice, wheat-flour, salt, vinegar, and so on. Have no hesitation; besides, there is an old servant whom you can get if you need him. Be at ease in your mind; I am, as it were, your father; do not be worried again. "Why?" you may wonder. I am old and advanced in years, but you are young and vigorous; all the time you have been working, you have never been deceitful, lazy, angry, or grumbling. I have never seen you, like the other laborers, with such vices as these. From this time forth you will be as my own begotten son."

The elder gave him a New Name and called him a son. But the poor son, although he rejoiced at this happening, still thought of himself as a humble hireling. For this reason, for twenty years he continued to be employed in scavenging. During this period, there grew a mutual confidence between the father and the son; he went in and out at his pleasure, though his abode was still a small hut.

Suddenly the father became ill, and knowing that he would die soon, said to the poor son, "Now I possess an abundance of gold, silver, and precious things, and my granaries and treasuries are full to overflowing. I want you to understand in detail the quantities of these things, and the amounts that should be received and given. This is my wish, and you must agree to it. Why? Because now we are of the same mind. Be increasingly careful so that there is no waste." The poor son accepted his instruction and commands, and became acquainted with all the goods. However, he still had no idea of expecting to inherit anything. His abode was still the original place, and he had yet to abandon his sense of inferiority.

After a short time had again passed, the father noticed that his son's ideas had gradually been enlarged, his aspirations developed, and that he despised his previous state of mind. Seeing that his own end was approaching, the father commanded his son to come, and also gathered all of his relatives and the kings, priests, warriors, and citizens. When they were all assembled, he addressed them saying, "Now, gentlemen, this is my son, begotten by me. It is over fifty years since, from a certain city, he left me and ran away to endure loneliness and misery. His former name was so-and-so and my name was so-and-so. At that time, in that city, I sought him sorrowfully. Suddenly, I met him in this place and regained him. This is really my son and I am really his father. Now all the wealth which I possess belongs entirely to my son, and all my previous disbursements and receipts are known by this son." When the poor son heard these words of his father, his joy was great at such unexpected news, and thus he thought, "Without any mind for these treasures, or effort on my part, this wealth has now come to me."

World-honored One! The very rich elder is the Tathagata, and we are all as the Buddha's sons. The Buddha has always declared that we are his sons. But because of the three sufferings, in the midst of births-and-deaths we have borne all kinds of torments, being deluded and ignorant and enjoying our attachment to things of no value. Today the World-honored One has caused us to ponder over and remove the dirt of all diverting discussions of inferior things. In these we have hitherto been diligent to make progress and have got, as it were, a day's pay for our effort to reach nirvana. Obtaining this, we greatly rejoiced and were contented, saying to ourselves, "For our diligence and progress in the Buddha-law what we have received is ample." The Buddha, knowing that our minds delighted in inferior things, by his tactfulness taught according to our capacity, but still we did not perceive that we are really Buddha's sons. Therefore we say that though we had no mind to hope or expect it, yet now the Great Treasure of the King of the Law has of itself come to us, and such things that Buddha sons should obtain, we have all obtained.

(Saddharmapundarika Sutra 4)

5
THE GOD OF THIS WORLD

THE LONE AND DREARY WORLD

(Adam and Eve are shown full view for the first time. They are clad in animal skins that cover their bodies to their knees. The lone and dreary world is represented by desert scenery. They both walk away from the Garden of Eden. Adam stops to look back. Eve looks at Adam and then forward. They both walk away from the Garden. The scene changes. Adam kneels at his stone altar, spreading his hands to heaven and piously invoking the Lord.)

NARRATOR: We now go with Adam and Eve into the lone and dreary world. Brethren and sisters, this represents the Telestial kingdom, or the world in which we now live. Adam, on finding himself in the lone and dreary world, built an altar and offered prayer, and these are the words that he uttered:

Being in a world alone ("lone") without the presence and guidance of Eternal Beings who serve us and assure our happiness, has surely created of mortality the makings of a "dreary" place. But without experiencing this kind of situation, we would never know the great significance and importance of trusting in the laws that will eventually assure us everlasting joy.

As previously addressed, the garments in which the participants are placed at the beginning of the endowment represent the corrupt mortal bodies we all must endure during the days of our probation. These "days of probation" have nothing at all to do with proving ourselves worthy of anything by way of any supposed earthly accomplishment or standard. We were **all** guaranteed happiness through the covenant our Creators made with us upon our creation. The Gods did not create us with the possibility or end that we might be destined to a final state of misery—Men are, that they might have joy (2 Nephi 2:25). "Probation" simply makes reference to the time we are meant to perform a *critical assessment and evaluation* of the situation in which we have been placed, and to *prove to ourselves* whether or not it satisfies the Creators' promise of lasting happiness. Also, it gives us a chance to prove who we are as individuals and that the type of happiness we desire for ourselves completely satisfies our individuality.

We lived for eons of time (in mortal years) in a pre-mortal state on the planet of our Creators. There, we established an eternal foundation of *who we are* and found out what it was going to take to provide us with those things necessary to maintain this foundation. In other words, we knew what was going to make us happy long before we came to this "lone and dreary world." We were able to understand and conclude these things about ourselves with the help of our Creators, who with Their experience, lovingly provided the information and examples we needed to make the determination. Deep down inside each one of us, we know who we *really* are. We can wear masks and act how others expect us to act, but when we act contrary to the established foundation of who *we really are*, we feel uncomfortable and unhappy. As mentioned before, all of us might want to have Celestial propensities and the same desires as our Creators (thus enabling us to be granted the powers They possess), but when it comes right down to it, how many of us truly want to spend the rest of eternity serving the needs of others? This life is the time to prove to ourselves that accepting our individual *selfishness* is proper and supported by the eternal laws of happiness.

In seeking the state of eternal emotional balance we call "happiness," human beings yearn to understand the natural environment in which they find themselves, usually by supernatural or 'spiritual' means. Though we are left without the ability to remember any experiences prior to our mortal birth, the spirit inside of us recognizes that something is missing, and we are left in the unpleasant situation of longing to feel "happy." We seek any means necessary, outside of our natural surroundings, which obviously are not bringing us much joy, to find this happiness for which our soul intuitively yearns. The results of this search have led us to the delusional comforts that come from the religions, beliefs, hypotheses, speculations, and precepts of mankind—all of which began through the individual search to find a semblance of balance and understanding in a "lone and dreary" world.

The first thing the rational mind begins to convince itself of is, "There must be a better life than this one!" However, mortals are limited to the available experience and resources in their surroundings. In the absence of better information, humans began to worship the sun, the moon, the stars, animals, natural conditions such as thunder, rain, and clouds, and any other part of their surroundings beyond their control. These "Gods," as they presumed, seemed to have control over their destinies in a grand but random scheme. Belief in these imaginary gods gave some respite to the human desire to justify that life wasn't so bad, as they supposed, since they believed (for example) that it was providential if the "God of Thunder" willed their village to burn to the ground by a bolt of his Divine lightning. Thus, "God" was thought to be a presence in control of everything, leaving humankind to be acted upon by these imagined deities, and thereby relieving them of personal responsibility for the misery in which they found themselves.

In time, mortals began to voice their minds as to the conditions of their lives through prayer by conversing with their imagined, unknown and unseen gods. True prophets correctly understand that these gods of man's vain imagination are Satan, *Lucifer*, or the devil (meaning their own flesh). With this in mind, Joseph interpolated this part of human nature into the form and presentation of the endowment with the following dialogue:

ADAM: Oh God, hear the words of my mouth. Oh God, hear the words of my mouth. Oh God, hear the words of my mouth.

(As Adam prays, Lucifer approaches from behind out of the shadows.)

LUCIFER: I hear you. What is it you want?

Well after the organization of the LDS Church in 1830, Joseph Smith finally revealed what is now known as the "First Vision" to the Church. In this vision, he was told that all churches were an abomination to our Creators. Even so, just as at certain times in history when the people demanded a king (and so, reluctantly, were given one), so, too, Joseph encountered followers who demanded a church, and he felt compelled to oblige. To the extent that he did this, Joseph acted as the devil's advocate. In this piece of dialogue, and in numerous other parts of the endowment as well, Joseph openly reveals the *real truth*, yet the people failed then as they do now, to see and understand these obvious simple explanations of the mysteries of God hidden within the outward presentation of the endowment.

The verbalization of thoughts and ideas by talking into space—otherwise known as prayer—with the idea of personal benefit to the individual thus engaged, is little more than self-delusion, self-hypnosis, and a conversation with one's own will; or in other words, *Lucifer* (or their own flesh). How could Joseph have been any plainer concerning prayer than he was here in this segment of endowment? Yet the people will continue to have their prayers, their churches, and their priesthoods.

(Although Adam has already encountered Lucifer in the Garden of Eden, he fails to recognize him at this appearance.)

ADAM: Who are you?
LUCIFER: I am the god of this world.
ADAM: You, the god of this world?
LUCIFER: Yes. What do you want?
ADAM: I am looking for messengers.
LUCIFER: Oh, you want someone to preach to you. You want religion, do you? ~~I will have preachers here presently.~~ **There will be many willing to preach to you the philosophies of men mingled with scripture.**

Adam fails to recognize or be alarmed by Lucifer because he appears as any other man. Here, and in immediate subsequent dialogue with Lucifer, we have many powerful hints in which Joseph clearly gives away the true nature of Lucifer's identity—even that *Lucifer* is not a particular being, but rather *any* given man or woman acting out the desires and beliefs of his or her flesh. (It is important to note that Eve has no part in the communication with Lucifer or any role to play in this part of the endowment. As explained previously, Adam represents a *specific* part of us, the **SUPEREGO**, which is usually the human emotional part that seeks for and participates in religion.) Earlier in the endowment, mankind was given "dominion…over the whole earth," effectively making man the "*god of this world*"; therefore, in calling himself the "*god of this world*" above, Lucifer identifies himself as "mortal men." Furthermore, the character portrayed as Lucifer earlier in the *Garden of Eden*, identified himself to Eve as her "brother," when Eve likewise questioned who he was.

Adam's prayer represents humankind's desire to make sense of this "*lone and dreary world*." As he prays for God to "*hear the words of my mouth*," he is eventually answered by the **_only_** god who hears and answers the verbalizations which mortals call prayer—Lucifer, the flesh. Our flesh desires to comprehend the world and the fallen state in which we find ourselves. And, as explained above, "Lucifer" (we, our lonesome and dreary selves) came up with religion to accomplish this.

As indicated by much of the following dialogue and the great amount that has been deleted and changed by the modern LDS Church, no religion (including the LDS church) wants to see itself as controlled and driven by "Lucifer." However, this is exactly what Joseph Smith had in mind by writing this part of the presentation in the way that he did. Needless to say, all religions belong to Lucifer—the need and will of the flesh to make sense of what is not understood—and the LDS Church is no exception. Few, if any, Mormons understand this or any of the other truths behind the symbolism of the temple endowment they revere.

The following includes numerous comments interspersed among items deleted from the original endowment by the modern LDS Church:

~~(Lucifer turns his head as a preacher approaches.)~~

~~**LUCIFER:** Good Morning sir!~~
~~**PREACHER:** Good morning!~~

~~(The preacher turns and looks into the camera.)~~

~~**PREACHER:** A fine congregation!~~
~~**LUCIFER:** Yes, they are a very good people. They are concerned about religion. Are you a preacher?~~

This deleted script typifies the perverse perception we have of our own and our neighbors' righteousness. In the dialogue, we (the congregation) are "*very good people*" by the standard set by religious institutions and leaders. This is further exemplified by those whose "righteousness" has permitted them to be present in receiving the endowment (as pointed out by Lucifer). Even beyond that standard, we are content that people are "good" if they do not have some visible indication of "evil," even as all pursue their individual fleshly desires, thus being considered "very good" according to *Lucifer's* standards.

~~PREACHER: I am.~~
~~LUCIFER: Have you been to college and received training for the ministry?~~
~~PREACHER: Certainly! A man cannot preach unless he has been trained for the ministry.~~

Deleted dialogue identifies the false notion that the gospel can be learned, accepted, and taught by book learning, as if to represent that *knowing* the scriptures is the same thing as *understanding* the *true* gospel. For the learned, the academics of perpetual study precedes the delusion that familiarity with scripture somehow equates to understanding, following, or deriving Divine authority to preach or expound on them.

~~LUCIFER: Do you preach the orthodox religion?~~
~~PREACHER: Yes, that is what I preach.~~
~~LUCIFER: If you will preach your orthodox religion to these people and convert them, I will pay you well.~~
~~PREACHER: I will do my best.~~

In reality, a thin line separates the broad spectrum of all religious beliefs, each of which is perverted by the very nature of the limitations presented by the written word. Joseph Smith said that the Bible is correct insofar as it is translated correctly, but this might more accurately be stated: insofar as it is "understood" correctly. No embellishment of language within the written word will ever ultimately lead to a full and proper understanding of the gospel. Certainly, all organized religions are little more than their own uniquely-contrived hybrid of "orthodoxy."

There is no greater form of hypocrisy that exists among humankind than that which would lead one to believe that his or her personal or denominational view, opinion, or belief in God is so accurate that it might warrant subscribers and payment for this information. Using reason or common sense, how does the requirement to pay a tithe or financial offering translate to the certainty of salvation in Heaven or redemption with God? The long-dead prophets of religious writ are the only ones to whom it is ascribed the certainty of knowing the truth and mysteries of God enough to declare them; yet which of the venerated men of scripture exacted a toll before preaching or showing the way of God? Indeed, these were killed for preaching without a license from the people, because the *real truth* they taught was outside the "orthodox" religions of their times.

Those who persuade believers that they should be paid or receive tithes for their labors are nothing more than successful entertainers and illusionists, tickling the flesh and misdirecting the emotions of their listeners for their own personal benefit. Thus is the state of all "orthodox religious" leaders. Whether by monetary stipend, salary, or the emotional power gained over their followers, these *sectarian ministers* are indeed *paid well* as they *do their best* to give religion to the people who are seeking it.

Jesus was one who specifically stated that what he had to give the people would relieve them of their stress and burdens *for free*. He instructed *his ministers* quite differently than how Lucifer instructs his own:

> And as ye go, ***ye shall*** **preach, saying, The kingdom of heaven is *now* at hand *and the sword of truth hangeth over this people, and except they repent, they shall in no wise enter into this kingdom. And this kingdom is within the hearts of the people, but their hearts are sick and diseased with the leprosy of false doctrine they have received from their leaders; and they walk as the lame and are dead to all things that are righteous and good; and in this way the angels of the devil have power over them. Behold, I am the way, the truth and the light, even those things which I have given unto you shall*** heal the sick, cleanse the lepers, raise the dead ***and*** cast out devils. ***And these things ye shall do to their souls in similitude of what I have done unto their bodies. Be not ye like those who make the people sick; for their leaders charge a price for that with which they poison the people.*** Ye have freely received; ***therefore,*** freely give. ***And*** neither ***shall ye*** provide gold, nor silver, nor brass in your purses, neither two coats, neither shoes, nor yet staves for your journey. ***And if they who receive freely of you do not provide you with that in which ye are in need, then they will not retain that which ye shall give them for they are not worthy of it and understand not that*** the workman is worthy of his meat. ***And ye shall have no*** scrip ***from which ye shall read to the people. For that which ye shall say shall be given unto you of the Holy Ghost in the moment that ye have need to say it.*** (Matthew 10:7–10, correct translation.)

~~(Lucifer guides the preacher to Adam and Eve, who stand nearby.)~~

~~**LUCIFER:** *(Indicating Adam.)* Here is a man who desires religion. He is very much exercised and seems to be sincere.~~

In our search for the meaning of life, we become lost in the conceit of our own journey, easily forgetting the various and similar situations of our fellowman. In doing so, we abandon the gospel of equality with the substitute opiate of organized religion, which dulls the senses to the gospel that Christ taught. From <u>The Sealed Portion</u> we learn that even Adam, for awhile, fell prey to the letter of the law, while Eve, guided by common sense and a "tingling in her flesh," persuaded Adam to finally concede to what was necessary for their progression.

The relationship of the character "Lucifer" to the preacher also illustrates what is pointed out in another important text that was promised to humanity by Nephi in the Book of Mormon. It was that John the Beloved would be commanded to make his own words clear in the latter days:

And it came to pass that the angel spake unto me, saying: Look! And I looked and beheld a man, and he was dressed in a white robe. And the angel said unto me: Behold one of the twelve apostles of the Lamb. Behold, he shall see and write the remainder of these things; yea, and also many things which have been. And he shall also write concerning the end of the world. Wherefore, the things which he shall write are just and true; and behold they are written in the book which thou beheld proceeding out of the mouth of the Jew; and at the time they proceeded out of the mouth of the Jew, or, at the time the book proceeded out of the mouth of the Jew, the things which were written were plain and pure, and most precious and easy to the understanding of all men. And behold, the things which this apostle of the Lamb shall write are many things which thou hast seen; and behold, the remainder shalt thou see. But the things which thou shalt see hereafter thou shalt not write; for the Lord God hath ordained the apostle of the Lamb of God that he should write them. And also others who have been, to them hath he shown all things, and they have written them; and they are sealed up to come forth in their purity, according to the truth which is in the Lamb, in the own due time of the Lord, unto the house of Israel. And I, Nephi, heard and bear record, that the name of the apostle of the Lamb was John, according to the word of the angel. (1 Nephi 14:18–27)

This has happened as part of the "restoration of all things," which commenced with the "Bearer of Christ." This incredible explanation is given in the text of the book known as 666, The Mark of America, Seat of the Beast—The Apostle John's New Testament Revelation Unfolded, hereafter referred to as 666, The Mark of America. In this book, John reveals the true meaning of his Revelation when he explains the beasts with "heads" and "tails," and what "locusts" and "scorpions" with "tails that sting" actually are. The disclosure (which means **APOCALYPSE** in Greek) of John's prophecy supports Joseph's own hidden explanation that *Lucifer* is indeed the god of this world and *his ministers* are the leaders of organized religions.

~~(As Lucifer presents the preacher to Adam and Eve, he steps back and observes the ensuing conversation. The preacher is made to sound sincere, although misguided and credulous. Adam appears humble, faithful and immovable in his determination to serve God. He is not swayed by the preacher, and is astounded by the doctrines espoused by the preacher.)~~

~~**PREACHER:** I understand you are inquiring after religion.~~
~~**ADAM:** I was calling upon Father.~~

In this instance, Adam represents those few who are not swayed by religion, but instead depend upon their *common sense* (the Holy Spirit) to guide them in what they choose to believe and disbelieve. Keep in mind that the "Glory" of God (our Creators) is intelligence; or in other words, Light and Truth. In this example, Adam was figuratively searching for this *Light and Truth*, which, when received, always makes *complete sense*, leaving no other questions to be asked in the mind of the recipient. In the presentation of the endowment, Joseph specifically instructs the actor playing Lucifer to remind all those in the congregation behind Adam, who are receiving the endowment, that *they* are the ones who have accepted Lucifer's religions and doctrines. This is done by specifically having the Lucifer character answer the following question given by Peter: "**PETER:** *How is your religion received by this community?*" Here, Joseph instructs the actor to look at and extend his arm in a gesture towards all those receiving the endowment and say: "**LUCIFER:** *Very well—excepting this man (referring to Adam). He does not seem to believe anything we preach.*"

Joseph knew that the LDS people in his day were corrupted by the very religion they were desirous to espouse. It should always be remembered that Joseph's primary mission was to restore the fullness of the gospel of Jesus Christ, *only* through the means of the Book of Mormon, and not to establish a church. He was instructed by Moroni as follows:

> *He* (Moroni) *said there was a book deposited, written upon gold plates, giving an account of the former inhabitants of this continent, and the source from whence they sprang. He also said that the fullness of the everlasting Gospel was contained in it, as delivered by the Savior to the ancient inhabitants;* (Joseph Smith—History 1:34, underlining added.)

The "fullness of the everlasting gospel" has nothing to do with "mysteries" and "religion," but all to do with how we treat each other as taught by "the Savior to the ancient inhabitants" in chapters 12, 13, and 14 of 3rd Nephi. Religion and mystery are the antithesis of truth and create an endless diversion and dialogue through which participants find their value in useless discussion, ritual, and the perpetuation of contrived commandments. In presenting the endowment in figurative symbolism, Joseph is telling the people what he could not tell them outright. Like all people led by the enticements of the flesh (Lucifer), the LDS people have looked "beyond the mark" of the true gospel and "sought for things that they can not understand." Reiterating for profound emphasis, well does their own scripture testify of their works as it does the Jews before them:

> *But behold, the Jews were a stiffnecked people; and they despised the words of plainness, and killed the prophets, and sought for things that they could not understand. Wherefore, because of their blindness, which blindness came by looking beyond the mark, they must needs fall; for God hath taken away his plainness from them, and delivered unto them many things which they cannot understand, because they desired it. And because they desired it God hath done it, that they may stumble.* (Jacob 4:14)

The temple endowment is only part of the "many things" delivered unto the LDS people "which they cannot understand." Because of their desire to observe the endowment as a law and commandment, they have "stumbled" in their lack of a deeper understanding of it and its purpose. Hardly mentioned from any Mormon pulpit are any of the words which Christ "delivered to the ancient inhabitants." In place of the *true* gospel are the commandments of the Church and the precepts of men (their leaders). The LDS Church teaches its members that they must respect and honor the leaders of the "Only True Church," attend church regularly, pay a tithe to it, and go to the temple often—none of which can be found in "the fullness of the everlasting Gospel as delivered to the ancient inhabitants.

~~**PREACHER:** I am glad to know that you were calling upon Father. Do you believe in a God who is without body, parts, and passions; who sits on the top of a topless throne; who His center is everywhere and whose circumference is nowhere; who fills the universe, and yet is so small that He can dwell in your heart; who is surrounded by myriads of beings who have been saved by grace, not for any act of theirs, but by His good pleasure? Do you believe in this great Being?~~
~~**ADAM:** I do not. I cannot comprehend such a being.~~
~~**PREACHER:** That is the beauty of it. Perhaps you do not believe in the devil, and in that great hell, the bottomless pit, where there is a lake of fire and brimstone into which the wicked are cast, and where they are continually burning but are never consumed?~~
~~**ADAM:** I do not believe in any such place.~~
~~**PREACHER:** My dear friend, I am sorry for you.~~
~~**LUCIFER:** *(Speaking to Adam.)* I am sorry, very very sorry! What is it you want?~~

Such flowery and abstract language creates the spirit of "ever learning and never able to come to the knowledge of the truth" (see 2 Timothy 3:7). Seeing through the seduction of such a diatribe, Adam remains firm in his *common sense*, which, stated in other terms, is the same as saying that he listens to and follows the *Holy Spirit* or *Holy Ghost*. Oddly enough, while the LDS members do not believe in the description of God just illustrated, the very nature of their prayers reflect belief in a God which indeed does possess these mysterious attributes.

ADAM: **But** I am looking for messengers from my Father.

Now comes a part of the endowment that announces the truth in such an extraordinarily simplified way that it is astonishing that it still remains a mystery to all those who have received the temple endowment. By Adam "calling upon Father," he is trying to make sense of the new world in which he finds himself and which he does not understand. He is weighing the new information against his *common sense*, i.e., his *Holy Spirit*, that which he had learned and knew in the *Garden of Eden*. The endowment now reveals a mystery of God that makes *complete sense*, yet destroys every conception ever imagined by human mortals about the true nature and character of God: Elohim, who represents our Creators, *does not* answer prayers, *does not* personally intercede in the lives of mortals, *is not* omnipresent, and has put the functioning and handling of all aspects of this solar system in the hands of His chosen One—Jesus, the Christ (Jehovah).

The participants of the endowment have just witnessed the interaction between Adam and Lucifer and the surprising manner in which Adam's prayer was answered. They further demonstrate their misunderstanding by overlooking the manner in which God governs His creations, even when it is plainly portrayed in the presentation. In the following text of the endowment, given as a series of reports by those assigned to do so, God sends Jehovah and others to the world to "*see if Satan is there*" and learn what Adam is doing. The religious dogmas held by those attending the endowment would lead them to think that somehow God hears them individually, and that what they just saw enacted in the presentation of the endowment is some kind of stylized dramatization of mysteries they are not supposed to understand.

The truth of the matter is, God was not present when Adam's prayer was answered. However, the "*god of this world*" was; and *Lucifer* is the *only* god who hears and answers the prayers of those who pray with their mouth and not by their actions. Christ taught us to pray by our actions. He taught us to "pray always." How can we pray always and still get anything done, if prayer actually meant to build an altar, get on our knees, and voice our needs and opinions to God all day long? Prayer in every sense of the word is a call to the Savior's mandate to love our neighbor as ourselves and to do unto others as we would have them do unto us, proclaiming the universal equality of all human beings by *the way* that we live.

Prayer has nothing to do with the vain repetition of words, which, in powerlessness, fade away unheard into space. While it *does* make us feel good to believe that we are being listened to by our Creators, an understanding of equality would ask: "Why would They listen to *our* prayers and ignore those of countless others whose plight in life is much worse than our own?" Why would They hear our plea in prayer of whether a job or a life's partner is the right choice, even as others are starving or dying in the horrors of war while supplicating the same God?

(The scene changes to a view of the Celestial Kingdom, where Elohim reigns from a white throne afront tall white pillars. He is radiant as before, and his voice resonates as he speaks with Jehovah, who stands before Him.)

ELOHIM: Jehovah, send down Peter, James, and John to visit the man Adam in the Telestial world, without disclosing their identity. Have them observe conditions generally; see if Satan is there, and learn whether Adam has been true to the token and sign given to him in the Garden of Eden. Have them then return and bring me word.
JEHOVAH: It shall be done, Elohim.

(Jehovah turns from Elohim and walks to the edge of the platform upon which he stands. He there meets Peter, James, and John, who await his command. They are dressed as the Jews were at the time of Christ.)

JEHOVAH: Peter, James, and John, go down and visit the man Adam in the Telestial world, without disclosing your identity. Observe conditions ~~generally. See if Satan is~~ there, and learn whether Adam has been true to the token and sign given to him in the Garden of Eden. Then return and bring us word.

PETER: It shall be done, Jehovah. Come, James and John; let us go down.

~~**JAMES:** We will go down.~~

~~**JOHN:** We will go down.~~

Another wonderful and liberating truth is revealed when one understands why Elohim commands Peter, James, and John to "*visit the man Adam in the Telestial world, without disclosing your identity.*" Here is the simple, yet incredible, explanation:

So long as humans exist in mortality, (while "*Satan is there*"—meaning that we have "fallen" and partaken of the "forbidden fruit"), a complete understanding of *real truth* is not intended to be a part of the plan set forth for us. This is so that we can have an existence where we can experience opposition to the perfect world from whence we came. As explained previously, "*cherubim and the flaming sword* (turn all away from) *the Tree of Life*." If the fullness of the truth was known, mortality would lose its probative value, in that we would not be able to weigh the difference between a perfect world controlled by the eternal laws of our Creators and one in which nature is left to itself to unravel into a controlled chaos. Without the "laws of God," free-willed beings are in control of everything, having "*dominion over…the whole earth*"—making *man* the "*god of this world.*" Though we may feel what is the right thing to do, we often act in opposition to our conscience. This is because of the power that we have been given to choose and act for ourselves, and the fact that we cannot remember anything of our past existence.

"*Without disclosing your identity*" is simply the mandate given to true prophets of God to teach the people in such a way that the *real truth* remains hidden from them. When prophets follow this divinely-mandated pedagogy, the people rarely understand the *true* reason for being left on an earth to themselves without the intervention of the Advanced Human Beings who put them here. Unable to remember, mortals naturally give in to the enticings of the flesh (Lucifer/Satan), and thus it is said that "he" rules over them.

Our probation period upon this earth proves that most free-willed beings will not exercise discretion if given power over others or over the laws of nature. This life is a time to prove to ourselves that we are *not* capable of being trusted with the power of a God. The analogy of an employee and how he or she acts and performs his or her job when the boss is not around gives a proper understanding of why most of us cannot be trusted with responsibility. Every human being who has been put into a position of power upon this earth in mortality has failed to treat all equally in righteousness. Well was it said that, though we have *all* been "called" (created) to be free-willed beings, few are "chosen" to control the "powers of heaven":

Behold, there are many called, but few are chosen. And why are they not chosen? Because their hearts are set so much upon the things of this world, and aspire to the honors of men, that they do not learn this one lesson—That the the rights of the priesthood (ascribed to the "Robes of the Holy Priesthood" as presented in the endowment) *are inseparably connected with the powers of heaven, and that the powers of heaven cannot be controlled nor handled only upon the principles of righteousness.* (D&C 121:34–6)

Later in the presentation of the endowment, Peter, James, and John are sent down, "*in their true character, as apostles of the Lord Jesus Christ.*" At that time, "*Satan*" is "*cast out.*" (This will be explained in greater detail later.) What is important to understand is that, while we are mortal, it is <u>expected</u> that "*…Satan is there,*" in order to "*learn whether Adam has been true to the token and sign given to him in the Garden of Eden.*" Mortality is the time that we, as free-willed beings, are being tested on how well we listen to and act on the sure feelings of our conscience (the token and sign [foundation of experience and learning] given to us in the *Garden of Eden*) or to see if we choose to follow the enticements of the flesh.

If we truly knew that *real messengers of our Creator* were among us (as they are), and if God and angels were allowed to be visible in the flesh, we would be prone to act appropriately. If we knew of Them, by virtue of Their continual presence we would be spurred to act appropriately, and would then know the *true* reason for our mortal state. This would invalidate the purpose of mortality by restricting the full exercise of our free agency to act according to our unrestricted mortal nature. Thus, "*their true identity*" is kept from us.

Another important truth that Joseph wanted to interpolate into this part of the presentation of the endowment is that all *true prophets* act and agree in the same way in all that they do. None would counter what another has done, and all agree to the plan of salvation and their role in allowing it to be followed properly. For this reason, here, and *only* here, the endowment presents James and John concurring with Peter by each agreeing, "*We will go down.*" Ordinarily, only *one* prophet is sent to a particular culture or people upon the earth at any given time in order to prevent the possibility of confusion. However (as the agreement of James and John figuratively shows), in every case, the teachings of a *true* prophet will agree with what all the others have taught. Once making his appearance among men, no true prophet would ever reveal his understanding of the mysteries of God (thus "*disclosing [his true] identity*") unless he was commanded to do so at the appropriate time for "*casting of Satan out of their midst*" or, in other words, revealing the truth in plainness.

It is important to review some of what has already been covered thus far and expound more fully upon the important *real truths* (reality) being taught at this point in the endowment:

God commands the One assigned to this solar system to send down "*Peter, James, and John without disclosing their true identity.*" Later, God will send down the same three men "*in their true character as apostles of the Lord Jesus Christ.*" The characteristic of these three is *figurative* only, and not required to exist within three literal beings, but rather is to be found only in the *one* chosen at any given time on the earth to teach and reveal the real truth.

The names "*Peter*, *James*, and *John*" are relevant to the figurative nature in which they are presented together. The publication of this book stands in as the figurative mission of "*Peter, James, and John.*" The author's name actually means "Bearer of Christ" on purpose. Only through this work has the *true* meaning of the temple endowment ever been properly revealed. This work has brought forth to the world the sealed portion of the Book of Mormon. Under the direction of John himself, the true meaning of his words hidden in the book of Revelation has been explained in plainness in the book 666, The Mark of America. This work stands alone with the ability to *awaken the memories* of the experiences and learning we received in the *Garden of Eden* from our Creators. Through common sense and a childlike attitude, the *Holy Spirit* (as it has been explained properly) within each individual will reveal that this work is indeed from a *true messenger* sent from God to cast Satan out from among you, as referred to in this part of the presentation of the endowment. (Always keep in mind that *everything* presented in the endowment is purely *symbolic* and *figurative* of some greater eternal truth.)

The purpose of mortality has been explained as the opportunity to experience existence without the intervention of the Gods or the institution of Their laws. This is so that in the end, by virtue of the nature of adversities experienced and recorded in the memories of our probations, we will ultimately agree with the sensibilities of our Eternal Parents and with the eternal plan and laws of happiness as they relate to our individual propensities. Thus consigned and reconciled, we will be able to resurrect to the environment (different kingdom/planet) which best befits our nature and happiness wherein we freely choose to follow those eternal laws without adversity or flaws within our nature, which we experienced with a "fallen" body of flesh and bone.

Keep in mind, it was God who planted the *Tree of Knowledge of Good and Evil* (which is the Veil under which we suffer and experience the vicissitudes of life), thereby becoming the source of *both* Good and Evil. Our Creators provided the opportunity for evil just as They did for good. However, as explained above, the nature of a Celestial Being is such that They will not tell us to do that which will bring us unhappiness; therefore, Elohim commanded Adam and Eve *not* to partake of evil fruit (that which brings us unhappiness) because our Creators cannot go against the very purpose of Their own existence.

Cherubim and the flaming sword have been explained, with the *flaming sword* symbolizing the refining fire of the word of God (the *real truth*) that comes from the words the prophets and others speak as they preach repentance without revealing the mysteries of God. Ultimately, these mysteries can only be known by the power and ministrations of the *Holy Ghost* (common sense and reality). *Cherubim* (the Veil, or our inability to remember anything previous to our current mortality) is in place to keep us from knowing or remembering the reality of our Creators and Their laws, so that we can truly experience the effects of Their absence without feeling compelled or coerced into following Their commands.

Peter means "rock." *James* means "to supplant," or better, "to take the place of or replace." *John* means "by the mercy of God." It is by the mercy and love of our Creator that the confusion of the lone and dreary world will one day be replaced by the eternal truths that will lead us to eternal happiness. These names characterize the *"true identity"* or character of all *true* messengers sent by God. Their job is to un-confuse and teach us the *real truth* (reality) upon which we can build a house; so that when "the rain descends, and the floods come, and the winds blow, and beat upon that house; it will not fall; for it was founded upon a rock" (see Matthew 7:25). This rock is *reality*.

Through the majority of our existence upon this earth, the *true messengers* of the Father are sent to the human race *"without disclosing their [true] identity."* This is so that we can learn from using our free agency and have the purpose of mortality fulfilled for our sakes. This means that they do not teach us in plainness, but rather in parables, allegories, and literary forms that humans do not readily understand unless they use their *common sense* (Holy Spirit). Thus spoke Jesus to his disciples in private:

> *And the disciples came, and said unto him, Why speakest thou unto them in parables? He answered and said unto them, Because it is given unto you to know the mysteries of the kingdom of heaven, but to them it is not given. ...All these things spake Jesus unto the multitude in parables; and without a parable spake he not unto them: That it might be fulfilled which was spoken by the prophet, saying, I will open my mouth in parables; I will utter things which have been kept secret from the foundation of the world.* (Matthew 13:10–11, 34–5)

In like manner as with *"Peter, James, and John,"* above, Joseph Smith *did not* disclose his true identity either, having been so commanded. For the very same reason, he did not reveal the true identity of "the angel" in earlier accounts of the First Vision until many years after he had established the "golden calf" for the people to worship—The Church of Jesus Christ of Latter-day Saints.

The purpose for not disclosing the truth to the world has been explained, but the presentation of the endowment goes further in revealing that, though the truth is not immediately available to us from human memory, there *is* a way we can receive it in our mortal condition. This "way" is presented when *"Peter, James, and John"* disclose their *true* identity to Adam as *"apostles of the Lord Jesus Christ."* Upon recognition of the "true messengers" he was looking for, Adam is no longer left to the confusion created by the doctrines and nonsense of the "orthodox religion" he was subjected to by Lucifer and his ministers. Confusion fades into clarity because, by the mercy of God (*"John"*), the false truths of orthodox religion and its many voices are supplanted (*"James"*) by the rock of truth (*"Peter"*). In like manner in these latter days, the world has been given the opportunity to hear the voice of *"Peter, James and John"* through this work as it establishes this final *marvelous work and a wonder* by taking away all stumbling blocks and teaching in plainness.

This was prophesied in the unsealed portion of the record by Nephi: (NOTE: Some important commentary of the following <u>Book of Mormon</u> verses is interspersed throughout.)

2nd Nephi 27

6 And it shall come to pass that the Lord God shall bring forth unto you the words of a book, and they shall be the words of them which have slumbered.

7 And behold the book shall be sealed; and in the book shall be a revelation from God, from the beginning of the world to the ending thereof.

8 Wherefore, because of the things which are sealed up, the things which are sealed shall not be delivered in the day of the wickedness and abominations of the people. Wherefore the book shall be kept from them.

9 But the book shall be delivered unto a man, and he shall deliver the words of the book, which are the words of those who have slumbered in the dust, and he shall deliver these words unto another;

10 But the words which are sealed he shall not deliver, neither shall he deliver the book. For the book shall be sealed by the power of God, and the revelation which was sealed shall be kept in the book until the own due time of the Lord, that they may come forth; for behold, they reveal all things from the foundation of the world unto the end thereof.

11 And the day cometh that the words of the book which were sealed shall be read upon the house tops; and they shall be read by the power of Christ; and all things shall be revealed unto the children of men which ever have been among the children of men, and which ever will be even unto the end of the earth.

The above is a full and complete description of the marvelous work and wonder which will be complete and ready for all those who will receive it by the year 2012. "Read upon the house tops" means it shall be made available to everyone upon the earth. "Read by the power of Christ" means it shall only be received by those who are of a broken heart and contrite spirit and have a sincere desire to Do Unto Others; i.e., to obey the gospel of Jesus Christ, and receive these things by the "Spirit of Christ," which simply means, their *common sense*. In other words, whether accepted by the world or not, everything brought forth in this work will make complete and perfect sense.

12 Wherefore, at that day when the book shall be delivered unto the man of whom I have spoken, the book shall be hid from the eyes of the world, that the eyes of none shall behold it save it be that three witnesses shall behold it, by the power of God, besides him to whom the book shall be delivered; and they shall testify to the truth of the book and the things therein.

This should leave no more question in anyone's mind as to why the translator of the sealed portion of Mormon's record was not allowed to have his OWN WITNESSES to the gold plates; and for those who have seen the plates, they are laid under a strict command that they shall never reveal the fact that they have. Can the "*eyes of none...save it be that three witnesses*" mean anything else? However, there *is* room for permission to allow others to see the plates (see verse below), as Joseph did the eight witnesses; but it was not necessary for Joseph to publish the testimony of the other eight, as most of them eventually rejected him regardless of what they had seen. Therefore, it does not matter then or now who witnesses the plates or gives testimony; the proud and blind who do not live the *true* gospel of Christ and have "his Spirit" with them, will reject it even if an angel of God came down and showed them. They would most likely convince themselves that the visitation was of the devil and a great illusion used to deceive them. Instead, if they had a *broken heart* and *contrite spirit*, it could lead them away from their "drunken state" of religious ignorance and the "lull of security" in which Satan has trapped them with materialism.

13 And there is none other which shall view it, save it be a few according to the will of God, to bear testimony of his word unto the children of men; for the Lord God hath said that the words of the faithful should speak as if it were from the dead.

14 Wherefore, the Lord God will proceed to bring forth the words of the book; and in the mouth of as many witnesses as seemeth him good will he establish his word; and wo be unto him that rejecteth the word of God!

15 But behold, it shall come to pass that the Lord God shall say unto him to whom he shall deliver the book: Take these words which are not sealed and deliver them to another, that he may show them unto the learned, saying: Read this, I pray thee. And the learned shall say: Bring hither the book, and I will read them.

This has NOTHING to do with the story surrounding the manuscript delivered to Professor Anton and his alleged response as passed around in Mormon intellectual circles through modern LDS dogma. This has to do with making the <u>Book of Mormon</u> available to all those who will accept it as truth ("deliver them to another") without seeing the gold plates. These shall give testimony to those who think they already know the truth ("the learned"), but who will reject it unless the gold plates are actually brought forth to prove the claim.

16 And now, because of the glory of the world and to get gain will they say this, and not for the glory of God.

17 And the man shall say: I cannot bring the book, for it is sealed.

18 Then shall the learned say: I cannot read it.

***19** Wherefore it shall come to pass, that the Lord God will deliver again the book and the words thereof to him that is not learned; and the man that is not learned shall say: I am not learned. **20** Then shall the Lord God say unto him: The learned shall not read them, for they have rejected them, and I am able to do mine own work; wherefore thou shalt read the words which I shall give unto thee.*

All those who think they know the truth ("the learned") will reject the Book of Mormon, because of their own pride and the precepts and doctrines of men which were taught to them throughout their lives. Those who accept the unsealed portion, the Book of Mormon, have tried endlessly to get others to accept it without much success in spite of the millions of copies in print. Thousands upon thousands of Mormon missionaries (the un-"*learned*") have already tried and will continue to try to get people to read the unsealed words, only to be rejected. The prophecy has already been established how ones who are "*not learned*" would attempt to share the book with those who are "*learned*," only to be rejected. Having assumed they were needed (as they supposed) to do "the Lord's work," these missionaries are rebuked when the Lord now declares, "*I am able to do mine own work*," i.e., "I don't need an 'unlearned' man to do it for me; I'll do it myself." How would it ever be possible, for those who do not understand all things, to accomplish that which is only known to the Lord and His true messengers?

***21** Touch not the things which are sealed, for I will bring them forth in mine own due time; for I will show unto the children of men that I am able to do mine own work.*

The Lord's "*own work*" did not begin until The Sealed Portion of the Book of Mormon—The Final Testament of Jesus Christ was translated and prepared for the world. For a space of time (beginning in 1830) the "*unlearned*" were allowed the opportunity to share the unsealed part with the "*learned*," only to be rejected because they could not bring forth any empirical proof to back up the claim of veracity. Missionary work represents the efforts of the "arm of flesh" and has nothing to do with "*mine own work.*" Were this not so, then a missionary could claim that he did the work of the Lord; therefore it would not "*show unto the children of men that [the Lord is] able to do [his] own work.*"

***22** Wherefore, when thou hast read the words which I have commanded thee, and obtained the witnesses which I have promised unto thee, then shalt thou seal up the book again, and hide it up unto me, that I may preserve the words which thou hast not read, until I shall see fit in mine own wisdom to reveal all things unto the children of men.*

23 For behold, I am God; and I am a God of miracles; and I will show unto the world that I am the same yesterday, today, and forever; and I work not among the children of men save it be according to their faith.

It is NOT a miracle when one man shows another a book and convinces him that it is true. It is not a miracle to have tens of thousands of missionaries canvas the world and proselyte for a few converts in comparison to the number of missionaries. The gospel of Christ is not a commodity that can be bought and sold for 10% of one's income. The "miracle" is in the way each person will receive The Sealed Portion at exactly the right time in his or her life when he or she is ready to receive it. It is only to those who demonstrate a "faith" that our Creators can reveal all things unto them; yea, even all Their mysteries, without the need for a church, leaders, or prophets, etc. And these will come to a complete understanding of all the mysteries of God. Only "according to their faith" shall the "angels" then be able to use whatever means they need to "show unto the children of men...that I can do mine own work." The Gods do not need, nor have They ever needed, the intervention of men who know nothing of the power and work by which miracles are performed. "Miracles" have always been those actions and phenomena that take place WITHOUT the conscious will or deliberate intervention of mortals by Beings assigned to oversee the progress of this earth and who possess the Advanced technology and knowledge to perform them. What is perceived as a "miracle" today, will be a simple reality in the future.

24 And again it shall come to pass that the Lord shall say unto him that shall read the words that shall be delivered him:
25 Forasmuch as this people draw near unto me with their mouth, and with their lips do honor me, but have removed their hearts far from me, and their fear towards me is taught by the precepts of men—
26 Therefore, I will proceed to do a marvelous work among this people, yea, a marvelous work and a wonder, for the wisdom of their wise and learned shall perish, and the understanding of their prudent shall be hid.

The unsealed portion of the record (Book of Mormon) did not in any way cause "*the wisdom of their wise and learned [to] perish,*" nor the "*understanding of their prudent [to] be hid.*" The "understanding of their prudent" is the understanding of the religious leaders and their followers, the likes of which seem to be sincere and forthright in their desire to teach good and honest things to others. To these types of people, the understanding will never be given to properly expound upon the mysteries of God and solve the conundrums that face the rational human mind about its existence. "Lucifer" (their own wisdom/the flesh) has deceived them. In contrast, this *marvelous work and a wonder* expounds upon and explains <u>all</u> the "mysteries of God" in their fullness. After one is exposed to this work and the answers it provides, many who once thought that their professors, their teachers, their politicians, their parents, and their religious leaders were wise, will think much differently of their supposed wisdom. In this sense, has not their wisdom perished?

27 And wo unto them that seek deep to hide their counsel from the Lord! And their works are in the dark; and they say: Who seeth us, and who knoweth us? And they also say: Surely, your turning of things upside down shall be esteemed as the potter's clay. But behold, I will show unto them, saith the Lord of Hosts, that I know all their works. For shall the work say of him that made it, he made me not? Or shall the thing framed say of him that framed it, he had no understanding?

There are many religious adherents and their "prudent" leaders who think that they are doing the right thing. They teach as "*good*" that which is *bad* when compared to the *real truth* given in the gospel of Christ in "Doing Unto Others" according to his words. They "turn things upside down." And though they might one day say, "Didn't I profess thy name and in thy name do many wonderful works?" (compare 3 Nephi 14:22), the Lord will profess that he never knew them. They will have no excuse, because the fullness of truth will be upon the earth; therefore, they will not be able to say that they "had no understanding," using as an excuse that they, and everyone else, were deceived by the parables, figurative speech, and stumbling blocks placed before them by the true prophets of God who did not disclose their true identity. Yes, the religions, governments, and works ("the thing framed") shall stand as a bright testimony of the works of "him that framed it."

This *marvelous work and a wonder* has produced a simple plan (**The Worldwide United Foundation**) that would eliminate poverty and inequality throughout the world. Simply by reading and signing the Declaration therein (see **wwunited.org**), one would be counted as supporting a *Plan of our Creators* in supporting life upon this earth without taking away anyone's free agency. On account of the sheer simplicity of this request, do you think anyone will have an excuse for not obeying the gospel of Christ? Absolutely not!

28 But behold, saith the Lord of Hosts: I will show unto the children of men that it is yet a very little while and Lebanon shall be turned into a fruitful field; and the fruitful field shall be esteemed as a forest.

29 And in that day shall the deaf hear the words of the book, and the eyes of the blind shall see out of obscurity and out of darkness.
30 And the meek also shall increase, and their joy shall be in the Lord, and the poor among men shall rejoice in the Holy One of Israel.

Those receptive to this work were once "*blind*," but now their eyes begin to "*see out of obscurity and out of darkness.*" They were once "*deaf*," but now they "*hear the words of the book.*" Their meekness has increased and their joy is surely in what has been given them, not by any "arm of flesh," but by the Lord ("mine own work"). The implementation of the Worldwide United Foundation (WUF) plan would make any "*poor among men…rejoice,*" knowing that there is ONE appointed to this solar system who will someday invoke the guarantee promised to all of us by our Creators before entering this mortal state. We will then be able to experience the equality—as well as have everything else—needed to pursue happiness, according to each of our individual desires of happiness.

31 For assuredly as the Lord liveth they shall see that the terrible one is brought to naught, and the scorner is consumed, and all that watch for iniquity are cut off;
32 And they that make a man an offender for a word, and lay a snare for him that reproveth in the gate, and turn aside the just for a thing of naught.

When Advanced Human Beings come here from other solar systems with Their technology and power, what will the "*terrible one[s]*" of this earth do then? What will the powerful do when they lose all their power? What will the rich and merchants of the earth say when their money is no longer of any value? All those who mock common sense and defy the right of an individual human being to live unmolested according to the dictates of his or her own conscience will be consumed by the reality brought to this planet by Those who have already learned the lessons of mortality long, long ago. The world will then know what is "just," and all that is a "thing of naught" shall be recognized for what it is—naught.

———————

(Peter, James, and John turn and leave, and the scene changes to the lone and dreary world. Peter steps out from behind a large rock, followed by James and John; they approach Adam, Eve, et al.)

PETER: Good morning.

LUCIFER: Good morning, gentlemen.

PETER: What are you doing here?

LUCIFER: ~~Teaching religion.~~ Observing the teaching of these people.

PETER: ~~What religion do you teach?~~ What is being taught?

LUCIFER: ~~We teach a religion made of~~ the philosophies of men, mingled with scripture.

Religion and scripture are fertile ground to capture the imagination of the people and make them captive to the lusts of their own ego. Because mortals cannot remember the truth, nor are they taught it in its fullness during the *second state* of mortality, all kinds of speculations, opinions, and false beliefs are perpetuated as they organize themselves into religions, groups, classes, and nations.

PETER: ~~How is your religion received by this community?~~ How is this teaching received?

As already stated, Lucifer now spreads his arm out, gesturing towards the seated participants ("this community"), who are all members of an organized religion established by the will of the people and their wont for religion. Ironically, only the LDS members of modern times and the Jews of ancient times can/could participate in the sacred temple endowment. Each of these groups believe[d] that they, and they alone, are/were the chosen people of God. The true prophets mock this attitude by having Lucifer gesture to those present in the endowment session. By this, in countless temples all over the world, Joseph Smith allows those thus deceived to step blindly into the trap they have set by their own egos with the following words from the "god of this world":

LUCIFER: Very well, ~~excepting this man. He does not seem to believe anything we preach~~ except this man does not seem to believe what is being taught.

(Peter, James, and John approach Adam and Eve.)

PETER: *(To Adam.)* Good morning. What do you think of ~~the preaching of these gentlemen?~~ this teaching?
ADAM: ~~I cannot comprehend it.~~
PETER: ~~Can you give us some idea concerning it?~~
ADAM: ~~They preach of a God who is without body, parts, or passions; who is so large that He fills the universe, and yet is so small that He can dwell in my heart; and of a hell without a bottom, where the wicked are continually burned but are never consumed. To me, it is a mass of confusion.~~ I am looking for messengers from my Father to teach me.

PETER: That is good. ~~We do not wonder you cannot comprehend such doctrine.~~ Have you any tokens or signs?

The religions of men only lead to confusion. If the truth is not taught in its fullness, (and at this point Peter, James, and John are *not "disclosing their identity"*), mortals who do not listen to their conscience and hold the "signs or tokens" they received in the Garden of Eden as "sacred," will believe in the religions and philosophies of men, though they are often confusing to the rational mind.

Only *Adam*, in contrast to the people receiving the endowment in the temple, is confused by religion. Peter observes the confusion and metaphorically asks Adam if the doctrine he has heard makes sense to him according to what he *feels* is right in his rational mind.

(Lucifer steps up to the side of Peter and interjects his query.)

LUCIFER: ~~Do you~~ have **you** any money?

At this point, a brief discussion of money is valuable. The sealed portion of the gold plates contains a portion of the endowment as given by Adam to his children, and therein, as here, mention is made of the use of money, although at the time, Adam's children had no idea what money was.

Money is the means by which humans convert their labor into units of value other than the thing for which their immediate labors produce, allowing them the liberty to "spend" these units of labor at other times and places for wants and needs at the convenience of the person who has "earned" the money. This sounds good, but the problem is that money, by its very nature, is created to remain in scarce supply, fluctuates in value by arbitrary means, and is obtained by labors which are valued differently according to the society in which it circulates; many have even found "legal" ways to obtain money without laboring at all.

By its very nature, money creates a profound system of inequality among God's children and causes many to suffer from the lack of basic needs because they do not have the energy, ability, desire, or capacity to compete adequately for "pay" against their fellow human beings. This is particularly devastating to the weak when a society assigns monetary values to all goods and services it produces and compels everyone to compete for the limited money needed to purchase these things. Money creates a sophisticated system of slavery around which all are compelled to labor or die. John refers to this condition in his book of Revelation, where he reveals that all would eventually be compelled to receive the "mark of the beast" (money) in their hand—meaning that all would be forced to use this medium of exchange in order to obtain the necessities of life.

It is by the seduction of money that people are drawn away from the *real truth*, thus being withheld from further understanding. Any religion of the world that supports the payment of tithes and offerings, the passing of the plate, or teaches any similar doctrine that God requires a donation of money in order for one to demonstrate righteousness, is a religion of Lucifer. Christ offered the *real truth* for free to all those who would accept it. Nowhere in his teachings did he ever give a commandment that a tithe or donation be paid as a penance towards God, or be required in order to comply with any of His commandments. HOWEVER, the *true prophets*, who were not allowed to "*disclose their true identities*," allowed the people to convolute the truth as they wished, thereby following Lucifer in the belief that their money would buy them entrance into some fantasized kingdom of God. If Christ taught that the kingdom of God is within you, then how much does it cost, and to whom do you pay, in order to enter within yourself for the truth?

Peter, James, and John next reveal a profound principle when they respond:

PETER: We have sufficient for our needs.

This statement corresponds perfectly with John's explanation in <u>666, The Mark of America</u> as found in the book of Revelation, wherein it is explained that those who have the "*mark of the beast*" in their *forehead* (those who have money, how it is obtained, and the things that it can buy on *their minds* constantly) cannot also have the "*mark of the Father*" in their forehead at the same time. (John taught that the reference to "666" is merely a reference to money. For more about this, see <u>666, The Mark of America</u> as previously mentioned.) Although all people on the earth have the "mark of the beast" in their right hand, Peter's response above reveals a profound example of how we may learn to cope within a system in which money is required to exist, and still leave room for the "mark of the Father" in our foreheads. We do this by living within our own personal needs and paying no attention to what others may have. Otherwise, by constantly desiring to be equal with them monetarily, this (according to the original Ten Commandments) is coveting.

LUCIFER: You can buy anything in this world for money.
PETER: *(To Adam.)* Do you sell your tokens or signs for money? You have them, I presume.
ADAM: I have them, but I do not sell them for money. I hold them sacred. I am looking for the further light and knowledge Father promised to send me.
PETER: That is right. We commend you for your integrity. Good day. We shall probably visit you again.

This dialogue is some of the most sobering in the entire endowment. Having "*sufficient for our needs*" means that Peter, James, and John used no more of their mortal physical and mental capacities than necessary to properly exist. Adam, by his response, likewise ratifies that he has not prostituted his mind, body, and energy for money, but reserves these faculties that he also might have room for the "*mark of the Father*." Almost all, including the "good" people present in the endowment ("this community"), sell themselves for money so as to have more than they need or to get gain.

When a person in mortality is engaged in the constant pursuit of money and worldly goods, the mind is centered on these things and leaves no capacity for it to remember the things that are recorded on the spiritual level (those things given in the pre-mortal existence). It is very hard to listen to your conscience when the very nature of profit and worldly success is diametrically opposed to doing unto others as you would have them do unto you.

In the larger context of the dialogue taking place between Peter, Adam, and Lucifer, Adam is confused by religion and its preachers, and is looking for something that makes sense to him. Peter's comments ("*We do not wonder that you cannot comprehend such doctrine*") is an acknowledgement that religion with its doctrines and commandments makes no sense. Peter then asks Adam if he has any tokens or signs. As used above, a "**token**" is the capacity or state of existence in which works are performed and experience gained. The "**sign**" is the demonstration of these works. Figuratively speaking, Adam's response communicates to Peter that he does not remember himself as a pre-mortal being (token) nor any of the experiences associated therewith (sign). This, Adam gives figuratively by saying that he "*hold[s] them sacred*." For the same reason, the spirit (ghost) inside of us is known as the *Holy* (sacred) *Ghost*. We cannot fully recall everything that is recorded upon our spirit because of a wise purpose instituted by our Creators. Anything the Gods do is considered sacred or holy. Therefore, the experiences we recorded when we were with our Creators in our first estate constitute what has been figuratively referred to as the *Holy Ghost* or Spirit, as it has been explained. Adam will later disclose that he cannot give the name of this **token** (the First Token of the Aaronic Priesthood), for it is the *New Name* he received in his pre-mortal state, which he cannot remember. However, in a later part of the endowment, Adam readily gives the name of the next token (the Second Token of the Aaronic Priesthood) as his *own given name*, representing his ability to remember his works and experiences in mortality.

Upon observation of these acknowledgements between Peter and Adam, Lucifer steps forward with an offer to sell them the "truth"—this being his greatest enticement and power: even that money can buy truth and happiness. In essence, Peter is asking Adam what he understands about truth, and Lucifer interjects that truth can be purchased with money. This is symbolic of the fact that any truth espoused by Lucifer always has a price, whether it be in tithes, donations, passing the plate, stipends, tuitions, dues or whatever other means is required from the members of the orthodox religions of the world in order to feel worthy of God's truth. In whatever form it is given, it is still payment to "Lucifer," and satisfies the human propensity to be recognized in society according to its traditional standard. Thus, organized religion allows its members justification of their worthiness to the God in whom they believe simply by the payment of money. It is much easier for one to pay some money to feel good than it is to feel good because one is doing the right thing.

In answer to Lucifer's inquiry, Peter responds in figurative style with a statement definitive of the lifestyle of any "*true messenger of God*," whether they disclose their true identity or not: "*We have sufficient for our needs*." There is no true messenger of God who would live beyond the very basic necessities of food, shelter, and clothing. They would not drive luxury cars or even any car if possible. They would not dress in suits and ties nor would they be successful men in Lucifer's world of business. They would truly only "*have sufficient for [their] needs*," living as Christ lived—nothing more, nothing less. Finally, and most importantly, they would never, ever <u>require</u> one to pay a tithe or an offering to "God" as a prerequisite of worthiness on one's journey to knowing and understanding the truth. Tithes and offerings given by human beings belonging to the orthodox religions of the world go directly to the "*god of this world*," who demands them and proclaims: "*You can buy anything in this world for money*."

Adam, though confused by religion, does not pay any money for something that should come free to all equally. When Peter asks Adam if he sells his "*tokens or signs for money*," he is figuratively asking if Adam is willing to purchase his *oil* (understanding of truth) from those who "sell" it for money (orthodox religions and their ministers). To Adam, such a consideration is nonsense, but to "*this community*" to whom the endowment is being presented, it is received "*very well*."

The figurative irony that Joseph gave between Adam and the congregation, both of which are supposedly searching for the truth, has been amplified in the way the LDS Church has evolved. No person can enter into an LDS temple and receive the endowment unless he or she is a FULL tithe payer. Ten percent (10%) of one's income must be paid for the quintessential endowment of truth offered by the LDS Church. There is no allowance for those who cannot pay a full tithe, nor does any amount of voluntary service to the Church equate to monetary value. Therefore, do the LDS people sell their signs and tokens for money? You bet they do—in their tithes and offerings!

Their leaders have misinterpreted the scriptures—which already suffer the perversions of time, translation, and the choice of texts by those who assembled them—turning the Church into a "golden cash cow" to fulfill their corporate and personal needs. These needs include opulent temples, conference halls and church buildings, as well as lavish personal houses, luxury cars, and fine clothes, all purchased under the guise that tithing is necessary for the personal salvation of the member and to spread the gospel to other people. The members are deceived into believing that their tithes go to "God" for the building up of His kingdom on earth, which claim is similarly made by every other orthodox religion.

The correct translation of the words of Malachi as restored through the *Urim and Thummim* finally reveals the *real truth* of what this ancient prophet had to say to religious leaders who take tithing from the people: (The plain and precious parts are restored and shown in ***bold italics***.)

> ***But*** even from the days of your fathers ye ***have corrupted*** mine ordinances, and have not kept them ***as I have commanded you***. Return unto me, and I will return unto you, saith the LORD of hosts. But ye said, Wherein shall we return? ***Do we not fulfill the law required of us in our tithes and offerings? Behold, ye wicked servants:*** Will a man rob God? Yet ye have robbed me. But ye say, Wherein have we robbed thee? ***Ye have robbed me*** in ***the*** tithes and offerings ***that ye have taken of the people for yourselves. And because ye have done this*** ye are cursed with a curse, ***and the***

> *windows of heaven have been closed so that ye receive no rain upon the earth, which would bring the good fruits of the field forth, even the fruit that giveth eternal life. But ye receive no rain,* for ye have robbed me, even this whole nation. Bring ye all the tithes *and offerings back* into *my* storehouse, that there may be meat in mine house *for those who are hungry. Yea, your temples and your synagogues have used up the meat. Your substance and priestly apparel have not covered your nakedness as ye suppose, but have taken from the widow and the fatherless and the stranger. Yea, bring back that which ye have robbed from me* and prove me now herewith, saith the LORD of hosts, if I will not open you the windows of heaven, and pour *upon* you a blessing, that there shall not be room enough to receive it. *For without the rain from heaven, how shall the vine receive her nourishment? Behold, except I do this, the leaf shall fall off from the vine, and the fig from the tree before its time.* (Malachi 3:7–10)

Nowhere in the words of Christ to the Jews at Jerusalem or to the people gathered in the land of Bountiful, did he ever make *tithing* a part of his gospel—nowhere! However, those who need a "golden calf" to worship require tithing to sustain the continual appetites created by this need. This is because they have leaders that lead them with "priesthood" authority—the same priesthood represented by Lucifer's apron. These leaders justify the demand for money as an integral component of the individual members' faith in order to promote their brand of "orthodox" truth. Many successful and popular human beings are LDS. Why? Because it is the easiest religion for them to follow. All a person has to do, no matter how rich, no matter how hard they "*grind the faces of the poor*" to make a profit, or no matter what political view they ascribe to, is to pay 10% of their income, say they believe in the leaders of the LDS Church, and go to church each Sunday. Then they will gain, as they believe, the "greatest of all God's kingdoms"—the *Celestial* reign and glory. Yes, it only costs 10% of one's increase to become a God!

Real truth will always be free. Why? Because all the truth we need to know is already embedded deep in our subconscious. We cannot remember, but when our heads are free from the cares of this world, it allows our inner "Holy Spirit" to seep into consciousness with flashes of familiarities of the truth and of those things that brought true pre-mortal happiness. When we finally hear the truth—if we are truly seeking it out of belief that we lack it—it will just make sense. "Making sense" is just remembering things that we presently cannot recall because of the limitations of our mortal brains that cannot bring up the record of prior existences.

(Peter, James, and John exit. Lucifer stares into the camera.)

LUCIFER: Now is the great day of my power. I reign from the rivers to the ends of the earth. There is none who dares to molest, or make afraid.

"The god of this world"—the enticements of the flesh—rules without the fear that man might come to an understanding of the gospel of equality. Selfishness is a more powerful master than "doing unto others" and loving one's neighbor as oneself. Unless man is willing to accept what ALL have in common; i.e., the need for food, clothing, shelter, health care, and the education necessary to accomplish these things for ALL equally, then human suffering will continue. This makes the idea of eternal happiness that we yearn for inside (which God has promised) seem unattainable. Will common sense ever prevail? Will man ever succumb to the promptings of the *Holy Spirit* of common sense and equality? The power of the flesh over mortal affairs appears firmly entrenched until such time as when those Beings return who will usher in worldwide peace. They will do this according to the timetable and laws which have always been and which insure the happiness of all of God's children. Until that time, it will remain "the great day of *Lucifer's* power!"

There is no doubt that desires of the flesh—i.e., money, success, degrees, material goods, looks, sex, entertainment, and sports—rule every aspect of human life *"from the rivers to the ends of the earth."* The curses brought upon us by participating in mortality give the flesh (Lucifer) its power. There are *"none who dare"* to attempt to challenge or change the course of human nature in desiring these things. There are none who dare to change the way humans think about themselves and others and the way they conduct their lives. Who dares challenge the people of this world to open up to the idea (become *"afraid"*) that their lifestyles and fleshly desires may actually be the cause of all of their problems? Who dares stand against the prevailing view that one's own family is far more important than that of a neighbor or a stranger? Who dares molest the economic beast that has devoured the world and caused the rich to become richer and the poor to become poorer, creating inequality and despair? Who dares stand up against the fleshly desires of worldly success, academic degrees, family bonds, materialism, and the freedom to succeed in spite of what this success may do to another?

The *"great day of [Lucifer's] power"* is the time of mortality in which our flesh is allowed unrestricted control over our thoughts and actions. There is only ONE who dares confound him. This ONE will un-confuse Adam and cast Lucifer out of his own kingdom and domain. This ONE is the *true messengers* of God who finally *disclose their true identity* and teach the people the *real truth*.

In 1831, Joseph prophesied concerning the great innovations, technology, and advancements that would come when the "devil shall have power over his own dominion." (See below.) Before and up to circa 1831, what progress had humanity made towards satisfying the lusts and "will of the flesh?" Very little. But now that this *"is the great day of my power,"* the lusts of the flesh are being fulfilled unlike any other time in the history of the world, through the technological and scientific advancements allowed in these latter days. Well did Joseph's prophecy state:

> *And again, verily I say unto you, O inhabitants of the earth: I the Lord am willing to make these things* (the real truth) *known unto all flesh; For I am no respecter of persons, and will that all*

men shall know that the day speedily cometh; the hour (1831) *is not yet, but is nigh at hand, when peace* (my spirit) *shall be taken from the earth, and the devil shall have power over his own dominion.* (<u>D&C</u> 1:34–5)

Who would attempt "*to molest or make* (others) *afraid*" by convincing them that the technology and advancements the human race has made are from Lucifer and not from God?

Only those who *bear* the name of Christ.

~~**PREACHER:** Shall we ever have any apostles or prophets?~~
~~**LUCIFER:** No. However, there may be some who will profess revelation or apostleship. If so, just test them by asking that they perform a great miracle, such as cutting off an arm or some other member of the body and restoring it, so that the people may know that they have come with power.~~

Is it any wonder why this was removed from the dialogue? Of course any righteous man asked to perform such miracles would decline to satisfy the curiosity of men in such a manner, even if they *could* oblige the request. The calling of a *true messenger* from God is only to proclaim the pure and simple gospel of Jesus Christ, which is: Do unto others as you would have them do unto you (Love your neighbor as yourself). They strive to teach the absolute equality of ALL men before God—nothing more, nothing less. Though many *true* prophets are endowed with certain knowledge and power, the use of this "power" is not required. Seeing miracles performed did not give the people any more surety of the divinity of Christ during his mortal time than they have during the lifetime of any *true messenger*. The only thing that will ever convince a self-thinking, free-willed being is his or her *common sense* (the power of the *Holy Ghost*).

The religions of the world perceive a "*great miracle*" as some supernatural intervention in healing, or any supplementary task, the accomplishment of which they cannot understand. Lucifer's instruction is to not believe anyone proclaiming the truth unless they can show forth such a miracle. However, the *miracle of truth* is not in magic, but rather in transformation. Real truth is intended to show people all things as they were, are, and are to come, so that they are brought to a state of understanding, thereby eliminating "miracles" as we think of them. No miracle would be considered as such if one understood how it was performed; the miracle therefore remains in the mystery of how it is performed. True messengers who *disclose their true identity* will not speak in parables as Jesus did; they will perform nothing that is not understood ("miracles") in order to capture the attention of potential followers. In fact, they are not looking for followers at all—but rather, speak truth in such manner that those looking for it may find *them*. They will not be wearing an "*apron...of [their] priesthood*," say anything that is confusing, or charge people money for the truth. Everything they say will make perfect sense.

The "*miracle*" a *true messenger* of the Father demonstrates is the figurative healing of *the blind who do not see and the deaf who do not hear*. In other words, they remove the stumbling blocks so that people do not stumble in their efforts to understand *real truth*. There is no religious leader on this earth who can do this. It can only be done by *true messengers* whose teachings oppose the **God of This Earth**.

6
TRUE MESSENGERS OF GOD

(The scene changes to the Celestial Kingdom. Peter, James, and John approach Jehovah with their report.)

PETER: Jehovah, we have visited the man Adam in the Telestial world as thou didst command us. We found Satan there, ~~with his ministers, preaching all manner of false doctrine and~~ striving to lead the posterity of Adam astray **with all manner of false doctrine**. But Adam has been true and faithful to the token and sign given him in the Garden of Eden, and is waiting for the further light and knowledge you promised to send him. This is our report.

Here again, the modern LDS leaders have deleted any reference to ministers and the preaching of false doctrine. In this attempt to pacify their sister orthodox religions, they have demonstrated their ignorance of the true endowment. A *true* messenger of God is not a trained minister who has been taught what to say and how to administer to the people. While the LDS people strain to profess that their leaders are not "trained" in what they do and say, the fact is, they are trained in all things. They are mandated in everything they do by the strict guidelines of church administration which includes detailed handbooks that outline when and what to do in all aspects of LDS leadership. They are trained just as much as any religious leader of other orthodox religion by even more comprehensive methods. From the time they attend Primary as a young child, all the way through seminary, missions, and a lifetime of calls to increasingly responsible positions, the LDS Church insures that the best-trained and most thoroughly indoctrinated individuals are given leadership positions over the members.

JEHOVAH: It is well, Peter, James, and John. *(Jehovah turns and approaches Elohim.)* Elohim—Peter, James, and John have been down to the man Adam in the Telestial world. They found Satan there,

~~with his ministers, preaching all manner of false doctrine and~~ striving to lead the posterity of Adam astray **with all manner of false doctrine**. But Adam has been true and faithful to the token and sign given him in the Garden of Eden, and he is waiting for the further light and knowledge you promised to send him. This is their report.

ELOHIM: It is well. Jehovah, instruct Peter, James, and John to go down in their true character as apostles of the Lord Jesus Christ, to ~~the man Adam and his posterity~~ **Adam and Eve and their posterity** in the Telestial world, and to cast Satan out of their midst. Instruct them to give unto ~~Adam and his posterity~~ **Adam and Eve and their posterity** the Law of the Gospel as contained in the ~~Book of Mormon and the Bible~~ **Holy Scriptures**; also **give unto them** a charge to avoid all lightmindedness, loud laughter, evil speaking of the Lord's anointed, the taking of the name of God in vain, and every other unholy and impure practice; and cause these to be received by covenant. Instruct Peter, James, and John further to clothe ~~Adam and his posterity~~ **Adam and Eve and their posterity** in the Robes of the Holy Priesthood, with the robe on the left shoulder, and to give unto them the Second Token of the Aaronic priesthood, with its accompanying name, **and** sign, ~~and penalty~~. The have them return and bring me word.

The following is a part of the above dialogue as it was originally written by Joseph Smith (the changes from the current endowment are shown in black text):

> …the Law of the Gospel as contained in the Book of Mormon and the Bible, (which shall) charge (them) to avoid all (types of) lightmindedness and loud laughter (that lead to) evil speaking of (those who have been) anointed by the Lord (this day to become Priests and Priestesses unto the Most High God), and every other unholy and impure practice (that would cause them to take) the name of God in vain, and cause these to be received by covenant.

JEHOVAH: It shall be done, Elohim. *(Jehovah turns, and approaches Peter, James and John.)*
Peter, James, and John, go down in your true character as apostles of the Lord Jesus Christ to ~~the man Adam and his posterity~~ **Adam and Eve and their posterity** in the Telestial world. Cast Satan out of their midst. Give unto them the Law of the Gospel as contained in the ~~Book of Mormon and the Bible~~ **Holy Scriptures**; also a charge to avoid all lightmindedness, loud laughter, evil speaking of the Lord's anointed, the taking of the name of God in vain, and every other unholy and impure practice. Cause them to receive these by covenant (the same changes should be inserted as given above in the original endowment created by Joseph). Clothe them in the Robes of the Holy Priesthood, with the robe on the left shoulder, and give unto them the Second Token of the Aaronic Priesthood, with its accompanying name, **and** sign, ~~and penalty~~. Then return and bring us word.
PETER: It shall be done, Jehovah. Come, James and John; let us go down.

(The scene changes again to the lone and dreary world. The three apostles boldly approach Lucifer.)

PETER: I am Peter.

JAMES: I am James.

JOHN: I am John.

LUCIFER: Yes, I thought I knew you. ~~*(He turns to the Preacher.)* Do you know who these men are? They claim to be apostles. Try them!~~

~~*(The Preacher approaches Peter.)*~~

~~**PREACHER:** Do you profess to be apostles of the Lord Jesus Christ?~~

~~**PETER:** We do.~~

~~**PREACHER:** This man told me that we should never have any revelation or apostles, but if any should come professing to be apostles, I was to ask them to cut off an arm or some other member of the body and then restore it, so that the people might know that they came with power.~~

~~**PETER:** We do not satisfy men's curiosity in that manner. It is a wicked and an adulterous generation that seeks for a sign. Do you know who that man is? He is Satan!~~

No person who has been born into a mortal body, besides Christ, has ever been given power over the elements necessary to perform so-called "miracles." Only those Celestial Beings from other solar systems who have been assigned to this earth to help guide its course and destiny can perform such things; and whenever any seeming miracle has been or is performed, it is executed by such a Being in concert or harmony with a mortal who does not have this power but is instructed to demonstrate a supernatural power for the sake of those who witness it. Miracles are never performed for the personal benefit of any one person or group, but as is necessary for the larger benefit of all humans according to principles of equality.

A "miracle" is simply an event that takes place, which we do not understand...yet! To Celestial Beings, there is no such thing as a "miracle." Christ performed miracles (to his displeasure because the people paid more attention to the miracles than to his message) by command of the Father, which were done in an effort to get people to pay attention to what he had to share with them. Those that Jesus did perform were simply a demonstration of his knowledge and ability to do something that did not occur on a regular basis in his day. Let's say, for example, that Lazarus had collapsed and died of a heart attack. If Christ would have performed CPR and revived him, how would the people have reported the incident to others? They could have said, "*By his touch and through the breath of his own soul, Jesus brought Lazarus back to life!*" When in reality, had Jesus showed others how to perform CPR, these others would be performing the same *miracle*. Such is the way all presumed "miracles" are performed.

In the figurative endowment presentation, Peter is now demonstrating the power he has been given by the command he received from Jehovah to "*cast Satan out*." Peter does this by revealing the *real truth* (reality). Then he informs the preacher that the person whom he (the preacher) thought was God and from whom he was receiving instruction was actually Lucifer… "*He is Satan!*"

~~**PREACHER:** What? The devil?~~
~~**PETER:** That is one of his names.~~
~~**PREACHER:** He is quite a different person from what he told me the devil is. He said the devil has claws like a bear's on his hands, horns on his head, and a cloven foot, and that when he speaks he has the roar of a lion!~~
~~**PETER:** He has said this to deceive you, and I would advise you to get out of his employ.~~
~~**PREACHER:** Your advice is good; but, if I leave his employ, what will become of me?~~
~~**PETER:** We will preach the gospel unto you, with the rest of Adam's posterity.~~
~~**PREACHER:** That is good. *(He turns to Lucifer.)* I would like to have a settlement. I want you to pay me for preaching.~~

Here we are shown what happens to most people who are taught the *real truth*, recognize it as such through *common sense*, and desire to leave the influence of the false doctrines, myths, vain imaginations, and foolishness they have believed in all of their lives. *True messengers* implore us to leave that in which we have believed all our lives and allow them to teach us the *true* gospel of peace, which is encompassed in the way that we treat each other.

Instead of simply accepting that they have been deceived and pouring out the "old wine" in preparation to receive the "new," and walking away from Lucifer by getting "*out of his employ*," this part of the endowment supports the idea that most of us cannot leave tradition, worldly associations, and learning, because we are too accustomed to following the enticements of our flesh (*Lucifer*). Most people cannot leave their pursuit of money, worldly honor and glories, materialism, and their ties and bonds with family and friends. They end up confronting their own flesh ("*He turns to Lucifer*") in trying to reconcile their new understanding with that which they are used to and still want to believe to be true. They want the "*pay*" they were promised by the flesh; i.e., the power, the glory, and the friendship and acceptance of the world. They turn to their fleshly (extrinsic) needs more than to their spiritual (intrinsic) ones. They expect the same recompense that the flesh had once promised and which they received while following its enticements.

~~**LUCIFER:** I am ready to keep my word and fulfill my part of the agreement. I promised to pay you if you would convert these people, and they have nearly converted you! You can get out of my kingdom; I want no such men in it!~~

No one who accepts and is converted to the *real truth* will ever be embraced by a world controlled by Lucifer. Those who *think* they are following God, but who are successful in and loved by the world, forget the poignant words of Jesus:

These things I command you, that ye love one another. If the world hate you, ye know that it hated me before it hated you. If ye were of the world, the world would love his own: but because ye are not of the world, but I have chosen you out of the world, therefore the world hateth you. (John 15:17–19)

No one wants to be "hated" or ostracized by their family and friends. Therefore, very few will walk away from the enticements of the flesh (Lucifer) without wanting to be satisfied by them (be paid). The very reason why LDS Church authorities decided to change certain aspects of the original temple endowment was for no other purpose than to please the world so it would not hate or ostracize Mormons. Christ spoke poignantly of what would happen as one accepted the *real truth* over the falsehoods of the world's traditions and religions:

But whosoever shall deny me before men ***because he is afraid of what others might do to him***, him will I also deny before my Father which is in heaven ***and he shall not have peace in this world, nor the kingdom of God that is to come. Because of the things which shall come to pass because of the preaching of my gospel, some*** think not that I am come to send peace on earth ***as is promised by the Father; yea, they think that*** I came not to send peace, but a sword ***to divide them from their families. They think this because the things which I have taught them*** set a man at variance against his father, and the daughter against her mother, and the daughter in law against her mother in law. And a man's foes ***have become*** they of his own household. ***But I have not taught them anything that taketh them away from their families. But if they receive not the peace of the Father in their families, then they listen to my words and follow me and become worthy of a greater peace given them of the Father.*** He that loveth father or mother more than ***that which I have given him*** is not worthy of ***the peace I offer. Even so, the father and the mother have been charged with the care of the son and daughter. But if the son or daughter bringeth no joy to them, why then should they be brought down to hell with their children? Behold,*** and he that loveth son or daughter more than ***that which I have given him, also*** is not worthy of ***this peace. Behold, the cross which I bear for the world is that I have no family; for they who do the will of my Father in heaven are my father, my mother, my brother, sister, son and daughter. For these bring the peace to me that I seek.*** And he that taketh not his cross, and followeth after me, is not worthy of ***the same peace I receiveth from the Father. Yea,*** he that findeth his life ***in the things of this world*** shall lose it ***to these things and shall have no peace. But*** he that loseth his life ***in those things which I have given them of the Father*** shall find ***this peace of which I speak***. (Matthew 10:33–9, corrected version.)

(~~As the preacher turns sadly and leaves,~~ Lucifer approaches Peter.)

LUCIFER: ~~Now,~~ what are you going to do **now**?

PETER: We will dismiss you without further argument.

LUCIFER: Ah! You have looked over my kingdom, and my greatness and glory. Now you want to take possession of the whole of it. *(Lucifer turns, and stares into the camera—indicating he is speaking to the initiates.)* I have a word to say concerning these people. If they do not walk up to every covenant they make at these altars in this temple this day, they will be in my power!

PETER: Satan, we command you to depart!

LUCIFER: By what authority?

Wherein does Lucifer have "*power*" over us? Wherein does Peter have "*authority*" over Lucifer? The answer to both is one and the same and can be found in a correct understanding of the *true* gospel and atonement of Jesus Christ. This "power" and "authority" resides in "doing unto others," loving your neighbor as your self, and in proclaiming the perfect equality of all humans—or not. Living in accordance with the simple message of this gospel does indeed *cast Satan out*. Only when one is proclaiming these things alone, does one give evidence of a *true messenger* of God. This is the gospel Jesus taught. We either decide to choose to live this gospel, or Lucifer retains power over us.

The authority Lucifer called for is nothing more than the expression of Priesthood ego, self-delusion, or an attempt to use magic to send Lucifer on his way. Religious leaders and zealous laymen alike have attempted to use empty words and imaginary priesthood *power* and *authority* to exorcise demons and cast them out of those who are believed possessed. Science has proven unequivocally that there is no such thing as demonic possession. But there is certainly such a thing as human beings following the natural course of their flesh (Lucifer) and causing great harm to others, either directly by their actions or indirectly by their *failure* to act. The only thing that can temper our fleshly desires (cast Satan out) is to give in to the gospel of Doing Unto Others As We Would Have Them Do Unto Us.

The covenant of the gospel will be given to the people next, after Satan is cast out of their presence (after the *real truth* is taught). Living the tenets of the gospel of Jesus Christ literally allows a person to wade through the quagmire of confusion created by the religions of the world into a clear pool of living water that freely flows from the source of all truth—the *Holy Spirit of God and His Kingdom*, which is found inside each of us. It is this inner source of *common sense* (the authority) that Peter uses to command Lucifer to depart.

When we are taught things that are easily confirmed by our *common sense* and which solve the "mysteries of God," then we are literally being *redeemed from the fall of Adam*, whose "fall" is an expression of his inability to remember what he knew before when he was an equal member of the Godhead (Michael). Christ's atonement has been referred to as the *ultimate sacrifice* that also redeems us from the *fall of Adam*. All this means is that Jesus taught *real truth* (reality) to his disciples. His teachings thwarted the designs of organized religion and it's ministers who had convinced the people that they needed religion to be saved. To the chagrin of the religious leaders, once the people were taught the truth, they left religion and no longer trusted in the supposed "power" and "authority" of the pretended priesthoods established to aggrandize one person over another. Jesus taught the people that the "kingdom of God is within you." He threw down all tradition previously believed by the people (the Law of Moses) and incorporated the tenants of *true* religion into how one person treats another.

The doctrine that the knowledge of *real truth* redeems us from the fall is taught perfectly in the Book of Mormon. Unfortunately, it is unseen by the Mormon people, who listen more to their current leaders than they do to what was written and preserved for their instruction. Before a *true messenger* of God can perform his duties of "casting Satan out," he must have a complete and full understanding of all truth. The brother of Jared received this knowledge, and learned that because of what he now understood, he was *redeemed from the fall* and had the ability to help redeem others:

> *And the Lord said unto him: Believest thou the words which I shall speak? And he answered: Yea, Lord, I know that thou speakest the truth, for thou art a God of truth, and canst not lie. And when he had said these words, behold, the Lord showed himself unto him, and said: Because thou knowest these things ye are redeemed from the fall; therefore ye are brought back into my presence; therefore I show myself unto you. Behold, I am he who was prepared from the foundation of the world to redeem my people. Behold, I am Jesus Christ. I am the Father and the Son. In me shall all mankind have life, and that eternally, even they who shall believe on my name; and they shall become my sons and my daughters.* (Ether 3:11–14)

One will notice that the Lord told the brother of Jared that he was redeemed from the fall "*because thou knowest these things.*" The Lord went on to include all the people with whom the brother of Jared would share what he now knew. The sentence (*Because thou knowest these things ye are redeemed...*) begins with the singular pronoun "thou," but proceeds with the plural pronoun "ye," indicating that all those who would believe on the brother of Jared's words ("ye") would also be redeemed in the same manner.

Moroni would later abridge what the brother of Jared knew of the mysteries of God in what has now been published as The Sealed Portion. By simply reading the abridgment given by Moroni, one will find that the *real truth* indeed will set one free from all religion and all leaders, and inspire a personal path of intrinsic exploration that will lead one to the "kingdom of God." The main theme of The Sealed Portion is Doing Unto Others What You Would Have Them Do Unto You.

Lehi gave his own presentation of the figurative *Holy Endowment* in his counsel to his young son, Jacob. In his incredibly eloquent prose, Lehi also explains the atonement that Christ would perform for the world:

Adam fell that men might be; and men are, that they might have joy. And the Messiah cometh in the fulness of time, that he may redeem the children of men from the fall. And because that they are redeemed from the fall they have become free forever, knowing good from evil; to act for themselves and not to be acted upon, save it be by the punishment of the law at the great and last day, according to the commandments which God hath given. Wherefore, men are free according to the flesh; and all things are given them which are expedient unto man. And they are free to choose liberty and eternal life, through the great Mediator of all men, or to choose captivity and death, according to the captivity and power of the devil; for he seeketh that all men might be miserable like unto himself. (2 Nephi 2:25–7)

Jesus the Christ taught people the *reality* of being human. He taught them everything that anyone would ever need to know to distinguish between *good* and *evil*. Whatever we would do to another that we would like done to ourselves, is *good*; and whatever we do to another that we would *not* like done to us, is *evil*. It could not be any easier to understand. As we interact with others appropriately, we find the peace promised us. More importantly, when we finally realize that <u>*all*</u> there is to the future experiences we will have in eternity is our interactions with each other, it becomes clearly apparent what the atonement of Christ is really all about. It is about loving ourselves appropriately and then loving each other in the same way as we love ourselves. Through forgiveness, we learn to love ourselves and others. Through acceptance of each other's free agency to "*act for ourselves*," we can live at peace with the unique manner of life that others might decide to live, which might not be agreeable to our own. This simple and clear way of life is "straight and narrow" and completely contrary to all organized religion and every other worldly principle promoted by the mortal human race. Following the opposite "broad way" (Lucifer/the flesh) will surely lead us into captivity, where we are all miserable. Thank God, there are *true messengers* sent to teach us the *real truth* and *cast Satan out* of our midst!

PETER: *(With his right arm raised to the square.)* In the name of Jesus Christ, our Master.

(Lucifer is visibly shaken as he turns and leaves. Peter waits until he has left, and then approaches Adam.)

PETER: Adam, we are true messengers from the Father, and have come ~~down~~ to give ~~unto~~ you the further light and knowledge He promised to send you.
ADAM: How shall I know that you are true messengers?
PETER: By our giving unto you the token and sign you received in the Garden of Eden.

(Peter takes Adam by the right hand in the First Token of the Aaronic Priesthood.)

ADAM: What is that?

PETER: The First Token of the Aaronic Priesthood.

ADAM: Has it a name?

PETER: It has.

ADAM: Will you give it to me?

PETER: I cannot, for it is the New Name, **and I have made a covenant not to disclose it,** but this is the sign *(Peter raises his right arm to square)*, ~~and this represents the execution of the penalty~~ *~~(thumb of right hand drawn across the throat)~~*.

As previously explained, the "New Name" represents the experiences and knowledge we gained in our pre-mortal state of existence that we cannot remember. For this reason, Peter cannot give it to Adam, because as a mortal, he cannot remember his first estate any more than Adam can.

After our creation as individual human beings with the power to exercise personal free agency, our existence and learning process required monitoring by others who had already experienced the same process and learned from it. These "others" perform many things on our behalf that are necessary to allow us the opportunity to progress. In our pre-mortal and mortal states of existence, we were and are continually being acted upon and monitored. This monitoring is accomplished by the ministering of angels and other Celestial Beings who serve us and oversee our progression in these first two estates. The *Aaronic Priesthood* has reference to those states in which we figuratively receive the *tokens* associated with Beings who act in our behalf. The first token, called *The First Token of the Aaronic Priesthood*, we received in our pre-mortal state; and the second token of the same priesthood we receive in our mortal state. The name given to us in our mortal state, which is concurrent with *The Second Token of the Aaronic Priesthood*, is our first given name, which is familiar to us, and which we currently *can* remember. Therefore, it is the figurative representation of the experiences and works we do in mortality. In contrast to this, the *"New Name"* symbolizes that which we received in our pre-mortal state, and is therefore a name we are unable to reveal because we are not allowed to remember our pre-mortal existence while in mortality.

The tokens of the *Melchizedek Priesthood* are received to represent those states in which *we do all things for ourselves* and choose for ourselves the degree of happiness in which we feel most comfortable. Progressing to this stage of our existence, we finally understand all of the mysteries of God and are able to commune with our Creators and make decisions for ourselves based on what we have learned in our first two estates; thus, determining what is best for each of us individually. In summary, the *Aaronic* (lesser) *Priesthood* represents the state of existence in which all that we experience is provided equally for each of us through the actions of Celestialized Servants. In our pre-mortal lives and during mortality, we are provided equal opportunity and experience through the efforts of others who oversee our progression in these two states of existence. Whereas, the *Melchizedek* (higher) *Priesthood* represents the state in which we are finally prepared to make our individuality and personal choices known. These *higher* choices separate us and make us Gods of our own kingdoms, whether that is to be a *Telestial*, *Terrestrial*, or *Celestial* glory. While in the figurative story of the people of Israel, *Aaron* was the one who was appointed to administer in the outward ordinances relevant to all people in equality, but it was *Moses* who communed directly with God himself and wanted all the people to do the same. Joseph explained it this way:

> *The power and authority of the lesser, or Aaronic Priesthood, is to hold the keys of the ministering of angels, and to administer in outward ordinances…The power and authority of the higher, or Melchizedek Priesthood, is to…have the privilege of receiving the mysteries of the kingdom of heaven, to have the heavens opened unto them, to commune with the general assembly and church of the Firstborn, and to enjoy the communion and presence of God the Father, and Jesus the mediator of the new covenant.*   (D&C 107: 20, 18–19)

As explained earlier in the endowment, the head represents the *kingdom of God*, or our interaction with our Creators. On our Creators' planet, our spirits were first introduced into a new body (thus the *New Name*) so we could begin our lives as free-willed beings. Since all of our spirit matter resides in the location of our head, it is appropriate to have the head represent this. The *execution of the penalty* for not keeping our first estate, or better, for not obeying (*Law of Obedience*) our Creators and choosing not to come to earth (*Law of Sacrifice*) and pass through mortality to learn good from evil, or happiness from unhappiness, is that we will be cut off from the kingdom of God forever, never being able to progress.

To reiterate, all of the spirit beings created on the planet of our Eternal Parents came to this solar system. However, not all of them accepted the plan of the Father and agreed to support it. With great mercy, our Creators allowed those rebellious ones to come here and participate in mortality. After doing so, if they *still* reject the plan and believe there is a better way, even after experiencing mortality for themselves, they will be subjected to what is known as "the Second Death." This is when the Creators who gave them the ability to have and record experience as a spirit (become a human being), disassembles this spirit. It is at this time that the realization of this "penalty" will be had. However, it is not really a *penalty* because these will no longer exist to experience anything; therefore, they are mercifully not punished at all.

ADAM: Now I know that you are true messengers sent down from Father. *(Speaking directly into the camera to the audience.)* These are true messengers. I exhort you to give strict heed to their counsel and teachings, and they will lead you in the way of life and salvation.

All things *make sense* when a true messenger teaches us the truth by *disclosing his true identity*. He can answer any question and can truly lead us to an understanding of things that make perfect sense. A true messenger of God (Peter) will teach things that are confirmed by the *Holy Ghost inside of us*. As we are taught the mysteries of God that have been hidden from the foundation of the world, all things will begin to come together and make sense, and we will know with a surety that those who teach us these things are "*true messengers [of our] Father [sent to] lead [us] in the way of life and salvation.*"

We can be assured that a *true messenger from the Father* is teaching us, if what is taught speaks to our hearts—our *common sense*—which will subconsciously agree with all we know but cannot remember because of our incapable mortal brains. The feeling of "making sense" is simply our consciousness coming into balance with our subconscious (which is our spirit that has recorded all of our previous experiences). Adam is finally convinced that Peter is a *true messenger* because everything that Peter teaches him *makes perfect sense*, whereas the traditions, beliefs, religious teachings, and exhortations of *Lucifer's* preacher confused him.

NARRATOR: The officiator will represent Peter at the altar.

The altar to which the endowment now refers is simply symbolic of *the actions and works of man in mortality*. It is the *same altar* that Adam built and upon which he prayed to God and was answered by Lucifer. It is the *same altar* that will be represented throughout the remainder of the endowment and upon which all the covenants are made. The analogy of an "altar" is used by John in his Revelation. The term "altar" always means *the manner in which mortals offer their works*, or rather, *that which is representative of the works of mortal hands*. The following is an excerpt from John's explanation of his book of Revelation:

Revelation 6:9 *And when he had opened the fifth seal, I saw the souls of them upon the earth who were slain upon the altar for the word of God, and for the testimony which they held.*

An altar is something built by mortal hands for the purpose of making an offering upon it, usually dedicated to a Deity. When one obeys the commands of God, one is effectually dedicating his or her works "upon the altar" before God, figuratively exclaiming, "Here, O my God, are my works that I have fulfilled and dedicated to Thee!" Therefore, being "slain upon the altar" means that one has sacrificed one's life "for the word of God" by keeping His commandments. In the same spirit, Jesus said:

He that findeth his life shall lose it: and he that loseth his life for my sake shall find it. (Matthew 10:39)

John is referring to all those upon the earth who have "lost their lives" in dedication to obeying the commands of God. It is truly a great sacrifice to live the gospel of Jesus Christ in a world that rejects it. The gentle and reassuring spirit of Psalms explains:

I will say unto God my rock, Why hast thou forgotten me? Why go I mourning because of the oppression of the enemy? As with a sword in my bones **[i.e., being slain]**, *mine enemies reproach me; while they say daily unto me, Where is thy God? Why art thou cast down, O my soul? And why art thou disquieted within me? hope thou in God: for I shall yet praise him, who is the health of my countenance, and my God. Judge me, O God, and plead my cause against an ungodly nation: O deliver me from the deceitful and unjust man. For thou art the God of my strength: why dost thou cast me off? why go I mourning because of the oppression of the enemy? O send out thy light and thy truth: let them lead me; let them bring me unto thy holy hill, and to thy tabernacles. Then will I go* **unto the altar of God**, *unto God my exceeding joy: yea, upon the harp will I praise thee, O God my God. Why art thou cast down, O my soul? and why art thou disquieted within me? Hope in God: for I shall yet praise him, who is the health of my countenance, and my God.* (Psalms 42:9–11; 43:1–5)

Isaiah reiterates the purpose and symbolism of altars:

At that day shall a man look to his Maker, and his eyes shall have respect to the Holy One of Israel. And he shall not look **to the altars, the work of his hands**, *neither shall respect that which his fingers have made, either the groves, or the images.* (Isaiah 17:7–8)

Moses was commanded to construct an altar to specified dimensions. This is symbolic of the commandments of God being specific in their purpose, which Jesus gives as the greatest law and commandment of all the prophets—do unto others what you would have them do unto you. Ezekiel borrows the symbolism to reiterate that the law of God is exact, and thus should our works be exact as we offer them upon an altar before the Lord:

The altar of wood was three cubits high, and the length thereof two cubits; and the corners thereof, and the length thereof, and the walls thereof, were of wood: and he said unto me, This is the table that is before the LORD. (Ezekiel 41:22)

Ezekiel continued in his teachings by figuratively expressing that we should purge ourselves of sin (which is anything we do to another that we wouldn't want done to us) and purify our lives throughout mortality (*seven days*), which is our symbolic offering upon the altar to God:

Seven days shall they purge the altar and purify it; and they shall consecrate themselves. (Ezekiel 43:26)

Revelation 6:10 *And the four and twenty elders cried with a loud voice, saying, How long, O Lord, holy and true, dost thou not judge them that dwell on the earth and avenge their blood, which has been spilt upon the altar?*

In other words, the prophets who have been sent to teach the people what they should do to serve God properly, are asking how long the Lord will allow the earth to remain in a state where living the word of God is such a tremendous sacrifice.

(666, The Mark of America, pgs. 156–8.)

(At this point the film or the play is concluded. The remainder of the endowment is conducted from an audio recording.)

THE LAW OF THE GOSPEL

PETER: A couple will now come to the altar. *(Witness couple comes to altar as before.)* Brethren and sisters, this couple at the altar represents all of you as if at the altar, and you will be under the same obligations as they will be. We are required to give unto you the Law of the Gospel as contained in the ~~Book of Mormon and the Bible~~ **Holy Scriptures**; to give unto you also a charge to avoid all (types of) lightmindedness (and) loud laughter (that lead to) evil speaking of (those who have been) anointed (by) the Lord (this day to become Priests and Priestesses unto the Most High God), and every other unholy and impure practice (that would cause you to take) the name of God in vain, and to cause you to receive these by covenant. (NOTE: The appropriate changes have been made to reflect Joseph Smith's original endowment.)

Again, Moroni's instructions to Joseph were simple and clear:
He said there was a book deposited, written upon gold plates, giving an account of the former inhabitants of this continent, and the source from whence they sprang. He also said that the fullness

of the everlasting Gospel was contained in it, as delivered by the Savior to the ancient inhabitants; Also, that there were two stones in silver bows—and these stones, fastened to a breastplate, constituted what is called the Urim and Thummim—deposited with the plates; and the possession and use of these stones were what constituted 'seers' in ancient or former times; and that God had prepared them for the purpose of translating the book. (Joseph Smith—History 1:34–5)

Joseph's primary mission was to give the people of the earth another testimony of the *fullness* of the *only true and unadulterated* gospel of Jesus Christ as it was given by his *own mouth* to the Nephites and Lamanites and recorded, translated, and published as 3rd Nephi, chapters 12, 13, and 14. The original translation from the gold plates did not give the Savior's words exactly as they are currently published in the Book of Mormon. However, Joseph was instructed to interpolate into his translation the "orthodox" accepted version of the same things Jesus taught to the Jews. (This "orthodox version" is the King James translation of the Bible.) This was done to help the people of today (who are more familiar with the words of Christ given in the New Testament) accept the "fullness of the everlasting gospel." It is for this reason only that 3rd Nephi 12, 13, and 14 parallel, almost exactly word for word, the KJV of the book of Matthew, chapters 5, 6, and 7—which is the closest description of the *only true and unadulterated* gospel ever given by Jesus, the Christ.

Living this *true gospel* is the *only* requirement the participants in the endowment covenant to obey in the "lone and dreary world," as given at this point by Peter. This gospel is found in its fullness in the Bible and reiterated in the second witness, the Book of Mormon. Jesus preached *no other gospel* and gave the same words in perfect harmony to the peoples of both continents. In their ignorance, uninspired leaders failed to recognize the simplicity of Christ's message and created churches and structured their religious beliefs by adding to or taking from his words in order to promote their own doctrines and precepts as the "gospel."

This is particularly true of LDS leaders, who, having blinded eyes, ignorantly changed the *only true and unadulterated* gospel to include the book of Doctrine and Covenants and their own modern-day revelations (thus the change to "Holy Scriptures" in the text above), which they believe also represents *the **fullness** of the gospel of Christ*. If this were so, Moroni would not have told Joseph Smith that the gold plates contained the **fullness** of the *everlasting Gospel*, but would have given some permission or idea about the need for continuing revelation. This so-called principle of "continuing revelation" is that upon which the Brigham Young version of the LDS Church bases its authenticity and continued authority. The *true* gospel is an *everlasting* Gospel because it *never changes*—NEVER! This simply means that it cannot be added to or taken away from by any implied authority of men or any other message.

The **Law of the Gospel** cannot be made any clearer than in the words of Jesus, alone, that are found in the Bible and the Book of Mormon, which irrevocably tie all humans to a plain understanding and obedience to the same.

Jesus spoke plainly of the fullness of the everlasting Gospel:

Therefore all things whatsoever ye would that men should do to you, do ye even so to them: for this is the law and the prophets. ...Thou shalt love the Lord thy God with all thy heart, and with all thy soul, and with all thy mind. This is the first and great commandment. And the second is like unto it, Thou shalt love thy neighbour as thyself. On these two commandments hang all the law and the prophets. (Matthew 7:12; 22:37–40)

The gospel is based upon eternal laws and was set up among free-willed human beings to guide us to treat others as we would want to be treated. As previously explained and symbolically performed in the Initiatory Ordinances, all participants receiving their own endowment were first anointed to become *Priests and Priestesses*, and now the prerequisite of obedience to the gospel is established in a series of steps leading to that end. Since Peter is about to clothe the participants in the "Robes of the Holy Priesthood," it is appropriate that the "charge" of obeying the gospel be given. This includes the avoidance of all things that one might do to speak ill of, make fun of, mock, or in any other way mistreat *"those who have been anointed by the Lord this day to become Priests and Priestesses unto the Most High God."* <u>Every</u> <u>person</u> receiving the endowment was anointed to become a Priest or Priestess during the initiatory ordinances. Therefore, this strict covenant to obey the **Law of the Gospel** has to do with the way we treat others and nothing to do with speaking evil of Church Leaders, except as they, too, are our neighbors.

"Taking the name of God in vain" has nothing to do with cursing or misusing the name "God" in daily speech. It simply means that when we take upon ourselves the name of Christ/Jesus/God, that we covenant to *act* appropriately as They would, and that we do not do so in vain, or without real purpose, not intending to do as we pretend to do in the name of God. As you may remember, the figurative expression *"name"* has already been explained as meaning *works*, meaning that, to our Creators and the prophets, a person is known by what he or she does, not by what one says or believes. Therefore, if we pretend to be believers and followers of Jesus Christ and do not act according to the mandates given in the fullness of his gospel, we have taken *his name upon us in vain*, and as the original commandment states:

Thou shalt not take the name of the LORD thy God in vain; for the LORD will not hold him guiltless that taketh his name in vain. (Exodus 20:7)

Well again did Jesus say of those who "take his name in vain":

Not every one that saith unto me, Lord, Lord, shall enter into the kingdom of heaven; but he that doeth the will of my Father which is in heaven. Many will say to me in that day, Lord, Lord, have we not prophesied in thy name? and in thy name have cast out devils? and in thy name done many wonderful works? And then will I profess unto them, I never knew you: depart from me, ye that work iniquity. (Matthew 7:21–3)

If we choose to obey the **Law of the Gospel** and take upon ourselves the *name of God*, then we will do "*the will of [our] Father which is in heaven*"…and His *only* will for us is to do unto others what we would have them do unto us—nothing more, nothing less—anything more or less than this is done in *vain*.

This is the *fullness* of the covenant we make to God at this point in the endowment, and prepares us for that which is to follow.

PETER: All arise. *(All patrons stand.)* Each of you bring your right arm to the square. *(This is done.)* ~~You and~~ each of you covenant and promise before God, angels, and these witnesses ~~at this altar~~, that you will observe and keep the Law of the Gospel and this charge as it has been explained to you. Each of you bow your head and say, "Yes."
PATRONS: Yes.
PETER: That will do. *(All patrons sit down.)*

Bringing the "right arm to the square" is an indication of righteous works in contrast to bringing the "left arm to the square" as an indication of unrighteous works (more will be explained about this later). Bowing one's head is a sign of humility and submission. In humility and submission we covenant to obey the **Law of the Gospel** as described in Matthew 5, 6, and 7, and 3rd Nephi 12, 13, and 14.

THE ROBES OF THE HOLY PRIESTHOOD

PETER: We are instructed to clothe you in the Robes of the Holy Priesthood. Place the robe on your left shoulder. Place the cap on your head with the bow over the right ear. Replace the apron. Tie the girdle with the bow on the right side. Remove the slippers from your feet, and put them on again as part of the temple clothing. You may now proceed to clothe.

(Patrons open their clothing envelopes and dress as instructed.)

The *removal of the slippers* from the feet represents leaving the current path upon which we have wandered all of our life, and preparing ourselves to embark on a new one. Our feet carry us throughout our lives and carry the burden of all of our experiences, good or bad. "Removal of the slippers" has the same significance as Jesus washing his disciples' feet. He symbolically washed away all the learning and burden of the paths they had been following and showed them a new way to peace and happiness. "Baptism" is also symbolic of the "removal of the slippers" and "washing of the feet," as one is immersed completely into water (washing away the previous life) and brought out as a new, clean person. Before one can wear the *Robes of the Priesthood* properly, one must leave all else behind and become a new person.

As explained above, and for the *first* time since Joseph Smith began his work, the *true* meaning of the terms "Aaronic," "Melchizedek," and the "Priesthood," are now made known in this endowment exposition. With the explanation of the Priesthood, the whole plan of life can be understood as never before. If here in mortality and in our previous state we all equally receive of our Creators those things to help us progress as human beings (the *Aaronic* state), and we still are not sufficiently prepared to make a final choice of personal happiness for ourselves (the *Melchizedek* state), what greater commission could be placed universally upon us all than to love our neighbor as ourselves and to do to unto others as we would have them do unto us? This *great law*, upon being followed, will maintain peace and order among beings created with the ability to exercise free will. This law takes away any dominion one human might have over another—making all equal. Which mortal human, therefore, would be the *leader* or *teacher* of any other mortal but one blinded by his or her own vanity?

Once again the paradigm of truth shifts the mind—in this case, concerning the Priesthood, from the delusion that it refers to "authority" or "power," to an understanding that it refers to our "state of being." "Priesthood" is about where we are in our progression and the "name" we establish for ourselves, not the titles that we hold. This explanation of the priesthood should help clarify the nature of the laws that veiled mortals have been given to observe. These laws are best typified in the *Aaronic* condition by Christ's call to become as *little children*, meek, submissive, and full of love; in anticipation of a day when we will be able to make a final choice for ourselves in the *Melchizedek* state, when all things necessary for our progression will be sufficiently made known to us.

The "*Robes of the Holy Priesthood*" are symbolic of the works that we perform, the way we live our lives, the way that we think, and the intent and purpose for which we act by our free will according to the *Aaronic* or *Melchizedek* states of existence in which we find ourselves. Both men and women put on these robes, which negates any false doctrine that the woman is not entitled to the *same* priesthood *equally* with the man. At this point in the endowment, the participants are (figuratively) in their mortal, or second part of the *Aaronic* state, where all of our works are unrighteous at one time or another (usually most of the time). For this reason, the "robes of *our works*" are placed on the *left shoulder* of all of those receiving the endowment, and the sign is made by the *left* arm forming a square.

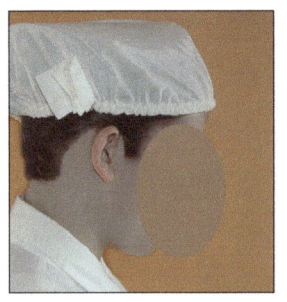

The cap that the male participants put on their heads represents the "Kingdom of God," or the existence where we were on a level equal to our Creators. As stated above, all of us are part of the "Holy Trinity." This Godhead balances the unrighteous works of the men who dawn the cap. This *Trinity* is represented by the three distinct bows, which at this point, are placed over the *right ear*. Directly across, on the other side of the cap, is a string that is tied to the three distinct bows found on the robes. This string represents the straight and narrow path, or straight line, which ties the "kingdom of God" to the *Robes of the Priesthood*, or our inner conscience to our individual propensities and actions as mortals. Some (as they suppose) call it the line of revelation coming from the kingdom of God to guide one in the correct and straight ways of priesthood "authority" (at least those without eyes that see), thereby giving the male an implied dominion, power, and authority over the female, as she does not have a similar cap, but is required to don a veil over her face when performing her works. Nothing could be further from the truth.

Oh, how foolish is the pride and vain imagination of the male ego! Joseph, with due reverence for the role that females take in the creation of life, made a mockery of the male perception of priesthood "authority" in this part of the endowment. Again, well did he say:

If I revealed all that has been made known to me, scarcely a man on this stand would stay with me. ...Brethren, if I were to tell you all I know of the kingdom of God, I do know that you would rise up and kill me. (Joseph Smith Jr.)

Not only did Joseph allow the women to put on the *exact same robes of the priesthood* as their male counterparts, but he also specifically instructed the males to wear the funny-looking caps in contrast to the females, who place beautiful veils over their faces. The cap symbolically *balances* the unrighteous, vain, and foolish imaginations of the hearts of men in receiving supposed *revelations from God* (the string), with the will of the Father, Son, and Holy Ghost (the bows). The female does not need a cap, but rather sees righteously *through the veil*. This means that the female usually perceives and has a propensity to care for others and treat others according to the tenets of the gospel of Christ instinctively. By her nature, the female more easily sees *through the veil* of the subconscious mind (where we once lived the fullness of the gospel with Celestial Mothers), whereas the male needs constant instruction (real or supposed revelation) and a continual reminder to overcome the male ego in order to live the gospel. In the *Garden*, for example, Adam wouldn't budge on breaking a commandment to make it possible that "man might be," while Eve intuitively understood what must be done in order to accomplish the charge given by God in order to progress.

As mentioned above, the string is balanced by the *Holy Trinity* directly on the opposite side of the hat. While wearing the robe on the left shoulder, or in other words, performing unrighteous works in mortality, the *Holy Trinity* is figuratively whispering in the *right ear* of the male participant, while the foolish man is getting false revelation (the *string going to the left shoulder*) from his veiled brain underneath the cap. In contrast, the women figuratively *see through the veil*, attributing no special revelatory power as the men assume of themselves.

(If the "Brethren" had understood fully that what Joseph was making them do was a representation of their foolhardiness rather than their inspiration, they *would* have killed him.)

Later, the participants will place the robe on the *right shoulder*, representative of their works performed, figuratively, in the *Melchizedek Priesthood* state of existence where all things are revealed and we are able to communicate directly with Celestial Beings. This was explained previously regarding receiving the *tokens and signs* of the lesser and higher priesthoods. Again, so that the true purpose of the priesthood can be well understood, the *Aaronic* (lesser) *Priesthood* represents the state in which that which is given, is given to all of us equally, and where all things are done for us equally (the rain falls upon all of us the same; we all have the same type of body;

we are all subjected to the enticements of the Telestial flesh). Whereas, the *Melchizedek* (higher) *Priesthood* represents the state in which we are finally prepared to make our individuality and personal choices known.

Under the *Melchizedek Priesthood*, we are in a state of existence where we can act in our own behalf and perform works according to principles of truth, understanding, and certainty, having the veil removed and understanding things as they really are. When the male is working in righteousness (robe on the *right shoulder*), his brain is giving him correct information (the *string* is on the *right* side connected to the robes of the priesthood), balanced by his unrighteous works (opposition) of the past. The *Holy Trinity*/the bows now overlook the *left shoulder*, symbolizing that the Father, Son, and Holy Ghost have "overlooked" our unrighteous works so that we may progress in happiness. This balancing act will always keep the male ego in check throughout the eternities. No matter what power and authority may be given to a male, he will always remember he was once a *male* who wore the cap with the string tied to his *left shoulder*—thus keeping him humble. In contrast to this somewhat jaded view of men at this part of the endowment representing our mortal existence, the women continue to be presented, figuratively, as never changing the beautiful way in which they perceive life and loving one's neighbor, as if they can actually see *through the veil*.

Continuing with the explanation of the temple attire, and as mentioned previously, the apron (which is always dark) represents the works we perform individually when our spirit is connected with a mortal body of flesh and bone. This is in stark contrast to the pure whiteness of the way we were first created. We are completely responsible for our own works (the apron), as contrasted against background of the white temple attire and garments which were given to us by Elohim, symbolizing our Creators' understanding of what we need to experience in order to progress to become like Them. Becoming "like Them" does not mean we will all be Celestial Servants, but indicates that we will experience an eternal joy of our own choosing, just as They do.

As mentioned above, at no time during the endowment did Elohim command us to put on an apron. Lucifer did. He was the one who created fear and shame, finding fault with Adam and Eve's condition and creating a false remedy: "***LUCIFER:*** *See, you are naked. Take some fig leaves and make you aprons. Father will see your nakedness. Quick! Hide!*" Without giving thought to what Elohim wanted us to do, we followed Lucifer's advice and obediently placed the *dark* apron over our *white* temple clothes and garments before receiving the necessary instruction from Jehovah.

On the other hand, we are not allowed to put on the robes of the priesthood *until* we are commanded to do so by Elohim. The "priesthood" symbolizes the works of God in our lives. As explained before, the *lower* priesthood (*Aaronic*) is connected with what our Eternal Parents and *ministering angels* do for us, and the *higher priesthood* (*Melchizedek*) is associated with what we do for ourselves. The robes are placed upon the participants at different stages of the endowment that represent different aspects of our Creators' work in our lives. These stages represent our pre-existence (*washing and anointing*), our pre-mortal existence (*Garden of Eden*), our mortal existence without the intervention of God in our lives (*the lone and dreary world*), the Millennial time when we will live upon this earth interacting with *God*, our Christ, and the angels; and finally, our resurrected, eternal state, where we exist in the degree of happiness that bests suits us (*entrance into the presence of our Creators* [Elohim] *through the veil*).

While we *are* responsible for our own actions and reactions within the different stages of our existence, we are *not* responsible for the processes and choices that preceded our awakening into existence—it was not our *free-willed* choice to be created. The eternal covenant of our Creators (or the laws by which They are required to perform Their own actions) is that the final state of existence for those they create (us) will *always* be eternal happiness; and it is *Their* responsibility, "Their work and Their glory," to assure us this happiness. To accomplish this end, a significant series of preparatory steps are necessary after each free-willed being is created. As part of this process, They created this earth, placed us in mortality, and purposefully allow us to exist without being able to remember Them or our interactions with Them.

It is in our current state of mortality that we *wear the Robes of the Priesthood on our **left** shoulder* in order to be "prepared to officiate in the ordinances of the *Aaronic* Priesthood," as Peter will soon instruct. Mortality and all things which occur upon this earth are directed by ministering angels who oversee the probationary period necessary in order for us to learn more about what does and does not make each of us happy. Later, in preparation for our *Millennial* existence, we will be instructed (as Elohim commands) to switch the Robes to the right shoulder "preparatory to officiating in the ordinances of the *Melchizedek* Priesthood." We will then become completely responsible for all of our actions and choices because of our ability to associate and commune with those Beings who have been hidden from our view—Christ and the angels from another solar system who shall be upon this earth during the *Millennial* part of our existence.

It is well to note that Lucifer's works (his power and *priesthoods*) are represented on *his* apron. His apron does not have nine leaves, as is the case of the endowment participants, but the symbols of education, business, and industry, upon which the foundation of his power on this earth is established. The robes of the priesthood are pure and white, as are the temple clothes and garments placed upon the participants in the beginning and throughout the presentation of the endowment, and have the same significance as the robes given to those who "overcome the world," figuratively represented by John the Beloved in his own unique endowment narrative of the mysteries of God:

Revelation 6:11 *And white robes were given unto every one of them who were sacrificed upon the altar; and it was said unto them, that they should rest yet for a little season until their fellowservants and their brethren who would also be killed upon the altar as they were should fulfill their works.*

Uninspired teachers would interpret the above passage as referring to those called of God, or in this case, who have *called themselves* to be missionaries, pastors, bishops, or administrators of God's word. They assume in a pious attitude of sacrifice and self-glorification, that these leaders must also be killed before the Lord comes again. Inasmuch as the true nature of "**slain or sacrificed upon the altar**" has now been properly revealed, John's later description of those given "white robes" puts the truth in proper perspective:

After this I beheld, and, lo, this great multitude, which no man could number, of all nations, and kindreds, and people, and tongues, stood before the throne, and before the Lamb, clothed with white robes, and palms in their hands;...And one of the elders spake unto me saying, Who are these who are arrayed in white robes? and from whence did they come? And I said unto him, Sir, thou knowest. And he said to me, These are they who came out of great tribulation, and have washed their own robes, and made them white in the blood of the Lamb. (Revelation 7:9, 13–14)

Clothing has always symbolized one's actions, deeds, and thoughts. Notice John was not told that Christ washed the blood out of the robes, but "*These...have washed their own robes and made them white in the blood of the Lamb.*" The works of Christ cannot save us unless we learn to do the same works he did, apply the principles he taught, and follow the example he set, and for which he lost his life, and lose ours in the same way.

Here John is telling us that those who follow the teachings and precepts of Christ will *rest* from all worldly trials and adversity that cause tribulation in one's life, supporting what he heard Jesus teach the people:

Come unto me, all ye that labour and are heavy laden, and I will give you rest. Take my yoke upon you, and learn of me; for I am meek and lowly in heart: and ye shall find rest unto your souls. For my yoke is easy, and my burden is light. (Matthew 11:28–30)

All must be allowed to live in mortality and prove themselves worthy to live in eternal worlds where they will not cause problems. Until one learns to always do unto another that which they would want done unto them, they will not be allowed to possess an exalted body that never dies and live on a planet which supports this type of body.

Those who learn and apply the gospel of Jesus Christ (given a *white robe*) will rest from tribulations and hell that others are experiencing in life. Nevertheless, mortality must be allowed to continue "*yet for a little season*" until all have been given ample opportunity to "*fulfill their works.*"

(666, The Mark of America, pgs. 159–60.)

The "girdle" or "sash," which resembles a long narrow scarf made of the same material as the robes, is tied around the waist or beltline of the robe, becoming an integral part of the temple clothing. It is nothing more than that which *binds* all of our works together and holds them securely in place so that we will never forget them. It is a symbolic representation of our spirit matter being able to record all of our experiences so that they will be remembered forever. In essence, this designed ability to have perfect recollection is the "*judgment bar of God*" before which we will all stand and be judged by our works. Can one imagine how long it would take God to literally stand each one of His billions of creations before Him to get their "day in court?" Therefore, "judgment" takes place in *our own minds*, as we recall all that we have done in our existence and stand before the "bar" of our own consciousness. This makes judgment immediate as we re-acquire all the memories "tied" to us, including those of the standards and laws we received from our Eternal Parents in our first estate, so that we may evaluate how we have fared with our free agency.

At this part of the endowment, the "tie" or bow of the sash is made on the *right side*, which means that our subconscious mind—or in other words, our spirit—has recorded and bound to us experiences of righteousness up to this point in our existence. The mercy of our Creator lies in the fact that the works we perform in mortality (symbolized by the green apron) are not counted against us, but are necessary to prove to ourselves who we really are. (This was explained above in reference to the parable of the *Prodigal Son*.) Thus, reconciliation with our Creator is made possible because the Veil that conceals our memories of the first estate makes it impossible to conduct our lives on a level playing field. Here in mortality, we are not able to make proper and conscientious choices with our free agency because of this Veil. The chaos of mortality was necessary in order to provide sufficient opposition to the righteousness of our original training, thereby programming into our beings the elements of counteracting force in order to discern that which creates happiness in all Eternal Beings. Consequently, these memories of our mortalities will be *tied in* with all parts of our existence (figuratively represented by the sash) and become our judgment bar, but not necessarily our "judgment day," as is now clarified.

Later, when we move the robe to the *right* shoulder and tie the bow on the *left*, figuratively exiting mortality as we now experience it, and begin to experience existence under new conditions on a *higher* level (*Melchizedek Priesthood*), the playing field will be leveled and fair, and we will have all things revealed to us. At that point, we can use our free agency to choose for ourselves what type of happiness we want. The sash is then tied on the *left* side, signifying that all of our unrighteous (*left*) choices play a part in the propensities of our egos, and are bound to us as part of determining for ourselves what kingdom of happiness we are best suited for. (More of this will be explained below.)

In summary, the main point of the sash or girdle is that it figuratively binds us to the memories and past actions of all that we have ever done since we were first created. These memories and actions will be tied into a perfect recollection of everything we have done so that we will have a proper understanding that will effect our choice of a kingdom—Celestial, Terrestrial, or Telestial—with each of these kingdoms having three differing degrees (figuratively shown as the nine leaves on the green apron as it has been explained before) in which we will dwell forever. These "degrees" simply mean differing personal perspectives of what brings joy to a person. We will eventually be separated and placed among those with whom we share the same desires of happiness. In this way, eternal peace can be maintained as we will associate only with those of the same mindset and who pursue the same experiences.

In our pre-mortal state we already developed certain human characteristics which helped our Creators determine how many planets They needed to create in our solar system to provide each of us with what would be best suited for our happiness. Every solar system in the Universe is based on the degrees of glory chosen beforehand by its future inhabitants. Some have less than nine, some have more, but it can be assured that in every solar system there will be sufficient planets where all humans will be guaranteed their free agency and have everything necessary to assure their eternal happiness.

THE SECOND TOKEN OF THE AARONIC PRIESTHOOD

PETER: A couple will now come to the altar. *(The witness couple kneels at the altar as before.)* With the robe on the left shoulder, you are prepared to officiate in the ordinances of the Aaronic Priesthood. We will now give unto you the Second Token of the Aaronic Priesthood, with its accompanying name, **and** sign, ~~and penalty~~. This token is given by clasping the right hands and placing the joint of the thumb (upon the first knuckle) between the first and second knuckles of the hand, in this manner.

As mentioned previously, Brigham Young was mistaken in his interpretation of the endowment in one of the most fundamental aspects of the rite—the placement of the thumb *in between* the first and second knuckles of the right hand rather than on the first knuckle. The original endowment gave the *Second Token of the Aaronic Priesthood* as follows: "This token is given by clasping the right hands and placing the joint of the thumb upon the first knuckle of the hand…"

This token is figurative of our mortal (second) existence, and is received through those assigned and properly called servants of God (Peter) in the state where a person has an imperfect body of flesh and bone. This is symbolically indicated by having the servant rest his thumb on the knuckle (a bone) of the body the participant receives in mortality. The way this is given is in contrast to the way we received the *First Token of the Aaronic Priesthood* from Elohim while we were still spirits in perfect bodies in the *Garden of Eden*. The *First Token of the Aaronic Priesthood* was figuratively given as though receiving it *without* mortal flesh and bone, as if we were in a spirit state (thus given in between the two knuckle bones as it was previously explained). Though we have always had some type of body to interact with our spirits whenever we have experienced a state of consciousness, it was imperative that Joseph clarify the distinction between these two states of existence and the associated signs and tokens figuratively received in each one.

(The officiator and the male witness join hands in the token, and slightly raise their hands to demonstrate it to the patrons.)

PETER: We desire all to receive it. All arise.

(As the patrons stand, the witness couple returns to their seats, and various temple workers circulate about the room administering this token as they did the former.)

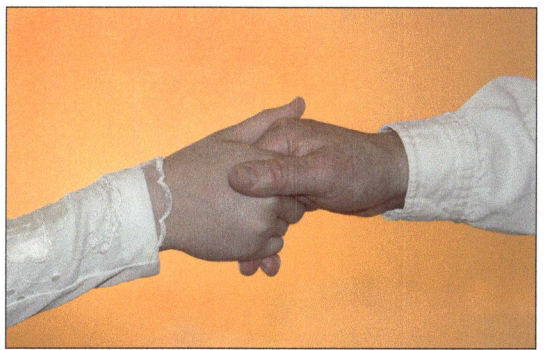

PETER: If any of you have not received this token, ~~you will~~ please raise your hand. The name of this token is your own first given name if you are going through the temple for your own endowment, or, if you are going through for the dead, it is the first given name of the person for whom you are officiating. The sign is made by bringing the right hand in front of you, with the hand in cupping shape, the right arm forming a square, and the left arm being raised to the square. This is the sign. *(The officiator demonstrates.)* ~~The execution of the penalty is represented by placing the right hand on the left breast, drawing the hand quickly across the body, and dropping the hands to the sides.~~ I will now explain the covenant and obligation ~~of secrecy~~ which are associated with this token, its name, **and** sign, ~~and penalty, and~~ which you will be required to take upon yourselves.

If I were receiving my own endowment today, and if my first given name were "David," I would repeat in my mind these words, after making the sign, ~~at the same time representing the execution of the penalty~~: I, David, **solemnly covenant before God, angels, and these witnesses**, that I will never reveal the Second Token of the Aaronic Priesthood, with its accompanying name, **and** sign, ~~and penalty~~. ~~Rather than do so, I would suffer my life to be taken.~~ All arise. *(All patrons stand.)* Each of you make the sign of the Second Token of the Aaronic priesthood by bringing the right hand in front of you, with the hand in cupping shape, the right arm forming a square, and the left arm being raised to the square. This is the sign. Now, repeat in your mind after me the words of the covenant, ~~at the same time representing the execution of the penalty~~.

I, _____, think of the first given name, **solemnly** covenant **before God, angels, and these witnesses** that I will never reveal the Second Token of the Aaronic Priesthood, with its accompanying name, **and** sign, ~~and penalty. Rather than do so, I would suffer my life to be taken.~~ That will do. *(All patrons sit down.)*

The *Second Token of the Aaronic Priesthood* is symbolic of how our spirit reacts when it is joined with an imperfect body in mortality. Keep in mind, we have come into existence through no conscious choice of our own, and this is completed for us (under the figurative *Aaronic Priesthood*) so that we can continue to progress as free-willed beings.

The *name* of this token is our *own given name* that we received from our mortal parents, and is representative of the works we do as *their* children (the children of mortal parents). The sign is made by the *left arm being raised to the square*, symbolic of the unrighteous acts we are offering up in the *cup of our right hand* (the things we perform)—those actions that we *believe* are righteous. (Thus, the sign is performed with the *right* arm and hand according to the limits of our mortal understanding, being shrouded in a veil of forgetfulness.) Unfortunately, all of our works are unrighteous and are figurative *fallen* actions associated with the environment in which we are placed during our mortal probation.

While still in mortality (the *Aaronic* state), none are qualified to lead or teach any other except the occasional *one* chosen by the powers that supervise this earth's progress. It is in the very nature of this state that personal righteousness in perfection will always be beyond our reach. We continue to think our works are righteous as they seem to be right-to-us and offer them as such (represented by our right hand in cupping shape as if we are offering something). Well was it written: "For all have sinned, and come short of the glory of God" (see Romans 3:23). In other words, all are unhappy sometimes, and incapable of complete happiness while in mortality.

The beauty of the *real truth* about our mortal existence is that, although we are all sinners and fall short, the situation is not by our own doing, and if there was nothing more to mortality, we would always have the excuse that IF only we had known the truth of all things, then we would have chosen a different path for ourselves. Well, shortly, there will be no more excuses. For this reason, Christ will reign upon this earth for a time and we will exist in *fallen*, imperfect bodies, having the fullness of the gospel given to us and all of the stumbling blocks removed. This is when we are to be clothed in the robes of the *higher priesthood* and when we will have the opportunity to live without having the excuse of, "I just didn't understand!" Though having viable justification with the robe worn on the *left* shoulder, we will have none when it is changed to the *right*.

The "covenant" associated with this token is, simply, that we accept our mortal actions (believing they are righteous when they are not) as part of the eternal plan—bound by eternal laws that allow us to progressively arrive at the purpose for which we were created, i.e., to experience eternal happiness.

It was not Joseph Smith who instituted the "obligation of secrecy" associated with this *token*, its *name*, *sign*, and *penalty*. Confused and confounded by what the endowment represented, it was Brigham Young who gave himself the literary license to make all things pertaining to the endowment a secret. This has driven discussion and the mystique of the endowment deeper underground. How anyone could believe that the endowment itself could somehow be kept "secret" (when literally millions have heard it) is baffling to the reasonable mind. Nevertheless, as in ancient times, people are willing to give staggering amounts of money to hear the *secret* (which no one understands), and religious authorities are more than willing to demand and accept payment from the members in order for them to attend the secret rites. Likewise, ancient temples were masterpieces of manipulative engineering and ingenuity, and the "secrets" therein amazed the patrons and guaranteed that the "faithful" would continue to flow through their doors and exchange their "coins" for salvation.

True Messengers of God will *only* do one thing for the people: teach them how to get along with each other. The basis of this type of teaching is the **fullness** of the gospel of Jesus Christ. These *messengers* have been taught the *real truth* and can share it with all those who inquire of them. Everything that they teach makes much more sense than any earthly religious doctrine or precept. By listening to a *true messenger*, one will no longer be deceived by the flesh (*Lucifer*) and will receive the *further light and knowledge Father promised He would send*. In other words, all of the mysteries of God will be revealed.

The *true* test of a *real* prophet who is *disclosing his true identity* is if he can explain all the mysteries of God in their fullness and have them *make sense*. As we hear the true explanations, no questions are left unanswered and everything makes sense to our subconscious mind. It is as if we ask them, "*How shall I know that you are true messengers?*" And they give to us "*the token and sign you received in the Garden of Eden.*" In other words, they bring to our memory all that we already know but have forgotten because of the Veil. Then we will understand the very last words of advice Adam gave to us:

These are true messengers. I exhort you to give strict heed to their counsel and teachings, and they will lead you in the way of life and salvation.

And the **only** counsel and teachings that will ever be given by a true messenger of God is this:

Learn To Love Yourself, And Then Love Your Neighbor As You Do Yourself.

Nothing more, nothing less!

7
THE TELESTIAL GLORY

PETER: We will return and report. Jehovah, we have been down to ~~the man~~ Adam **and Eve** and ~~his~~ **their** posterity in the Telestial World, and have cast Satan out of their midst. We have given unto them the Law of the Gospel as contained in the ~~Book of Mormon and the Bible~~ **Holy Scriptures**; also a charge to avoid all lightmindedness, loud laughter, evil speaking of the Lord's anointed, the taking of the name of God in vain, and every other unholy and impure practice, and have caused them to receive these by covenant. We have also clothed them in the Robes of the Holy Priesthood and have given unto them the Second Token of the Aaronic Priesthood, with its accompanying name, **and** sign, ~~and penalty~~. This is our report.

JEHOVAH: It is well, Peter, James, and John.

Elohim—Peter, James, and John have been down to ~~the man~~ Adam **and Eve** and ~~his~~ **their** posterity in the Telestial World, have cast Satan out of their midst, and have done all else that they were commanded to do.

ELOHIM: It is well. Jehovah, send down Peter, James, and John again to the Telestial World. Have Adam **and Eve** and ~~his~~ **their** posterity change their robes to their right shoulder, preparatory to officiating in the ordinances of the Melchizedek Priesthood, and introduce them into the Terrestrial World. Instruct Peter, James, and John further to give unto ~~Adam and his posterity~~ **them** the Law of Chastity, and **to** put them under covenant to obey this law, which is, that the daughters of Eve, and the sons of Adam shall have no sexual ~~intercourse~~ **relations** except with their husbands or wives to whom they are legally and lawfully wedded, ~~and to~~ give unto them the First Token of the Melchizedek Priesthood, or the Sign of the Nail, with its accompanying name, **and** sign, ~~and penalty~~. Have them return and bring me word.

JEHOVAH: It shall be done, Elohim.

Peter, James, and John, go down again to the Telestial World. Instruct Adam and **Eve and their** ~~his~~ posterity to change their robes to the right shoulder, preparatory to officiating in the ordinances of the Melchizedek Priesthood;

and introduce them into the Terrestrial World. Give **to them** ~~unto Adam and his posterity~~ the Law of Chastity, and put them under covenant to obey this law, which is, that the daughters of Eve, and the sons of Adam shall have no sexual ~~intercourse~~ **relations** except with their husbands or wives to whom they are legally and lawfully wedded. Give unto them the First Token of the Melchizedek Priesthood, or the Sign of the Nail, with its accompanying name, **and** sign, ~~and penalty~~; and return and bring us word.

PETER: It shall be done, Jehovah. Come, James and John; let us go down.

We are instructed to have you ~~change~~ **remove** the robe **and change it** to the right shoulder, preparatory to officiating in the ordinances of the Melchizedek Priesthood, and to introduce you into the Terrestrial World. You may now ~~make the change by removing~~ **remove** the robe **and make the change**.

(The patrons stand and remove their robes, replacing them on their right shoulders. The male patrons turn their cap, so that the bow is now placed over the left ear, and all tie the girdle on the left side. The patrons then sit.)

Before we proceed further with the proper explanation of this part of the endowment, the "penalties" must be explained further so that they are better understood. It is quite obvious that none other, before the explanation given in this book, had a clue to the penalties' importance in the eternal plan of our existence. Brigham Young's endowment incorporated the penalties and then changed them into pseudo "blood oaths;" the modern LDS Church has deleted them altogether; and the rest of the world sees them as cult-like ritualistic oaths. Yet without what they symbolically represent, our existence as free-willed human beings would be meaningless, leaving us no different than any other animal or life form that is unaware of happiness, and exists solely for the will and pleasure of its Creator. The penalties are paramount in understanding why humans are so different from any other life form in the Universe and why we can become as our Creators while other creations cannot.

The type of "penalty" we receive for simply becoming who we are and doing what is expected of any free-willed being is *not* a punishment of any kind. We were not created to be punished. We were created to experience happiness, which is best described as a free-willed being's ability to act as it desires with no outside coercion or force, with the experience of this action creating a perfect balance for the individual. The "penalties" figuratively expressed in the presentation of the endowment are better described as a *disadvantage* for breaking a rule, somewhat like a penalty imposed on a player for breaking a rule in a game of sport. The *game* can be viewed as our eternal existence, where the rules are explained to us in the beginning and the penalties for breaking them are outlined. However, in a sporting event, even though the player *chooses* to break the rules from time to time, either purposefully to gain an advantage or inadvertently in the course of the competitive nature of the contest, he or she is not banned from playing the game, but *disadvantaged* in some way to make the playing field fair for those who do not break the rules. However, within our existence, there are eternal laws (*rules*) set that *would* cause a player to be cast from the *game* and ban that individual from participating further in any form of the contest—this is what is known as the *Second Death*.

The penalties are each designed to specify certain *disadvantages* a human entity will experience based on the free agency of the being to pursue happiness as described above.

The first penalty given in the endowment has already been explained, and is figurative of a free-willed being's inability to progress, if, by a choice of free will, the being does not want to participate in the *game* that has always existed to assure the eternal experience of human happiness. This first penalty is associated with the experiences of our pre-mortal life, which we are not able to remember during our mortal existence. Thus, this penalty is given to us by our Creators (*Elohim*). Again, it is associated with the *Aaronic* Priesthood in which all things are done for us.

The second penalty is associated with the *Second Token of the Aaronic Priesthood,* or given to us in a state where all things are done for us without our ability to change things by our own will. It is given to us by assigned representatives (*true messengers of the Father*). During mortality, though it seems that we use our free agency regularly, *ministering Advanced Nomads of God's Eternal Love and Service,* unseen, oversee every aspect of our mortal existence. For this reason, human intellect and free-will is stifled appropriately so that the mortal race cannot destroy itself before we have the chance to experience what is needed, so that in the end, we can understand the necessity for the eternal laws and their penalties. While going through mortality, we wear the Robe of the Holy Priesthood on the *left* shoulder, which makes us eligible for our needs to be taken care of by Those who oversee our progression. Now, it might make one think that the *angels* are not doing a very good job of taking care of our needs; the wars, the inhumanity and vicissitudes that are happening every second of our mortal existence (not to mention the poverty, inequality, depression, and unhappiness), how can these things equate to *angels* overseeing things? However, keep in mind what mortality is for: It is to experience the *opposite* of what we experienced in the *Garden of Eden*. In this respect, the angels are doing a splendid job!

In our mortal bodies, some of us will come to the conclusion that being served all the time and having someone else provide every aspect of what is needed to experience our happiness is what truly makes us happy. These do not want the responsibility of thinking for themselves, or coming up with ways to entertain themselves. They simply want someone else to make them happy. These beings are those who will *wear the Robes of the Holy Priesthood* on the *left* shoulder throughout eternity. These are those who will be served in every capacity that will bring them happiness, having no responsibility except to be happy. These are those who will receive **Telestial** bodies in the final resurrection, which bodies will allow them to be served forever by the *angels of God*.

However, there is a *disadvantage* to having a Telestial body. This is the *penalty* presented symbolically in the endowment. It is *executed* by bringing the right hand (*those works that are right for those who are Telestial*) and placing it on the *left* breast and drawing the hand across the body and then dropping both hands to the sides. Ironically, and purposefully set up through the sense of humor often exhibited by the *Advanced Nomads*, this penalty is part of the Catholic sign of the cross, except that the universal sign of the cross incorporates *all the penalties* in one fluid motion—from the forehead across the throat to the stomach area then across the breast. Oh how fun it will be to see how often we "*wearers of the robe on our left shoulders*" have used our free agency to amuse those who serve us!

Feelings of emotion are generally associated with a sensation in our breast or bosom. Though our brain creates the sensation, the feeling seems to originate in this area. *Telestial* people will always feel an emotion of realization that they will never become as their Eternal Parents. Even though our Parents do not care what we choose to do with our free agency, and exist to serve all of us equally according to our individual desires of happiness, it is part of a human being's makeup to want to please one's parents. In essence, *Telestial* bodies have the ability to sense the unpleasant emotions and feelings associated with pure selfishness, or the need for others to care for them (thus the second penalty is given in the area of the breast). This is the *penalty* associated with the *Telestial* world chosen by those who will analyze their many experiences in mortality and determine that staying in a 5-Star Hotel and being catered to forever, is much better than making the beds and assuring there is plenty of food at the buffet table, or serving themselves in their own mansion. Though just one of the many LDS dogmas attributed to Joseph Smith, which he really did not say. If he *had* revealed all that he knew, he definitely would have said, "*If you could just get a glimpse of the Telestial Glory, you would kill yourself to get there. But if you do, you'll forever have the emotions associated with that kingdom.*"

The penalty associated with the *First Token of the Melchizedek Priesthood* will be explained at the appropriate time in reference to when it is presented in the endowment. This penalty has to do with the *disadvantages* that those who are **Terrestrial** will experience in that type of body. They will not have the disadvantage of an emotional feeling but will never have the ability to experience sex or the purpose for sex—the creation of new bodies—symbolized by the penalty of the womb (stomach area) being cut open. More on this later.

The most incredible part of the presentation of the penalties associated with the tokens of the Holy Priesthood is the penalty received with the *Second Token of the Melchizedek Priesthood*. There is none. Why? Because this token is associated with **Celestial** Beings and Their bodies, and there is no disadvantage to being a Celestial Being—worlds without end.

THE TERRESTRIAL WORLD

NARRATOR: We now enter the Terrestrial World. *(Additional lights are switched on.)*

The symbolism of entering the Terrestrial world in preparation for putting the robes of the priesthood on our right shoulders and receiving the tokens of the *Melchizedek Priesthood*, is to finally have the privilege of receiving the mysteries of the kingdom of heaven (the *real truth*), to have the heavens opened unto us, and to commune with the general assembly of all those who associate with Christ and are in his service. This will finally allow us the ability to enjoy the communion and presence of the *true God—the Father, and Jesus, the mediator of the new covenant*. (Compare the incomplete words as presented in the D&C 107:18–19, with what was explained previously.) In other words, we will associate with Beings that know everything there is to know about absolutely *everything* relevant to our existence.

The figurative *Terrestrial World* is the state of the world upon which we will live during the Millennial reign of Jesus Christ/Allah/Jehovah/Vashti/Krishna—or whatever other name the anticipated god of the religions of this world is known by the human race. (Ironically, most people at that time will simply recognize these Advanced Human Beings as Extra*terrestrials*.) This *Millennial reign* is symbolic of finally having someone around with power and authority to show us the right way to deal with each other as human beings. These are *resurrected* beings simply by the fact that they were once mortals who existed in bodies of a fallen nature (which were not eternal), but who now possess bodies with the ability to function to the full extent of their individual spirit's potential. Thus, They remember all things and have powers and abilities beyond our wildest imaginations, yet consistent with our own human potential to imagine. Their glory is Their intelligence, or in other words, *light and truth*.

Figuratively speaking, the *sign* that we have entered into a *Terrestrial* state of existence is that we will now recognize that our mortal works have been *un*righteous and offer them as such (done with the left arm in front of us forming a square with the hand in the shape of a cup). This is a sign of our ability to now distinguish our mortal works from the righteous works that we *should* have been doing all along in our mortal *fallen* state (done by the right arm forward, palm facing downward, the fingers close together and the thumb extended). In other words, we will come to recognize the difference between the way we *thought* was good in how we treated our neighbor, and the way we *really* should have treated them. The *right hand* with the palm facing *down*ward simply represents an acknowledgment that we still exist in a fallen, or a *lower* state than an exalted state in the kingdom of God during the time of the figurative Millennium. In this *sign*, the arm is brought forward <u>below</u> our head, whereas when we lived in the kingdom of God (the sign we received in the *Garden of Eden*) the sign was given <u>above</u> our head with our *right arm* forming the square. During the *Terrestrial* time, we have not reached the final stage of our existence, but will now experience mortality under the direction of a righteous government and its laws.

Once They have arrived on this planet in Their *glory*, these *extraterrestrials* will set up a righteous government upon this earth that has never been known before by mortal human beings (or at least not one that mortals can remember or have experienced in their history books). They will establish proper laws and positions of service, replacing the politicians, judges, and leaders of the whole earth. Their technology will far supersede any yet known to humankind, or any it will come up with before Their coming. With this, peace will be established and maintained throughout the world. The weapons of war and destruction possessed by humans at that time, though far more advanced than any yet known in earth's history, will be the equivalent of a peashooter to an atomic warhead. In fact, there will be no more weapons of destruction, as Their intelligence and technology will render obsolete and useless any technology invented to take the life of a human being.

Equality and freedom will come to all. They will implement the necessary technologies that will feed, clothe, house, heal, educate, and provide the means of happiness for every human being upon the earth—without requiring payment and without gaining in any way Themselves, except through Their personal pleasure in providing these things to all people equally.

Different areas of the earth will be constituted as distinct places where one might go to experience different and unique cultures and pursuits of happiness consistent with each individual's desires of happiness. Each person will be able to travel, at no cost, anywhere in the world in order to experience life within the boundaries of these different cultures. Having our physical needs met, we will finally be able to come to some conclusion of what truly makes each of us happy and in what environment we feel most comfortable.

During the *Millennium*, while mortals are experiencing human life like they never have before, the *glory of God* will be utilizing Their technology and understanding to transform the planets of this solar system into habitable environments, aligning them precisely where they need to be in conjunction with the life-giving Sun so that humans might one day reside there. Yet even though death and sickness will cease, and poverty and inequality will be a thing of the past, one thing will stand in the way of eternal and unlimited happiness: **The Law of Chastity**.

Though all things will be provided for, the ability to experience sex and all its facets will be a continual *curse* to the free agency and happiness of humankind. Jealousy, possessive and co-dependant natures, adultery, and broken hearts and promises will continue to plague this otherwise peaceful and serene state of existence. And after determining that this *one* thing is the *only* thing that stands in the way of complete happiness, it will take the free will and choice of mortals to *bow their heads and say*, "*Yes*, take this sexual desire and all it entails from me, because it is the *only* thing that keeps me from being consistently at peace and feeling a fullness of joy."

The *token* of this experience is in all we do (our works), which is figuratively expressed by what is done with our *right hand*. The part of our *work* that will be the hardest to give up and the most painful to our free will, is *right in the center* of all that we do in mortality—the essence of human desire—our sexual natures. It is a state of existence (token) in which its *center point* bears all the weight of *the cross* we are forced to bear in mortality. It is what was done (the absence of which, coming by way of a *virgin*) to create the *name*, the Son of God. It is figuratively called the *Sign of the Nail*, as a nail driven through our hand would cause us a tremendous amount of misery. It is the *only* thing about our existence during the Millennium that will cause us sorrow.

For those who will eventually reign in what is called the Terrestrial Glory or Terrestrial Kingdom of God, there is only one *disadvantage* (the penalty): There will be no sex or procreation.

Nowhere in the English language, or in any other language upon this earth, is there found a definition for the word "Telestial." However, there is a definition for the word "Terrestrial." Joseph Smith was instructed to use the word "Telestial" to make a distinct separation between our mortal experience <u>before</u> the coming of extra*terrestrial* beings (i.e., "the Second Coming of Christ"), and the mortal experience we will have <u>after</u> Their coming to this earth from another solar system. With the help of some witty *angels*, the word was created by simply removing from the orthodox English word "Te*rr*est*r*ial" (which means all things associated with life upon the earth), the letters associated with <u>r</u>esu<u>rr</u>ected beings ("r r r") and adding an "l" for "*Lucifer*." And thus was the existing word "Terrestrial" transliterated into the new word "Telestial." (Remember, it wasn't until *Lucifer* was cast out that *Peter*, *James*, and *John* were able to introduce Adam into the *Terrestrial* world.)

On the one hand, in a *Telestial* state, all things are controlled for us from a distant advanced solar system through the technologies and knowledge of Those who created our solar system and the earth on which we live. On the other hand, when those *Alien Beings* reveal Themselves to us, we will no longer be living as mortals under a Veil that isolates us from those who created this world and put us here. We will also have many *real truths* that They will share with us while residing among us.

"*Lucifer*" is the antithesis of *real truth*, as "Christ" is the bearer of *all* truth. Or better, because of our *flesh*, our brains haven't the ability or the capacity to be utilized properly by our spirit matter to remember anything past what we did yesterday in our current mortal state. Because of our innate human curiosity and our propensity to reason and figure things out, *Lucifer* has been able to call *his ministers* to preach the *beautiful*, but confusing, fantasies of orthodox religions, which include all the sciences and arts. This "preaching" satisfies our longing to make sense out of who we are and why we exist. But one can rest assured, that when Alien extra*terrestrials* appear from another solar system, mortals will definitely listen to what They have to say, which of course, will be the *real truth* that will replace *Lucifer*, *his ministers*, their *orthodox religions*, and all the other sciences and arts associated with them.

THE LAW OF CHASTITY

PETER: A couple will now come to the altar. *(The witness couple comes as before.)* We are instructed to give unto you the Law of Chastity. ~~This I will explain.~~ **which is that each of you shall have no sexual relations except with your husband or** ~~To the sisters, it is that no one of you will have sexual intercourse except with your husband to whom you are legally and lawfully wedded. To the brethren, it is that no one of you will have sexual intercourse except with your~~ wife to whom you are legally and lawfully wedded. ~~Sisters~~ **All** please arise. *(All ~~women~~ stand up.)* Each of you bring your right arm to the square. You and each of you covenant and promise before God, angels, and these witnesses ~~at this altar~~ that you will observe and keep the Law of Chastity, as it has been explained to you. Each of you bow your head and say, "Yes."

~~SISTERS~~ **ALL:** Yes.

PETER: That will do. ~~*(All women sit down.)* Brethren, please arise. *(All men stand up.)* Each of you bring your right arm to the square. You, and each of you, covenant and promise before God, angels, and these witnesses at this altar that you will observe and keep the Law of Chastity, as it has been explained to you. Each of you bow your head and say, "Yes."~~

~~**BRETHREN:** Yes.~~

~~**PETER:** That will do. *(All men sit down.)*~~

The above covenant to obey the **Law of Chastity** is the figurative expression of using our free agency to give up or only use our sexual nature according to the eternal laws associated with it.

Sexual pleasure comes from the human desire to procreate and create life. It is the purpose and blessing of being a Creator, and throughout eternity it is reserved *only* for those who can be trusted not to abuse it. It is the *only* selfish thing Celestial Beings possess that serves *only* Themselves and no other. It is the *advantage* They have over all the rest of us, who, when we had the ability of a God to create, abused it for our own purpose and pleasure, causing us misery.

Sexual pleasure and the need to experience and satisfy it are the greatest and the strongest human desires. Nothing brings more satisfaction and pleasure, uniting both the body and spirit in such away that both of their potentials are fully exercised and achieved. Only through an orgasm—the desired end of the sexual experience—does the mortal body have the ability to allow the spirit to exhibit its full potential—not in memory, not in learning, not in communication, but in the exalted feeling of complete satisfaction and joy. Only in this one thing can a mortal being realize what it is like to experience a complete fullness of joy associated with being a Creator.

To give up this ability and power will be the hardest decision any free-willed being will ever be required to make. However, unless one's desire of happiness is exclusively realized in the service of others, the power will be taken away. It is this that will cause many free-willed beings to take a final stand at the very end. (This is figuratively represented by *Lucifer* being released at the end of the Millennium to once again deceive the world for a short time.) It is the final battle to occur between mortals and their Creator: *"Why, God, can't we continually experience the ultimate joy associated with sex without having to create or serve others? It just doesn't make sense!"*

It will make sense eventually, but it will still be hard for many to accept. But accept it they must. For the eternal laws that govern our existence and the eternal Universe have always been and never change. No matter how rational our argument might be, these laws must always be followed—**always**—worlds without end.

THE FIRST TOKEN OF THE MELCHIZEDEK PRIESTHOOD
OR SIGN OF THE NAIL

PETER: We will now give unto you the First Token of the Melchizedek Priesthood, or Sign of the Nail, with its accompanying name, **and** sign, ~~and penalty~~. This token is received by bringing the right hand into this position: the hand vertical, the fingers close together, and the thumb extended; and the person giving the token placing the tip of the forefinger of his right hand in the center of the palm, and the thumb opposite on the back of the hand of the one receiving it, in this manner. We desire all to receive it. All arise.

(After the officiator and male witness demonstrate the token at the altar, temple workers circulate around the room to administer this token to the patrons.)

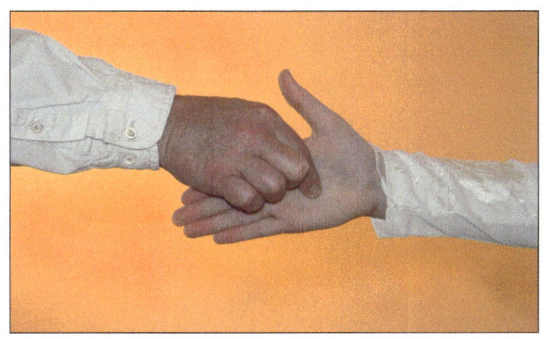

PETER: If any of you have not received this token, you will please raise your hand. The name of this token is "the Son," meaning the Son of God. The sign is made by bringing the left hand in front of you with the hand in cupping shape, the left arm forming a square; the right hand is also brought forward, the palm down, the fingers close together, **with** the thumb extended, ~~and the thumb is placed over the left hip~~. *(The officiator makes the sign.)* This is the sign. ~~The execution of the penalty is represented by drawing the thumb quickly across the body and dropping the hands to the sides.~~ ~~*(Officiator completes the action.)*~~

This **token** (state of existence) has been explained above as a time in our progressive human existence where we will live in a world where our works will be continually righteous (bringing the *right* hand vertical, the fingers close together, and the thumb extended); and the only part that will bring us any pain is in our continued capacity to experience sex. The token is given in the center of the palm, representing *the center* of our works during mortality. Being able to give up sex (**Law of Chastity**) is a realization we must make for ourselves and is the probationary purpose for living in a near-perfect world with the continued ability to experience it. As explained, though everything else will be provided for our individual happiness, our sexual desires will still bring us the same sorrow they bring us today.

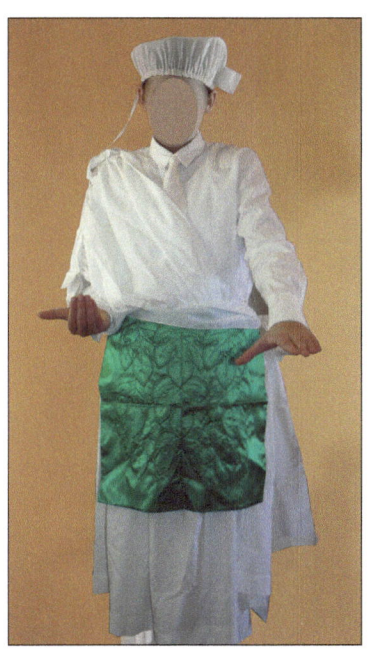

The **name** of this token is given as "the Son, meaning the Son of God," because he was the *only* human ever created *without* sex (complying with the **Law of Chastity** associated with the token). The virgin birth of Christ ("*the Son*") gives an appropriate conclusion as to how Celestial Mothers create bodies for Their children. Our modern technology demonstrates the ability of *asexual* procreation, and the advanced technologies known by Celestial Beings will perfect it. Figuratively speaking, God did not use the lust of the flesh to create His Only Begotten (mortal) Son.

The works (the *name*) associated with living an asexual life corresponds to an eternal *Terrestrial* existence. The disadvantage of this type of existence (the *penalty*) is figuratively presented by the sexual organs being removed from the individual in *drawing the thumb quickly across the body and dropping the hands to the sides*. Keep in mind that during the Millennium, we will still have imperfect bodies; and it is only when we receive our final (resurrected) body (if our chosen eternal body be *Terrestrial* or *Telestial*) that we will not be able to experience sex again.

The **sign**, also explained above, is a figurative realization that what we once thought was good was really bad, and what we thought was bad, was really good. For example, Joseph presented the irony of prayer and religion that humans believe are *good* and from God, when in reality they are *bad*—because they cause problems and are from *Lucifer*. (He presented this figuratively earlier on in the presentation of the endowment. We were warned this would happen:

> *Wo unto them that turn aside the just for a thing of naught and revile against that which is good, and say that it is of no worth! For the day shall come that the Lord God will speedily visit the inhabitants of the earth; and in that day that they are fully ripe in iniquity they shall perish. ...For behold, at that day shall he* (Satan) *rage in the hearts of the children of men, and stir them up to anger against that which is good.* (2 Nephi 28:16, 20)

> *Wherefore, take heed, my beloved brethren, that ye do not judge that which is evil to be of God, or that which is good and of God to be of the devil.* (Moroni 7:14)

PETER: I will now explain the covenant and obligation ~~of secrecy~~, which are associated with this token, its name, **and** sign ~~and penalty~~, and which you will be required to take upon yourselves. If I were receiving the endowment today, either for myself or for the dead, I would repeat in my mind these words, after making the sign, ~~at the same time representing the execution of the penalty~~:
I **solemnly** covenant **before God, angels, and these witnesses** in the name of the Son that I will never reveal the First Token of the Melchizedek Priesthood, or Sign of the Nail, with its accompanying name, **and** sign, ~~and penalty. Rather than do so, I would suffer my life to be taken.~~
All arise. *(All patrons stand.)*
Each of you make the sign of the First Token of the Melchizedek Priesthood, or Sign of the Nail by brining the left hand in front of you with the hand in cupping shape, the left arm forming a square; ~~also by bringing~~ the right hand **is also brought** forward, the palm down, the fingers close together, the thumb extended, ~~and by placing the thumb over the left hip~~. This is the sign.
Now repeat in your mind after me the words of the covenant, ~~at the same time representing the execution of the penalty~~:
I **solemnly** covenant in the name of the Son that I will never reveal the First Token of the Melchizedek Priesthood or Sign of the Nail, with its accompanying name, **and** sign ~~and penalty. Rather than do so, I would suffer my life to be taken~~. *(Patrons perform the action as the officiator guides them.)*
That will do. *(All patrons sit down.)*

All free-willed beings must be comfortable with the fact that, unless they are *Celestial Servers*, they will never experience sex again. During the Millennium, this will be revealed and taught properly, and when a person is ready to accept the degree of happiness in which he or she chooses to exist, that person can visit a *Celestial Office of Advanced Technology* (for want of a better term) where he or she will be given the body of their choice that will never again be "male" or "female." Nevertheless, with advanced technology and other medical progressions, one will be able to eliminate the sex drive at any time, but this will *only* happen by the *free will* and choice of that person, and *will not* be forced upon anyone until the time they receive their eternal body.

Revealing this token simply means that a person who does not accept the consequence of the *Terrestrial* kingdom and all associated with it, will *lose their life*. After experiencing free agency in a mortal body and the continued unhappiness that sex brings to most people, if one still cannot accept the fact that sex will be taken away from them forever, that one will experience the *Second Death* and will no longer exist in any form.

PETER: We will return and report. Jehovah, we have been down to ~~the man~~ Adam **and Eve** and ~~his~~ **their** posterity, have placed the robe on the right shoulder and have introduced them into the Terrestrial World. We have put them under covenant to observe and keep the Law of Chastity. We have also given them the First Token of the Melchizedek Priesthood, or Sign of the Nail, with its accompanying name **and** sign, ~~and penalty~~. This is our report.

JEHOVAH: It is well, Peter, James, and John.

Elohim—Peter, James, and John have been down to ~~the man~~ Adam **and Eve** and ~~his~~ **their** posterity, **and have done all that they were commanded to do.** ~~have placed the robe on the right shoulder, and have introduced them into the Terrestrial World. They have also put them under covenant to observe and keep the Law of Chastity. They have given unto them the First Token of the Melchizedek Priesthood, or Sign of the Nail, with its accompanying name, sign, and penalty. This is their report.~~

ELOHIM: It is well.

Jehovah, send down Peter, James, and John and instruct them to give to ~~the man~~ Adam **and Eve** and ~~his~~ **their** posterity in the Terrestrial world the Law of Consecration, in connection with the Law of the Gospel and the Law of Sacrifice, and to cause them to receive it by covenant; to give unto them the Second Token of the Melchizedek Priesthood, the Patriarchal Grip, or Sure Sign of the Nail, with its accompanying sign; and to teach them the Order of Prayer and prepare them in all things to receive further instructions at the Veil. Then have them report at the Veil.

JEHOVAH: It shall be done, Elohim.

Peter, James, and John, go down to ~~the man~~ Adam **and Eve** and ~~his~~ **their** posterity in the Terrestrial World and give unto them the Law of Consecration, in connection with the Law of the Gospel, and the Law of Sacrifice, and cause them to receive it by covenant. Give unto them the Second Token of the Melchizedek Priesthood, the Patriarchal Grip, or Sure Sign of the Nail, with its accompanying sign. Teach them the Order of Prayer and prepare them in all things to receive further instructions at the Veil. Then report at the Veil.

PETER: It shall be done, Jehovah. Come, James and John; let us go down.

Next will be revealed the greatest of all of the mysteries of God; that is, what exactly does it take for a human being to become a Celestial Being with all the power and the glory given to an Eternal Creator, Male and Female—worlds without end. Unfortunately for many temple goers who revel in the idea that receiving the endowment will bring them closer to becoming a God, the revelation of the meaning of the *Second Token of the Melchizedek Priesthood* and all associated with it, will likely prove that he or she is not capable, nor would it be his or her true desire, to become a *Celestial Eternal Servant*.

8
THE TERRESTRIAL GLORY

THE LAW OF CONSECRATION

(**NOTE:** The following words presented in black and strike-through are still currently used in the LDS Temple Endowment presentation. However, they were *not* part of the original endowment and have been marked below to emphasize that they should not have been included.)

PETER: A couple will now come to the altar. *(The witness couple comes forward, and kneels at the altar as before.)* We are instructed to give unto you the Law of Consecration ~~as contained in the book of Doctrine and Covenants~~ *~~(The officiator picks up a copy of the Doctrine and Covenants from the altar, and holds it up in view of all patrons.)~~* in connection with the Law of the Gospel and the Law of Sacrifice, which you have already received. It is that you do consecrate yourselves, your time, talents, and everything with which the Lord has blessed you, or with which he may bless you ~~to the Church of Jesus Christ of Latter-day Saints~~, for the building up of the Kingdom of God on the earth and for the establishment of Zion.

All arise. *(All patrons stand.)* Each of you bring your right arm to the square.

You and each of you covenant and promise before God, angels, and these witnesses at this altar, that you do accept the Law of Consecration ~~as contained in this, the book of Doctrine and Covenants~~ *~~(the officiator holds up a copy of the Doctrine and Covenants again)~~*, in that you do consecrate yourselves, your time, talents, and everything with which the Lord has blessed you, or with which he may bless you ~~to the Church of Jesus Christ of Latter-day Saints~~, for the building up of the Kingdom of God on the earth and for the establishment of Zion.

Each of you bow your head and say, "Yes."

PATRONS: Yes.

PETER: That will do. (All patrons sit down.)

In the original endowment penned by Joseph Smith, there was no mention of "the book of Doctrine and Covenants." This was interpolated by Brigham Young so that, again, he could incorporate his own understanding into what he thought the endowment meant. That being the case, then the first thing an honest person would ask is, "What is the **Law of Consecration** as described in the Book of Doctrine and Covenants?" If one reads everything written in the D&C where the word "consecrate" is given, one will soon realize that this Law has nothing at all to do with "*building up the Kingdom of God on the earth and for the establishment of Zion,*" which mandate would, of course, have directly benefited Brigham Young's vast *kingdom* he set up for himself and the church he formed. Brigham Young was one of the richest men west of the Mississippi at the time he died. His holdings, interests, and powers were massive. Little do the LDS members know that Brigham Young owned the largest brewery of alcoholic beverages in the Territory of Utah.

Brigham must have pre-supposed that the members of his church who received the endowment would not read the book of Doctrine and Covenants and find out for themselves what is said of the **Law of Consecration.** (The fact is, most of the people who followed him out West were illiterate and depended completely on what Brigham Young told them.) The *Law* as described in the D&C has all to do with providing for the poor and nothing to do with providing for the church, its leaders, or their lavish life styles:

> *If thou lovest me thou shalt serve me and keep all my commandments. And behold, thou wilt remember the poor, and consecrate of thy properties for their support that which thou hast to impart unto them, with a covenant and a deed which cannot be broken.* (D&C 42:29–30)

Unfortunately for the poor, millions of dollars are donated each year outside of the required 10% of the LDS member's income. These donations come from the estates of deceased members who have legally willed "*everything with which the Lord has blessed you*" to what they believe is the building of temples, churches, schools, and other church-owned ventures that have little, if any, benefit to the poor among them. They die believing this is their ticket into the *Celestial* Kingdom. They couldn't be further from the truth.

Though administering to the needs of poor should not be overlooked as the most essential part of the greatest of all commandments (Love Your Neighbor As Thyself); nevertheless, the *Second Token of the Melchizedek Priesthood* associated with the **Law of Consecration** has absolutely nothing to do with dedicating what one owns in this world to a Celestial purpose. It has all to do with consecrating who one is to this purpose.

The most important aspect to point out in this part of the endowment is the wording of the covenant of the **Law of Consecration.** Previously, we received three other *Laws* under which we were placed by covenant. Each of these laws and covenants is associated with a certain state of our existence: the **Law of Obedience and Sacrifice**—our pre-mortal state; the **Law of the Gospel**—our mortal state and *Telestial* degree of happiness; and the **Law of Chastity**—the Millennial state and *Terrestrial* degree of happiness. Now we are given a law and covenant that pertains *only* to the state of existing as a God in the *Celestial* degree of happiness.

However, the *Law of Consecration* is limited to those who are now, and those who will one day become, the Creators of other worlds and the perpetuators of life for all other free-willed human beings. These are those who will hold *The Book of Life* in their *right hands* and possess the powers and perform all the necessary functions to bring to pass the immortality and Eternal Life of humankind. Thus, these types of individuals *consecrate* all that They are and all that They do to perform the tasks required of Eternal Servants, which is simply *"building up the kingdom of God"* on this earth and all other earths that will be created through Their works. These are the Celestial Fathers, Mothers, and the angels who each perform Their labors to assure that life continues as it always has—worlds without end.

Since the law connected to performing these labors of continuing life (**Law of Consecration**) is related to the involvement of Celestial Beings in the different states of existence in which human beings find themselves, it can *only* be connected to two (2) of the three (3) other states (our pre-mortal state and mortal state before the Millennium), and has nothing to do with the **Law of Chastity** associated with the Terrestrial kingdom. This is explained further below.

It was previously pointed out that wearing the robes of the priesthood represents our works during the different stages of our lives—during the *Aaronic* state we are continually watched over and served by Celestial Beings—our Eternal Mothers in the pre-mortal state, and our Father and ministering angels in mortality. It is Their *consecrated* duty in these two states to make sure we are allowed all the experiences necessary in order for each of us to come to an individual and unique understanding of what makes each of us happy and what does not. They indeed *consecrate* all that They have and are, to this end.

When we changed the robes of the priesthood to our right shoulder, we became ready to do things for ourselves and act as we want to act without the continual involvement of Celestial Beings. In this *Melchizedek* state (during the Millennial reign), we will depend upon ourselves because of our *own* knowledge and understanding and will be responsible for all that we do. This knowledge and understanding will come because of our ability to interact and learn from the Advanced Humans who will reside with us upon the earth at that time. In essence, we will become Gods *without* the ability to produce children or the powers associated with the creation of planets and solar systems necessary for the continuation of human life throughout the Universe. However, in the eternities, those living in a *Terrestrial* state will retain the ability to grow plants and produce animals to serve the needs of their happiness.

Just as modern mortals can use hybrid breeding processes of both flora and fauna to create the perfect rose or the most playful puppy, *Terrestrial* people in their state of eternal existence will have the knowledge and power to utilize the elements of their planets to make their *very own kingdom* through the works of their own hands. Each of these will establish a kingdom uniquely satisfying the individual desires they envision for their personal happiness. *Terrestrial* people will not need *Celestial* people to serve them. They will serve themselves. *Telestial* people, on the other hand, do not want to serve themselves, but will remain dependant upon *Celestial* intervention forever, having all of their individual needs of happiness met by the powers and influence of Celestial Servants. Taking these things into account, it is easy to understand why the Celestial **Law of Consecration** is connected to our pre-mortal state and our *Telestial* state only, and has nothing to do with a *Terrestrial* state of existence.

The *Law of Consecration* is the hardest of all laws for mortals to live. After Jesus was murdered, his disciples were beside themselves for some time until they had the euphoric-shared-epiphany called "The Day of Pentecost." The record given in the New Testament relates a story where the apostles began to speak in tongues "as the Spirit gave them utterance." The editors of the New Testament, with the help of the distorted view of the author of Acts (who gave his personal interpretation of what he heard someone say about what another said he had heard about the event), distorted the presentation. They turned a simple day of finally coming to an understanding of what the mission of Jesus Christ was really all about, into a miraculous demonstration of speaking in other languages. In other words, the story of the apostles "speaking in tongues" really had all to do with them receiving an understanding of the mysteries of God as it is explained in the endowment, figuratively, by repeating the words (in tongues) *Pay*, *Lay*, *Ale*.

"Speaking in tongues" simply means that one is receiving the mysteries of God which mortals cannot comprehend. The "interpretation of tongues" is understanding the mysteries of God and presenting the *true meaning* to others in plainness, or in a language and words that are plainly understood. In that sense, this book is a correct interpretation of the "tongue" in which the temple endowment is written.

Once the apostles figured things out, the first thing they did was to try to incorporate *Celestial* principles of living into a mortal (Telestial) world. The **Law of Consecration** didn't work. Joseph Smith did the same thing once he experienced his own "Day of Pentecost." He tried to teach the people this *Celestial law*, only to have it fail, as it always will, unless those who are attempting to live it are <u>all</u> Celestial-destined people.

Any person who is not willing to sacrifice their money, their prestige, their ego, their wife, husband, sons, daughters, all of their material possessions, even all that they are, to the *proper* service of others, cannot be Celestial, and cannot comply with the law pertaining to that kingdom. Humans exist in mortality for thousands of years to prove to themselves that they are *not Celestial* Beings. *Telestial* maybe, *Terrestrial* probably, but certainly not deserving of Celestial powers. All Telestial and Terrestrial beings would misuse this power and would never be able to consecrate all that they have and are for the sake of others' happiness—worlds without end.

THE SECOND TOKEN OF THE MELCHIZEDEK PRIESTHOOD, THE PATRIARCHAL GRIP, OR SURE SIGN OF THE NAIL

Before explaining the *Second Token of the Melchizedek Priesthood, the Patriarchal Grip, or Sure Sign of the Nail*, the proper way in which humans receive true and correct knowledge must be revealed.

This **token** is given in conjunction with the Celestial Kingdom, or the degree of happiness of all those who are Celestial Beings. The token itself is given by clasping the right hands, interlocking the little fingers, and placing the tip of the forefinger upon the center of the wrist of the person receiving it. The way the token is given is directly linked to *why* the token is named what it is (*the Patriarchal Grip, or Sure Sign of the Nail*).

It has already been explained that the Melchizedek Priesthood is: "*To have the privilege of receiving the mysteries of the kingdom of heaven, to have the heavens opened unto them, to commune with the general assembly and church of the Firstborn, and to enjoy the communion and presence of God the Father, and Jesus the mediator of the new covenant.*" (D&C 107:19)

"God the Father" is represented by the word "Patriarchal." Being held in this Patriarchal Grip means that the person is *one* with the Patriarch and has a proper understanding of all that the Great Patriarch (the Father) is and does. This is the bulk of support represented in this token by the *clasping of right hands*. The word "grip" in the English Dictionary has as one of its meanings: "comprehension" (a proper understanding of something), as in the colloquialisms: "Come to grips with it!" "Get a grip!" Or in other words, "Accept it and understand why it is!"

Supported by this *grip*, one no longer has the weakness of the fleshly body, represented in the token by the weakest part of the human body, the little finger. (This finger is the weakest support in the human body; no bone, tendon, and muscle structure is as weak as the little finger—even a toe is stronger than this finger by itself.) Our sexual desires, which are necessary in order to create life (what a Celestial person does), are the *weakest* part of our mortal nature. This "weak-link" to our flesh is now *supported* and *interlocked* with the very purpose for this Celestial power. Celestial people do not misuse Their sexual nature in any way that would abuse the power They have been given. It was presented in the *First Token of the Melchizedek Priesthood* that our greatest fleshly weakness and *the center* of our works is our sexual natures. As we are taken in the Patriarchal Grip, this *weak* part of our works (what is done with the *right hand* during mortality) is supported (by the *clasping of the right hands* in the token) by all the knowledge and power associated with existing as a Celestial Being.

The symbolic point on the right hand where this ability (sexual experience) is received is no longer *the center* of our works (given in the middle of the right hand), but is given on our *right wrist*, which is the connecting point where our free will (our spirit—located in our brain) controls and gives power to the works of our hands. Everything that a Celestial Being does, all of Their works, all of Their desires, and the will of Their spirit, has to do with the production of life and its perpetuation—worlds without end.

One who chooses the *Terrestrial* Kingdom for their happiness receives the *penalty* of never being able to produce life (this is the disadvantage associated with that kingdom); but there is no penalty given in association with the Celestial Kingdom—thus no penalty is given in conjunction with the *Second Token of the Melchizedek Priesthood*. Celestial Beings enjoy sex and all it entails forever, but only because They do all things with an eternal and selfless perspective—yes, they have a *grip* on all that sex is meant to do, and understand the proper way it is experienced and understood by the *Patriarch* of all life on this earth—God, the Eternal Father.

The sign associated with this token is made by raising both hands high above the head, and while lowering the hands repeating aloud the words: "*Pay Lay Ale*; *Pay Lay Ale*; *Pay Lay Ale*." This is a representation of a person receiving an understanding of *all* the mysteries of God, which are hidden from the eyes and ears of all those who do not receive it in the proper way. Thus, the sign is figuratively spoken in a language that no one understands except those who receive an explanation of it from a *true messenger of the Father*. Ironically, the leaders of the LDS Church changed the original endowment and interpolated a meaning they assumed was meant by the words. They improperly translated the meaning as, "Oh God, hear the words of my mouth," repeated three times. It was Adam who had said these words earlier in the endowment that prompted a response from Lucifer. It will soon become apparent why those who pray with their voice will never understand the mysteries of God and will always be answered by *Lucifer*, the god of this world.

Early in the endowment, in the Telestial world, a presentation was given of the *improper* way to receive knowledge: raising both hands high above the head, and *without* lowering the hands, exclaiming, "Oh God, hear the words of my mouth. Oh God, hear the words of my mouth. Oh God, hear the words of my mouth." This has been explained as being the *improper* way to pray, or *False Order of Prayer*, and the fruits of this prayer have also been explained figuratively by Lucifer answering this type of invocation. Associated with knowing all the mysteries of God and existing as a Celestial Being is the ability to understand and pray properly in the *True Order of Prayer*, which will be explained in its entirety later.

"Pay Lay Ale" does not mean, "Oh God, hear the words of my mouth!" repeated three times. To the world, the mysteries of God will always be hidden, and given in a way that will never be understood; and unless an individual receives them through the *True Order of Prayer*, he or she will not be able to understand them. *Lucifer* answering our prayers is the figurative representation of the vain and foolish imaginations of the human heart which have tried to answer the questions of life's realities in vain. No mortal has ever discovered all the answers. No matter how advanced science becomes, the mysteries (knowledge and abilities) of Celestial Beings will remain hidden. Celestial Beings are distinguished from all others *by the way They pray*. In all things They pray in the *True Order of Prayer*.

"Pay Lay Ale" means, "Father, Son, Holy Ghost," or as the prophets have used to teach the people *without disclosing their true identity*, "Faith, Hope, and Charity." Only through these three attributes will the mysteries of God be revealed. In other words, having faith in the Father, a hope in Christ, and possessing charity (the Holy

Ghost) encompasses all that is required to know the mysteries of God. Knowing the mysteries of God is simply using *common sense* to put together the pieces of the eternal puzzle of life. To have common sense, one must first understand what it is. The general English definition for the word is:

> *Common sense (or, when used attributively as an adjective, commonsense, common-sense, or commonsensical), based on a strict construction of the term, is what people in common would agree: that which they "sense" in common as their common natural understanding. Some use the phrase to refer to beliefs or propositions that in their opinion they consider would in most people's experience be prudent and of sound judgment, without dependence upon esoteric knowledge or study or research, but based upon what is believed to be knowledge held by people "in common," so: the knowledge and experience most people have, or are believed to have by the person using the term.* (Wikipedia, the free encyclopedia. 28 January 2008 http://en.wikipedia.org/wiki/Common_sense)

Though the above definition seems concise and covers the general understanding of the term, it certainly does not mean an understanding of the *real truth* as is intended in the figurative expression of "charity" used by the prophets. As defined above, "common sense" could also be regarded as an *impediment* to understanding and accepting real truth. In mathematics, for example, human intuition often conflicts with the correct solution. But the greatest abuse and hindrance of what we would all like to accept as the "prudent and sound judgment" of our experience, is our personal prejudices.

Albert Einstein, a mortal renown for his own sensibility, said, "Common sense is the collection of prejudices acquired by age eighteen." How correct he was! It makes perfect *sense* to a Christian that homosexuals should die of AIDS as a punishment for their "sins." But it doesn't make much sense to a mother whose young child dies of the same disease or to a homosexual who prefers to live. It makes perfect *sense* to one lawyer that his position and arguments are valid and true. But to the opposing counsel, his position makes better sense. (In this case, it only matters what collection of prejudices the judge acquired by age eighteen that determines the truth of the case and which side wins.)

The greatest discourse ever given on common sense was that by Moroni, who paraphrased what his father Mormon had written concerning the subject. In this discourse, it is "*…given unto you to judge, that ye may know good from evil; and the way to judge is as plain, that ye may know with a perfect knowledge, as the daylight is from the dark night*" the correct form of "common sense." (See Moroni 7:15.) Instead of calling it "common sense," Moroni called it "charity," "the Spirit of Christ," "the Light of Christ," or "the Holy Ghost."

His discourse is profound. However, it is written in "tongues." Hiding therein from the eyes of all those who do not have *charity* or *true* common sense, is the mystery of what it takes for a human being to become a God, or in other words, a Celestial Being full of proper common sense, unaffected by preconceived notions or prejudices. Significantly, having the same *sense* of things in *common* with Celestial Beings is the essence of being held in the *Patriarchal Grip*. Throughout this discourse, every mention of "God" or "the Father" is directly associated with something to do with *faith*. "Christ," "Jesus," or "the Son" is associated with *hope*; and true common sense (*charity*) is associated with the "Holy Ghost" along with the other words given above. The discourse begins by Moroni outlining what is going to be discussed:

Moroni 7

1 *And now I, Moroni, write a few of the words of my father Mormon, which he spake concerning faith, hope, and charity; for after this manner did he speak unto the people, as he taught them in the synagogue which they had built for the place of worship.*

2 *And now I, Mormon, speak unto you, my beloved brethren; and it is by the grace of God the Father, and our Lord Jesus Christ, and his holy will, because of the gift of his calling unto me, that I am permitted to speak unto you at this time.*

3 *Wherefore, I would speak unto you that are of the church, that are the peaceable followers of Christ, and that have obtained a sufficient hope by which ye can enter into the rest of the Lord, from this time henceforth until ye shall rest with him in heaven.*

These "peaceable followers of Christ" obtained a hope through the words of Jesus given to Mormon's ancestors about 400 years before this discourse. Following the gospel of Christ will always make one "peaceable." Mormon goes on to explain that those whose "walk is peaceable" with others, are those who are doing the <u>right</u> thing. This will later be referenced in the presentation of the endowment when the <u>*True Order of Prayer*</u> is introduced and couples are invited to participate where, "*Only the best of feelings should exist in the circle. If any of you have unkind feelings toward any member of this circle, you are invited to withdraw so that the Spirit of the Lord may be unrestrained.*" Everyone who is not "walking peaceable" in this way walks contrary to how a Celestial Being would act, and cannot do "good" no matter what their "common sense" has convinced them is good.

4 *And now my brethren, I judge these things of you because of your peaceable walk with the children of men.*

5 For I remember the word of God which saith by their works ye shall know them; for if their works be good, then they are good also.

6 For behold, God hath said a man being evil cannot do that which is good; for if he offereth a gift, or prayeth unto God, except he shall do it with real intent it profiteth him nothing.

7 For behold, it is not counted unto him for righteousness.

8 For behold, if a man being evil giveth a gift, he doeth it grudgingly; wherefore it is counted unto him the same as if he had retained the gift; wherefore he is counted evil before God.

9 And likewise also is it counted evil unto a man, if he shall pray and not with real intent of heart; yea, and it profiteth him nothing, for God receiveth none such.

10 Wherefore, a man being evil cannot do that which is good; neither will he give a good gift.

11 For behold, a bitter fountain cannot bring forth good water; neither can a good fountain bring forth bitter water; wherefore, a man being a servant of the devil cannot follow Christ; and if he follow Christ he cannot be a servant of the devil.

12 Wherefore, all things which are good cometh of God; and that which is evil cometh of the devil; for the devil is an enemy unto God, and fighteth against him continually, and inviteth and enticeth to sin, and to do that which is evil continually.

13 But behold, that which is of God inviteth and enticeth to do good continually; wherefore, every thing which inviteth and enticeth to do good, and to love God, and to serve him, is inspired of God.

14 Wherefore, take heed, my beloved brethren, that ye do not judge that which is evil to be of God, or that which is good and of God to be of the devil.

Anyone who does not have a "grip on," or a full understanding of, what it requires to be a God <u>cannot</u> do good, because they lack the understanding required to do the "right" thing. If, for example, a person is being raped and murdered and one intervenes and stops the act, it very well could be that the hero is doing that which is *not* good and is of "the devil, an enemy unto God." Are there angels or not? If there are, and They do the work of the Father, as Mormon will explain below, why don't They intercede to stop every insidious act committed contrary to the *common sense* of humankind? Are these Celestial Servants not doing that which is "*good and cometh of God?*" Now in this example, it might very well be that the angels would work through the hero to accomplish Their work, *if* saving the victim from the seemingly terrible experience was truly what was the best thing to do for everyone. It is very hard to determine if our supposed "good works" are indeed the works of the devil (our fleshly desires), or if what we think are "evil" works, are actually the will of those who know what is best for us to experience. (Remember, it was "God" who planted the *Tree of Knowledge of Good **and** Evil*!) Mormon teaches the people that in many cases their "common sense" of right and wrong can fail them. He then reveals the sure way to judge:

15 *For behold, my brethren, it is given unto you to judge, that ye may know good from evil; and the way to judge is as plain, that ye may know with a perfect knowledge, as the daylight is from the dark night.*

16 *For behold, the Spirit of Christ is given to every man, that he may know good from evil; wherefore, I show unto you the way to judge; for every thing which inviteth to do good, and to persuade to believe in Christ, is sent forth by the power and gift of Christ; wherefore ye may know with a perfect knowledge it is of God.*

17 *But whatsoever thing persuadeth men to do evil, and believe not in Christ, and deny him, and serve not God, then ye may know with a perfect knowledge it is of the devil; for after this manner doth the devil work, for he persuadeth no man to do good, no, not one; neither do his angels; neither do they who subject themselves unto him.*

18 *And now, my brethren, seeing that ye know the light by which ye may judge, which light is the light of Christ, see that ye do not judge wrongfully; for with that same judgment which ye judge ye shall also be judged.*

19 *Wherefore, I beseech of you, brethren, that ye should search diligently in the light of Christ that ye may know good from evil; and if ye will lay hold upon every good thing, and condemn it not, ye certainly will be a child of Christ.*

Mormon reiterates the words of Christ in which we are commanded *not to judge*. If we follow the words of Christ in every way, then we are doing the "right" thing. In the example used above concerning the rape and murder of another, what would Christ have done? Would he have interceded, or would he have forgiven the perpetrator and allowed the act? His example in the flesh and the words of his gospel are all we need to know in order to understand how most human beings act contrary to a *Celestial common sense*, and is why they are not allowed to know the mysteries of God. Often what we *think* is a "good" act, is diametrically opposed to the gospel of Christ and what Jesus would do, and therefore, is actually an "evil" act. As we intercede and physically restrain and hurt the perpetrator, are we at peace? Are we demonstrating our "peaceable walk with all men" by our works, or are we justifying our actions because of the "collection of prejudices we have acquired by age eighteen?" Since it seems that none of us are doing what is right, the question arises, as it did to Jesus' disciples in his day: "Who then can be saved?" The correct translation of that passage of scripture explains and reads as follows:

Matthew 19

(Correct translation is given in ***bold italics***)

25 ***And*** when his disciples heard it, they were exceedingly amazed, saying, Who then can be saved?

26 But Jesus ***perceived their thoughts***, and said unto them, With men this is impossible; but ***if they will forsake all things for my sake***, with God ***whatsoever I speak is*** possible.

27 Then answered Peter and said unto him, Behold, we have forsaken all, and followed thee; what shall we have therefore ***in the kingdom of God***?

28 And Jesus said unto them, Verily I say unto you, That ye ***who*** have followed me ***and believed in me and obeyed the commandments of the Father in all things,*** in the ***resurrection*** when the Son of man shall sit in ***judgment of those who have rejected these things before*** the throne of ***the Father, then*** ye also shall sit ***in judgment***, judging the twelve tribes of Israel, ***because unto them I shall send you to preach these things***.

29 ***And because we have preached these things unto them, our testimonies shall be given before the Father, that they might be judged according to those things which we preached unto them, and our testimonies against them shall stand before the Father, even that they were given the chance to obey His commandments. And our testimonies and our words shall judge them before the Father, because they did not believe in that which we were sent to teach unto them***.

30 And every one ***of you*** that hath forsaken houses, or brethren, or sisters, or father, or mother, or wife, or children, or lands, for my name's sake, shall receive an hundredfold ***of the happiness that these things would have brought unto you in the flesh***. And ***you*** shall inherit everlasting life.

31 But many ***unto whom we preach these things, which*** are first, shall be last ***in the resurrection, because they refuse the commandments of the Father as we have given them.*** And ***many of them that shall receive this gospel after it hath been rejected by the Jews; yea, even the Gentiles, which are*** the last, shall be first ***to be resurrected unto everlasting life, because they rejoiced in the Father and kept His commandments***.

32 ***But in the end, all those who are first shall be last; and those that are last shall be first, for the Father shall save all of His children as soon as they are willing to keep His commandments which He hath commanded me to give unto them. And all shall be equally blessed of the Father, whether they were resurrected first or last, all shall be heirs of His kingdom and given that which the Father promised them in the beginning.***

Mormon continues his discourse explaining how it is possible to always do good:

20 *And now, my brethren, how is it possible that ye can lay hold upon every good thing?*
21 *And now I come to that faith, of which I said I would speak; and I will tell you the way whereby ye may lay hold on every good thing.*
22 *For behold, God knowing all things, being from everlasting to everlasting, behold, he sent angels to minister unto the children of men, to make manifest concerning the coming of Christ; and in Christ there should come every good thing.*
23 *And God also declared unto prophets, by his own mouth, that Christ should come.*
24 *And behold, there were divers ways that he did manifest things unto the children of men, which were good; and all things which are good cometh of Christ; otherwise men were fallen, and there could no good thing come unto them.*
25 *Wherefore, by the ministering of angels, and by every word which proceeded forth out of the mouth of God, men began to exercise faith in Christ; and thus by faith, they did lay hold upon every good thing; and thus it was until the coming of Christ.*

Herein is given the correct meaning of "faith" as given by all prophets, yet allowed to be misunderstood by humankind until they "exercise faith in Christ" so that the proper meaning can be revealed to them. "Faith" means to be "faithful" in keeping the words and commandments of Christ. Though allowed to be presented in the ways that humans are accustomed to understand it (i.e., believing in something unseen), when used by the prophets, "faith" means a demonstration of one's pure intent by doing what has been asked. Above, Mormon proclaimed that unless a person prays to God or makes an offering with "real intent, it profits him or her nothing." In other words, unless a person is "faithful" in keeping the commandments of Jesus Christ, in how that person "walks peaceably with the children of men," that person can pray and offer all the "righteous works" he or she wants (according to the personal collection of prejudices acquired throughout his or her life), but it is all in vain, profiting that person nothing, and thereby *taking the name of God in vain.*

Mormon indicates the proper way in which the *real truth* is given to mortal humans who cannot remember the truth and have been placed in a situation where they are <u>not supposed</u> to remember. In this state, *ministering angels* and prophets are the <u>only</u> source of real truth; and the way to know if one is being ministered to by an unseen angel or hearing *real truth* from the mouth of a *true* prophet, is to ascertain whether that person is being led to the words of Christ and is enticed to treat everyone around him or her better. Anything other than learning how to treat others better is given by false prophets, or are thoughts influenced by the "collection of prejudices a person has acquired."

Mormon continues his discourse presenting "faith" as "exercising faith" in doing the will of the Father (Pay/faith) in keeping the commandments given by Christ to his (Mormon's) ancestors:

26 And after that he came men also were saved by faith in his name; and by faith, they become the sons of God. And as surely as Christ liveth he spake these words unto our fathers, saying: Whatsoever thing ye shall ask the Father in my name, which is good, in faith believing that ye shall receive, behold, it shall be done unto you.

27 Wherefore, my beloved brethren, have miracles ceased because Christ hath ascended into heaven, and hath sat down on the right hand of God, to claim of the Father his rights of mercy which he hath upon the children of men?

28 For he hath answered the ends of the law, and he claimeth all those who have faith in him; and they who have faith in him will cleave unto every good thing; wherefore he advocateth the cause of the children of men; and he dwelleth eternally in the heavens.

29 And because he hath done this, my beloved brethren, have miracles ceased? Behold I say unto you, Nay; neither have angels ceased to minister unto the children of men.

30 For behold, they are subject unto him, to minister according to the word of his command, showing themselves unto them of strong faith and a firm mind in every form of godliness.

31 And the office of their ministry is to call men unto repentance, and to fulfill and to do the work of the covenants of the Father, which he hath made unto the children of men, to prepare the way among the children of men, by declaring the word of Christ unto the chosen vessels of the Lord, that they may bear testimony of him.

32 And by so doing, the Lord God prepareth the way that the residue of men may have faith in Christ, that the Holy Ghost may have place in their hearts, according to the power thereof; and after this manner bringeth to pass the Father, the covenants which he hath made unto the children of men.

Mormon describes how humans are taught the will of the Father, which, if heeded, will bring peace to all those who have "faith." A "chosen vessel" cannot be *chosen* unless the choosing is done by the angels who "minister unto the children of men." Though presumed "common sense" convinces people that religious leaders, spiritual gurus, psychics, mediums, and others who claim a connection *with God* actually have a connection with Him, the fact that none of these has been properly commissioned by a *real* ministering angel, is fact enough to disregard *everything* they tell you. The only thing that a *true messenger of the Father* ("chosen vessels") would ever tell you to do is: Obey the words of Jesus Christ. Do Unto Others What You Would Want Them To Do Unto You. Walk peaceably with each other. Everything else is vanity. The covenant the Father has made to human beings is that if they will just love each other as each wants to be loved, all will be happy.

But even if they can't love each other, our Creators still love them, and will keep Their covenant and prepare a mansion in Their kingdom where they won't have to be around those that take away from their happiness.

33 *And Christ hath said: If ye will have faith in me ye shall have power to do whatsoever thing is expedient in me.*
34 *And he hath said: Repent all ye ends of the earth, and come unto me, and be baptized in my name, and have faith in me, that ye may be saved.*

Repentance is simply getting rid of *the collection of prejudices we have acquired by the age of eighteen* and being reborn (baptized) as a little child who has no prejudices, but is full of true *common sense* (the light of Christ).

35 *And now, my beloved brethren, if this be the case that these things are true which I have spoken unto you, and God will show unto you, with power and great glory at the last day, that they are true, and if they are true has the day of miracles ceased?*
36 *Or have angels ceased to appear unto the children of men? Or has he withheld the power of the Holy Ghost from them? Or will he, so long as time shall last, or the earth shall stand, or there shall be one man upon the face thereof to be saved?*
37 *Behold I say unto you, Nay; for it is by faith that miracles are wrought; and it is by faith that angels appear and minister unto men; wherefore, if these things have ceased wo be unto the children of men, for it is because of unbelief, and all is vain.*
38 *For no man can be saved, according to the words of Christ, save they shall have faith in his name; wherefore, if these things have ceased, then has faith ceased also; and awful is the state of man, for they are as though there had been no redemption made.*
39 *But behold, my beloved brethren, I judge better things of you, for I judge that ye have faith in Christ because of your meekness; for if ye have not faith in him then ye are not fit to be numbered among the people of his church.*

Mormon knew that the true judgment of another is in their works—the way one lives his or her life. He knew that those who "exercise faith" in Christ become meek, and are those who are "*numbered among the people of his church.*" "His church" has always been those who keep his commandments, whether the membership therein is one person or two (and not necessarily those in any particular religious group or sect). Thus spoke Christ to his disciples saying, "*For where two or three are gathered together in my name, there am I in the midst of them*"; he then taught that we should forgive each other as many times as we sin against each other (see Matthew 18:20–2).

Mormon continues explaining "hope" (Lay/the Son):

40 A*nd again, my beloved brethren, I would speak unto you concerning hope. How is it that ye can attain unto faith, save ye shall have hope?*
41 *And what is it that ye shall hope for? Behold I say unto you that ye shall have hope through the atonement of Christ and the power of his resurrection, to be raised unto life eternal, and this because of your faith in him according to the promise.*
42 *Wherefore, if a man have faith he must needs have hope; for without faith there cannot be any hope.*
43 *And again, behold I say unto you that he cannot have faith and hope, save he shall be meek, and lowly of heart.*
44 *If so, his faith and hope is vain, for none is acceptable before God, save the meek and lowly in heart; and if a man be meek and lowly in heart, and confesses by the power of the Holy Ghost that Jesus is the Christ, he must needs have charity; for if he have not charity he is nothing; wherefore he must needs have charity.*

Mormon explained that unless we keep the commandments of God in treating each other good and being "meek, and lowly of heart," and in so doing, believe in Christ—in that we hope for a better world where <u>all</u> will experience eternal peace and happiness—all of our works and thoughts are vain and profit us nothing. If we know and understand these things (Pay/faith/Father and Lay/hope/the Son) we will have charity (Ale/Holy Ghost). In other words, we will start to recognize, by the power of our own spirit, what brings us peace and happiness. "The Holy Ghost" will bring to our remembrance the way we felt when we lived with Celestial Beings who always did unto others what They would want done unto Them. When we start to remember these things, we will begin to act differently and participate properly in the *True Order of Prayer*, receiving an understanding from the heavens of all the mysteries of God. Thus, with an eternal perspective (charity), we exercise faith in God and have a hope in Christ, which will cause us to act in the following way:

45 *And charity suffereth long, and is kind, and envieth not, and is not puffed up, seeketh not her own, is not easily provoked, thinketh no evil, and rejoiceth not in iniquity but rejoiceth in the truth, beareth all things, believeth all things, hopeth all things, endureth all things.*

46 *Wherefore, my beloved brethren, if ye have not charity, ye are nothing, for charity never faileth. Wherefore, cleave unto charity, which is the greatest of all, for all things must fail—*

47 *But charity is the pure love of Christ, and it endureth forever; and whoso is found possessed of it at the last day, it shall be well with him.*

48 *Wherefore, my beloved brethren, pray unto the Father with all the energy of heart, that ye may be filled with this love, which he hath bestowed upon all who are true followers of his Son, Jesus Christ; that ye may become the sons of God; that when he shall appear we shall be like him, for we shall see him as he is; that we may have this hope; that we may be purified even as he is pure. Amen.*

This "love of Christ" is the "Spirit of Christ," the "light of Christ," even true "common sense" that leads us to have "charity" and act like we should act in order to "walk peaceably with all men." If we are acting upon the common sense that is the "collection of prejudices we have acquired all of our life," we will never know the *true common sense* that will allow us to "be like him," so that we "see him as he is" and not shrink from his presence and the presence of the holy angels who will come with him.

"Charity" is an understanding of the *real truth* as it pertains to the mystery of God. Charity is not the action of a mortal mind influenced by outside forces such as parents, teachers, leaders, etc., who do not have charity; but is an action that comprises an understanding of things as they really are, as they really have been, and as they really are to come. In other words, it is an action of *real truth* as the Gods would see it. And the only way we know what the "Gods" are all about is from our past experiences with Them. This experience is embedded in the memory banks of our spirit makeup, or *Holy Ghost*. Thus, *charity* is always associated with the *Holy Ghost* and our actions that reflect what we have experienced before, but which we cannot remember. When we are told to have charity, we are simply being told to act like we did before, when we were influenced by Celestial Parents, Teachers, and Servants who actually *do* have charity.

Unfortunately, modern definitions of the term "charity" have corrupted its meaning and misled people into believing, quite ironically, that all one needs to do to demonstrate that one possesses *charity* is to bestow some portion of one's good will, either in goods or emotion, towards another in need. This usage and loose definition was first introduced by the Catholic Church and those who organized and eventually canonized what the world accepts as the New Testament of the Bible. The introduction of the meaning indicating the giving of one's goods or thoughts to benefit another is exactly what the leaders of the Catholic Church wanted their followers to accept and believe.

If a person gives money to a church, ostensibly to benefit the poor, or otherwise support the works of this church, it is viewed as a *charitable* donation. The giving of money in the form of tithes and offerings, or in restitution for committing a sin, has become a general form of an accepted standard of righteousness associated with charity. The reason why the leaders of organized religion emphasize this meaning of "charity" is because their followers *do not* have true charity, and there is no other reference in their accepted "word of God" (scripture) that would justify the taking of tithes and offerings for the benefit of the organization and leadership of their churches. Where in the scriptures does it say to support religious leaders and give money to build churches, temples, or synagogues and provide stipends and luxury for church officials? The word "charity" is not found anywhere in the Old Testament, nor is it found anywhere in the related teachings of Jesus Christ. Therefore, to influence *charitable* donations, religious leaders allow their followers to understand "charity" as selfless giving to God through them.

"Charity" has nothing whatsoever to do with giving to another mortal, but all to do with "giving to God." It is properly defined as "the pure love of God," and is held as the ultimate perfection of the human spirit. It both glorifies and reflects the true nature of our Creators through the actions of the one who has it, or who loves as our Creators love. It is a complete understanding of all that "God" entails, what our Creators do, how They think, and most importantly, what They expect of Their creations. It is a mortal human's reflection of all that "God" is—it is loving God. Conversely, throughout our existence, we receive God's love for us. Those who are Gods do exactly what They expect of us: They love everyone as They love Themselves, and do to us what They would have done to Them. Thus, They (the Gods) who experience eternal joy and happiness want the same for everyone else and will assure that it happens.

"Charity" is the pure love of Christ, or the pure love of God—nothing more, nothing less. But when these words are presented and read throughout accepted holy writ, the human mind, prejudiced by the corrupt teachings and understandings of religious and spiritual leaders, automatically considers it to be Christ's love or God's love for us. "Charity," as it is given by the prophets, has little to do with either Christ's or God's love towards humankind, but all to do with a human's love of Them! In every instance in the written word (except for a few expressions in Paul's words, which were edited and translated according to the Catholic hierarchy's own agenda), the "love of God" means the feelings that one should have *towards* God, and has nothing to do with God's love for men. John's writings couldn't be more clear:

> *For this is the love of God, that we keep his commandments: and his commandments are not grievous.* (1 John 5:3)

The word that was used to translate John's statement is the same word in Hebrew that is used when the word "charity" is given. The Latin word, from which the English derivative "charity" is taken, is *caritas*. In the Latin Bible, 1 John 5:3 reads:

*haec est enim **caritas** Dei ut mandata eius custodiamus et mandata eius gravia non sunt.*

Therefore, a more correct translation would have been:

*For this is **charity**, that we keep his commandments: and his commandments are not grievous.*

Though not translated correctly into the English language, Jesus did use the word "charity" in his teachings. In Luke 11:42, it is reported that Jesus said:

But woe unto you, Pharisees! for ye tithe mint and rue and all manner of herbs, and pass over judgment and the love of God: these ought ye to have done, and not to leave the other undone.

The Latin version reads:

*sed vae vobis Pharisaeis quia decimatis mentam et rutam et omne holus et praeteritis iudicium et **caritatem** Dei haec autem oportuit facere et illa non omittere.*

Therefore, a more correct translation would have been:

*But woe unto you, Pharisees! For ye tithe mint and rue and all manner of herbs, and pass over judgment and **charity**: these ought ye to have done, and not to leave the other undone.*

The problem in understanding what was really intended by the original author lies in the various translations of the Hebrew words. In Latin, there are various ways to express the word "love": *amo/amor, ardor, caritas, delecto, diligo, studeo, suavis,* and *voluptas*. If one goes through the Latin Bible and compares every instance where the Latin word indicating some form of deep devotion is translated into the English word "love," one will find that differing Latin forms are used at different times. This usage reflects the personal bias and understanding of the translator and is not necessarily the proper way that the word was intended. In Latin however, *caritas* is used to express "dearness," "regard," or "esteem" without any connotation of sensualism or eroticism, which the other words can emphasize.

"Charity," as intended by all the *true* prophets of God who used it, means that one knows and understands what God expects, thus the person *knows God*, and gives God what is due to Him. This is a demonstration of an individual's love of God, not of one's love for his or her neighbor. However, the only thing *due to* God is that we keep His commandments; and the *only* commandment He expects us to keep is to love our neighbor as ourselves, or have charity towards each other. This charity includes *understanding* each other and doing to each other what we would want done to us if we were in the same situation. Thus, "charity" is loving *as* our Creators love.

Those who understood the true meaning of "charity" used it correctly in the context of what they were trying to teach. Here are the words of Paul (and these few were fortunately not changed, edited, and mixed in with the doctrines of the church leadership), which reflect in context what "charity" is all about:

Put on therefore, as the elect of God, holy and beloved, bowels of mercies, kindness, humbleness of mind, meekness, longsuffering; Forbearing one another, and forgiving one another, if any man have a quarrel against any: even as Christ forgave you, so also do ye. And above all these things put on charity, which is the bond of perfectness. And let the peace of God rule in your hearts, to the which also ye are called in one body; and be ye thankful. Let the word of Christ dwell in you richly in all wisdom; teaching and admonishing one another in psalms and hymns and spiritual songs, singing with grace in your hearts to the Lord. And whatsoever ye do in word or deed, do all in the name of the Lord Jesus, giving thanks to God and the Father by him. (Colossians 3:12–17)

Paul reiterates that charity is knowledge of God, not what we think we know, but what is real truth and known of God:

Knowledge puffeth up, but charity edifieth. And if any man think that he knoweth any thing, he knoweth nothing yet as he ought to know. But if any man love God, the same is known of him.
(1 Corinthians 8:1–3)

The message of all *true prophets* of God is twofold: **1)** The people do not know anything as they ought to know because they are listening to and obeying leaders who do not know; and **2)** They are not obeying the law of the gospel by properly doing unto others as they would want others to do unto them. Throughout their words, *true* prophets reiterate that the only thing anyone has to do is obey the words of Christ, which teach us how to treat each other properly; and if one would do just that, the mysteries of God will start to unfold themselves. And what is the mystery of God? People don't know because they do not have *true* charity. They do not understand charity because they do not know the mystery of God. If they understood the true nature of our Creators, they would understand charity.

The last thing most *true* prophets are compelled to say at the end of their personal ministries was stated this way by Nephi:

Wherefore, ye must press forward with a steadfastness in Christ, having a perfect brightness of hope, and a love of God and of all men. Wherefore, if ye shall press forward, feasting upon the word of Christ, and endure to the end, behold, thus saith the Father: Ye shall have eternal life. (2 Nephi 31:20)

In Ether 12, we read that Moroni lamented because of the people's inability to have this charity:

And again, I remember that thou hast said that thou hast loved the world, even unto the laying down of thy life for the world, that thou mightest take it again to prepare a place for the children of men. And now I know that this love which thou hast had for the children of men is charity; wherefore, except men shall have charity they cannot inherit that place which thou hast prepared in the mansions of thy Father. Wherefore, I know by this thing which thou hast said, that if the Gentiles have not charity, because of our weakness, that thou wilt prove them, and take away their talent, yea, even that which they have received, and give unto them who shall have more abundantly. And it came to pass that I prayed unto the Lord that he would give unto the Gentiles grace, that they might have charity. And it came to pass that the Lord said unto me: If they have not charity it mattereth not unto thee, thou hast been faithful; wherefore, thy garments shall be made clean. And because thou hast seen thy weakness thou shalt be made strong, even unto the sitting down in the place which I have prepared in the mansions of my Father. And now I, Moroni, bid farewell unto the Gentiles, yea, and also unto my brethren whom I love, until we shall meet before the judgment-seat of Christ, where all men shall know that my garments are not spotted with your blood. And then shall ye know that I have seen Jesus, and that he hath talked with me face to face, and that he told me in plain humility, even as a man telleth another in mine own language, concerning these things; And only a few have I written, because of my weakness in writing. And now, I would commend you to seek this Jesus of whom the prophets and apostles have written, that the grace of God the Father, and also the Lord Jesus Christ, and the Holy Ghost, which beareth record of them, may be and abide in you forever. Amen. (Ether 12:33–41)

Any who approach a *true prophet of God* and ask what it is that they must do to find peace and happiness in this life—even all those who ask for personal advice for their own lives, or for instruction on how to respond to another—what do they expect to hear? Do they expect a prophet to guide them in all that they do? Do they expect them to take away free agency and command them in all that they do? Are they free-willed beings or not? Prophets *cannot* tell another what will make that person happy according to that individual's desire of happiness. But they *can* tell the people what was given them of ministering angels, and what has worked for them and many others. They will say, "You must have charity! If you do not, you will experience the hell reserved for the devil and his children, in which you belong because you are *not* happy."

The peace and happiness experienced here on this earth will be the exact same peace and happiness experienced in the worlds to come. Why would it be any different? The emotions and elations of joy will always be the same. This is salvation; this is eternal life. To be held in the *Patriarchal Grip* is to glorify God and have this Eternal Life as described by Christ himself:

Father, the hour is come that Thou shalt glorify Thy Son, and that Thy Son also may glorify Thee. And Thou art glorified through Thy Son because Thou hast given him power over all flesh, that he should give eternal life to as many as Thou hast given him. And this is life eternal, that they might know Thee the only true God, and Jesus Christ, whom Thou hast sent. I have glorified Thee on the earth by teaching the things that Thou hast commanded me to teach unto Thy children; that they might repent of their sins and do that which Thou requirest of them to prepare them to live in the kingdoms of glory that Thou hast prepared for them. Yea, I have finished the work which Thou gavest me to do. And now, Oh, Father, glorify Thou me with Thine own self, even with the glory which I had with Thee before the world was. I have manifested Thy name unto the men who Thou gavest me out of the world; Thine they were, and Thou gavest them me; and they have kept Thy word as I have commanded them. Now they have known that all things whatsoever Thou hast given me are of Thee and are not for mine own glory, but for Thine. For I have given unto them the words which Thou gavest me; and they have received them, and have known surely that I came out from Thee, and they have believed that Thou didst send me. (TSP 58:17–21)

We have the words of Christ. Feast on them! This is all that has been said by the prophets. Yet still, one is left to wonder why it is that one cannot understand the mysteries of God. The people do not understand because they do not have a pure love of God and of all men. If they did, they would understand the words of the prophets. If the reader of this book had *charity*, he or she would rejoice in the truth and what is revealed herein. Yet, there will be many who are offended by what is written and taught in this true explanation of the endowment. But what is taught herein that Christ did not teach? Therefore, if one is offended by these truths, so shall Christ offend this person. And if one is offended by Christ, then how great will be the anguish of that one when the *real truth* is revealed of him and the Gods, who created us.

God is a representation, not of one Celestial Being, but of many (thus the use of the name "Elohim"). Their love represents an understanding of what it was like to live in a perfect world where all things were provided for us and where we were respected and, in turn, respected each other's desire to do what we wanted, individually, to make us happy. "Charity," or the pure love of God, is that we all would *love* to exist in this type of world, surrounded by others who all *love* in the same way. Because we love God (which is really loving ourselves), we want to live like we once lived, where the foundations of all we recognize as happiness were established in our eternal souls. There we were happy—whether *Telestial*, *Terrestrial*, or *Celestial* in nature according to our individual desires of happiness—we were all equally happy; we all had a pure love of all that represents "God."

The *Patriarchal Grip, or Sure Sign of the Nail* cannot be explained more plainly than as presented above. However, Brigham Young and other *false prophets* who lack *charity*, incorporated their own interpretations as given below in the various ways the original endowment has been changed to memorialize and perpetuate their ignorance:

PETER: We will now give unto you the Second Token of the Melchizedek Priesthood, the Patriarchal Grip, or Sure Sign of the Nail, with its accompanying sign. **This token has reference to the crucifixion of the Savior. When he was placed upon the cross, the crucifiers drove nails through the palms of his hands; then, fearing that the weight of his body would cause the nails to tear through the flesh of the hands, they drove nails through his wrists. Hence, in the palm is the Sign of the Nail, and in the wrist, is the Sure Sign of the Nail, or the Nail in the Sure Place.** This token is given by clasping the right hands, interlocking the little fingers, and placing the tip of the forefinger upon the center of the wrist, in this manner. *(The officiator demonstrates this token with male witness.)* We desire all to receive it. All arise.

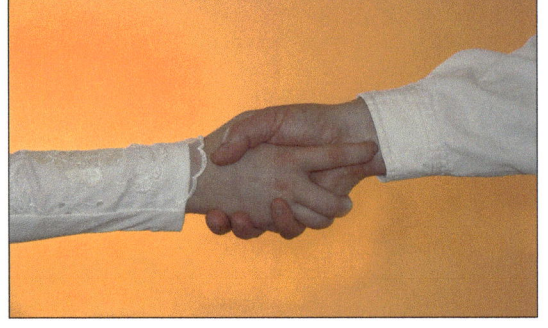

(As the witness couple returns to their seats, various temple workers administer the token as before, and each patron sits after receiving it.)

PETER: If any of you have not received this token, you will please raise your hand.

No where in any scripture can Brigham Young's version of Christ's crucifixion through the wrists be found. Because he had no idea what the *Patriarchal Grip* meant, Young came up with his own understanding, and made up his own truth that the Savior had nails driven through his wrists. He did not. He was crucified in the self-same manner as were others of his time.

PETER: This token has a name and a sign, ~~but no penalty is mentioned. However,~~ you will be under ~~just as~~ **the same** sacred obligation ~~of secrecy~~ in connection with this token and sign, as you are with the other tokens and signs

174   **Sacred, not Secret**

of the Holy Priesthood, which you have received in the temple this day. The name of this token will not be given ~~unto~~ **to** you at this stage of the endowment, but it will be given later on.

The sign is made by raising both hands high above the head *(the officiator demonstrates)*, and while lowering the hands repeating aloud the words:

~~Pay Lay Ale; Pay Lay Ale; Pay Lay Ale~~ **O God, hear the words of my mouth! O God, hear the words of my mouth! O God, hear the words of my mouth!**

~~(The hands are lowered in three distinct movements, one move for each word. [1] Pay--hands above head, [2] Lay--both arms dropped to the square, [3] Ale--both hands lowered to the height of chest.)~~

PETER: When Adam was driven out of the Garden of Eden, he built an altar and offered prayer, and these are the words that he **uttered** ~~used, which interpreted are~~: "Oh God, Hear the words of my mouth!" repeated three times.

All arise. *(All patrons stand.)* Each of you make the sign of the Second Token of the Melchizedek Priesthood, the Patriarchal Grip, or Sure sign of the Nail, by raising both hands high above the head, and while lowering the hands repeating ~~aloud~~ **three times** the words: ~~Pay Lay Ale; Pay Lay Ale; Pay Lay Ale~~

O God, hear the words of my mouth! O God, hear the words of my mouth! O God, hear the words of my mouth!

(As the patrons make the sign, they repeat the words with the recording as described before.)

PETER: That will do. *(All patrons sit down.)* Brethren and sisters, with the robe on the right shoulder you are prepared to be taught the True Order of Prayer, and to be introduced at the Veil.

9
THE CELESTIAL GLORY

With the robe on the right shoulder, a person is acting on his or her *own* accord, and is completely responsible for his or her own actions. This has been explained above as a *Melchizedek* state of existence where all have the privilege to commune with Celestial Beings who exist to help us determine what happiness means to each of us individually. Human beings will have this opportunity during the Millennial period (represented by a *Terrestrial* state), at which time Eternal Beings from other planets will be among us to help us learn how to properly live the gospel of Jesus Christ. *Living* this gospel is what it means to *pray* in the *True Order of Prayer*. Thus, we are prepared to be taught this *true order* and to be introduced at the Veil.

We were taught that the *False Order of Prayer* is expecting to receive "further light and knowledge" by building an altar with our own hands, prostrating ourselves before God (as if He wants us to do this), and by our words, calling upon God to deliver. Through this method, we can be deceived by our own mind or by those who profess to be "trained in the ministry," who likewise are deceived by their own minds, and give us their religions, opinions, and perceptions. In contrast to this ubiquitously-accepted form of prayer, the *True Order of Prayer* teaches us the *proper* way to pray and receive the *further light and knowledge*, or better, a correct understanding of the mysteries of God. (The sign of this is given with our arms raised above our heads and lowered, as in the act of receiving.)

Our *common sense* begins to tell us that the *True Order of Prayer*, or the correct way to pray, is through our actions. Thus, this *proper* prayer is given by the demonstrated *actions* of the participants *without* the participants saying a word. Except for saying, "Pay Lay Ale," no one speaks a word, but all participants perform the actions that represent each state of existence in which humans have been, presently are, or will be involved. These actions are done by *faith*, *hope*, and *charity*, given to us through the *Father*, *Son*, and *Holy Ghost*; thus, the only words spoken represent these three things.

Throughout the scriptures we are counseled to "pray always"; not sometimes, or three or five times a day, not just in the morning, at midday, and evening, but *always*. The *True Order of Prayer* can and should be done "always" and is directly connected to our works. "Praying always" means that we are always engaged in good works. Jesus taught his disciples the correct way to pray in this manner:

(The ***plain and precious*** parts of Luke, chapter 11, verses 1–13, have been restored through the Urim and Thummim and are annotated with ***bold italics***.)

1 And it came to pass, that, as he was ***teaching the people, he said unto them, Ye seek me that ye might be baptized as John also baptized you because he preached of me. But ye shall not be baptized of me by water; for behold, I have come to baptize you with fire, which is the Holy Ghost, which ye cannot receive unless ye pray as John has instructed you. And*** when he ***had*** ceased ***teaching the people these things,*** one of his disciples said unto him, Lord, teach us to pray, as John also taught his disciples, ***that we might receive the Holy Ghost***.
2 And he said unto them, ***John taught his disciples that they should do good works, and in this way they should pray. But the people could not receive these things because of their traditions. Therefore, ye shall pray according to your traditions that ye might be led to good works. Verily, I say unto you,*** When ye pray, say, Our Father ***who*** art in heaven, Hallowed be thy name. ***Bless us that we may know and do Thy works, that*** Thy kingdom ***may*** come ***among us, and that*** Thy will be done ***on*** earth, as ***it is done*** in heaven.
3 ***Ask not for that which ye can consume upon the lusts of your hearts, for the Father knoweth all things in which ye are in need, therefore, if ye ask for that which He already hath blessed you with, ye ask in vain only to consume it upon the lust and vanity of your hearts. Ask only that He*** give us day by day our daily bread.
4 ***And the will of the Father is that ye love one another*** and forgive ***them of their*** sins; for ***it is His will that*** we also forgive every one that is indebted to us. And ***if we love another and forgive them of their trespasses against us, then we shall have the Holy Spirit, which is sent from the Father to*** lead us ***in the path in which we should go. For without the Holy Spirit it is easy for you to be led into temptation. But if ye do the will of the Father upon this earth as it is done in heaven, then ye shall*** not ***be led*** into temptation; ***and ye shall be delivered*** from evil. ***And by your works, make ye therefore a friend of the Holy Spirit that ye might have always that which ye are in need of***.
5 And he said unto them, ***Your heavenly Father will not fail to give unto you of His Spirit whatsoever ye ask of Him. And he spake a parable concerning the Holy Ghost, saying***, Which

of you, ***then***, shall have a friend, and shall go unto him at midnight, and say unto him, Friend, lend me three loaves ***for I have been slothful and have not of what thou hast of which to give unto my friend;***

6 For a friend of mine in his journey is come to me, and I have nothing to set before him, ***and he is hungered and has asked of me bread.***

7 And he from within shall answer and say, Trouble me not ***with your problems, for because of thy slothfulness thou lackest that which would feed thee and thy friend. Behold, my*** door is now shut, and my children are with me in bed; ***therefore***, I cannot rise and give thee.

8 ***Behold***, I say unto you, Though ***his friend*** will not rise and give him ***of his bread***, because he ***has not done those things required of him as a good*** friend; ***but if he asketh forgiveness and promises that he will do those things required of a friend, and if he asketh with*** importunity, ***behold, his friend*** will rise and give him as many ***loaves of bread*** as he needeth.

9 And I say unto you, ***Ye cannot have the Holy Spirit as your friend if ye do not the will of the Father, who giveth unto you His Spirit as ye do His will. And if ye are doing His will, then if ye*** ask, it shall be given you; ***if ye*** seek, ye shall find; ***if ye*** knock, it shall be opened unto you.

10 For every one that asketh ***in righteousness, showing by his works that he is a friend of the Holy Spirit, he shall receive***; and he that seeketh ***shall find***; and to him that knocketh it shall be opened ***unto him***.

11 ***And if a man is not a friend of the Holy Spirit, he is still a son of God. And*** if a son shall ask bread of any of you that is a father, will ***you*** give him a stone? or if he ask a fish, will ***you*** give him a serpent ***instead of*** a fish?

12 Or if he shall ask ***of you*** an egg ***so that he might be nourished***, will ***ye*** offer him a scorpion ***that will torment him***?

13 If ye then, being evil, ***because ye do not the will of the Father, and ye*** know how to give good gifts unto your children ***so that they might be benefited thereby***, how much more shall your heavenly Father give ***good gifts through*** the Holy Spirit to them that ask him ***in righteousness***?

The *real truth* teaches us that praying *with words*, on our knees, with our eyes shut and our arms extended towards heaven, asking God to hear the words of our mouth and give us further light and knowledge, is the *False Order of Prayer*. Again, the participants who are engaged in the *True Order of Prayer* perform specific actions and **do not speak**, except for the words, "Pay, Lay, Ale," as it has been explained above.

Joseph Smith arranged the original endowment so that "Peter" was instructing in the *True Order of Prayer*. After the endowment was corrupted by modern leaders, Peter, to whom Adam had already told the people to pay attention to and obey, is NOT the one officiating and giving the actual prayer when the participants are gathered in the circle formed for the *True Order of Prayer*. In the original endowment there was no officiator. Peter taught the *True Order of Prayer* by having the participants in the circle perform all the signs and penalties given throughout the endowment, and then he introduced the participants to the Veil without doing anything else. Brigham Young made the changes that reflect his propensity to contaminate the truth with his own understanding.

Brigham instructs the "officiator" (with the help of some very humorous angels) to pray by bringing his "left arm to the square, right hand forming a cup" (always indicating unrighteous works being presented as righteous ones) and to *decide the prayer's form and content. He speaks a few sentences at a time, which are repeated in unison by the patrons in the circle.* Young grievously abused this part because he didn't understand what the *True Order of Prayer* was actually all about. As a result of this profound ignorance, he further introduced "prayer rolls" and mandated that the officiator (for quite some time in all temple ceremonies of the LDS Church) ask for vengeance upon those who killed Joseph and Hyrum. Thus, Young completely corrupted the instruction of the *True Order of Prayer*, not only by having people speak words, but, through no conscious thought of their own, vainly repeating the words of the one who "officiates" over them. This provides a vivid demonstration of the general attitude of LDS people, who blindly follow their leaders and listen to and repeat their words—even if "Peter," the one to whom everyone is supposed to be "giving heed," is now nowhere to be heard. As also marked appropriately at the beginning of this chapter, all the parts given by the "officiator" were introduced by Brigham Young and were not part of the endowment presentation originally established by Joseph.

The *True Order of Prayer* is the way that all humans will "pray" for all generations of time and throughout all eternity. "Prayer" is a demonstration of our works. Whether these works are those we performed in our pre-mortal state in the figurative *Garden of Eden*, those we performed during mortality in the figurative *Telestial* World (or the world in which we presently live), those in the figurative *Terrestrial* World during the Millennium, or those works performed in the *Celestial* World, our *prayers* are an accountability (a *sign*) of all of our works. This is the reason why <u>all</u> the *signs* of the priesthood are given <u>with</u> their accompanying *penalties* in the circle created by those receiving their endowment.

The participants are equally dressed and form a perfect circle, symbolizing the eternal equality that all of us possess in common. After all of our works have been represented by the signs and penalties given, the participants are instructed to unite with each other in the circle. Each brother is asked to take the person at his left in the *Patriarchal Grip*, and then all participants raise their left arm to the square and rest it on the right shoulder of the person to their left. Each of us is represented by couples consisting of the male on the right and the female on the left. This represents the final state of all those who will become the Celestial Fathers and Mothers residing in the Celestial worlds. The "grip," as it has been explained previously, illustrates the way in which male and females are connected forever in the work of bringing forth new life and assuring that this life culminates in happiness.

Each man represents an Eternal Father, and the woman to his left, his Eternal Mate. Joseph made sure that it was well known from whom each man and woman receives his or her support, respectively. The man places his left arm forming the square (his free-willed propensity to "sin") upon the shoulder of the woman. The woman receives her support from her *Father*, represented figuratively by her placing her left arm forming the square on the *right* arm of the man to her left. In this eternal way, no male will ever claim dominance or inequality over the female. Without the support of a female, all males would be useless, having no ability to provide the materials and care for the bodies needed to house the spirit elements. The woman, on the other hand, finds no support from a man who is not her Eternal Father; and she looks *only* to Him for her support. This is a unique demonstration of a woman's propensity and desire to have children and perpetuate Eternal Life when the man doesn't perceive things (*see through the veil*) as she does. This same thing was figuratively demonstrated by Eve wanting to partake of the fruit so she could have children in spite of Adam's opposing determination.

In other words, the Gods do not need males to produce new life, but They do need women. Eternal women support the men with whom They choose to do the work of the Father. These Eternal Mothers get no support from Their partners or from the men whom They choose to oversee the eternal progression of Their children. Contrary to *Telestial* marriage relationships here on earth, in which men are expected to support their wives in all things, Celestial Males are constantly involved in Their own work, which becomes the "work of the Father" for Their own children, and haven't the time or capability to give support to a Celestial Female. These women get Their support from Their own Eternal Father as They do His work, which is to bring about the immortality and Eternal Life of other humans. This support comes from having all things provided for Them to be able to create bodies and care for newly-created humans. This support is not provided by the Celestial Males with whom these women share a Celestial planet, but is provided for by Their mutual Creator—"Elohim," who created *both* the Celestial Males and Females. As humans become Celestial Servants, they depend on their Creators to provide them with the knowledge and power they will need to perpetuate life for other *new* humans, who will, in turn, become dependent on them—in their *own* worlds without end. However, once one is Celestial and becomes an Eternal Father or Mother, this person has all the powers and knowledge given to them to make them completely independent of any other intercession or help. Thus, they now become *one* with the Father in all things.

All those who are not Celestial will still exist in an eternal affiliation with others who share the planet on which they reside. In these worlds there will no longer be any bad feelings or misgivings between the inhabitants, as all will understand who they are and why they exist, and more importantly, why they have freely chosen that particular kingdom. All will understand the mysteries of God that pertain to them and their planet (their degree of glory or kingdom), and in one accord, will experience peace and happiness there as they have learned to "*pray always in the True Order of Prayer*" by doing unto others what they would have others do unto them—which is *always* living the gospel of Jesus Christ. After all humans have performed their works, or rather, gained their experience in the different stages of human development (performed figuratively by the signs given in the *True Order of Prayer*), they are ready to be presented at the Veil and enter into the presence of our Creators, which is symbolic of inheriting the proper part of the Kingdom of God according to our individual desires of happiness.

THE PRAYER CIRCLE AND THE TRUE ORDER OF PRAYER

PETER: A few **of you, including** couples, will please come forward and form a circle around the altar.

(The audio recording stops and the officiator says in his own words a statement to the following effect.)

OFFICIATOR: We would like to invite the witness couple, **to take their place at the head of the altar, and an equal number of brothers and sisters to join us in the circle**. Any receiving their own personal endowment, and any who are about to be married **are especially invited** to join us in the prayer circle at this time.

(The tape recording again resumes.)

NARRATOR (Peter): Only the best of feelings should exist in the circle. If any of you have unkind feelings toward any member of this circle, you are invited to withdraw so that the Spirit of the Lord may be unrestrained. In the circle we make the signs of all the tokens of the Holy Priesthood.

(Patrons make each sign as they are mentioned by the narrator.)

We will begin by making the Sign of the First Token of the Aaronic Priesthood. This is done by bringing the right arm to the square, the palm of the hand to the front, the fingers close together, and the thumb extended. This is the sign. The name of this token is the New Name received in the temple today. ~~The execution of the penalty is represented by placing the thumb under the left ear, the palm of the hand down, and by drawing the thumb quickly across the throat to the right ear, and dropping the hand to the side.~~

We will now make the Sign of the Second Token of the Aaronic Priesthood. This sign is done by bringing the right hand in front of you with the hand in cupping shape, the right hand forming a square, and the left arm being raised to the square. This is the sign. The name of this token is your first given name if you are going through the temple for your own endowment, or if you are going through for the dead, it is the first given name of the person for whom you are officiating. ~~The execution of the penalty is represented by placing the right hand on the left breast, drawing the hand quickly across the body, and dropping the hands to the sides.~~

We will now make the Sign of the First Token of the Melchizedek Priesthood, or Sign of the Nail. This is done by bringing the left hand in front of you with the hand in cupping shape, the left arm forming a square. The right hand is also brought forward, the palm down, the fingers close together, **with** the thumb extended, ~~and the thumb is placed over the left hip~~. This is the sign. The name of this Token is "the Son," meaning the Son of God. ~~The execution of the penalty is represented by drawing the thumb quickly across the body, and dropping the hands to the sides.~~

We will now make the Sign of the Second Token of the Melchizedek Priesthood, the Patriarchal Grip, or Sure sign of the Nail. This is done by raising both hands high above the head, and while lowering the hands repeating ~~aloud~~ **three times** the words: ~~Pay Lay Ale; Pay Lay Ale; Pay Lay Ale, signifying, "Oh God, Hear the words of my mouth!"~~
O God, hear the words of my mouth! O God, hear the words of my mouth! O God, hear the words of my mouth!

We have here a list of names of persons who are sick or otherwise afflicted, whom we are requested to remember in our prayer. We will place ~~the~~ **this** list upon the altar, and request the faith of those present in behalf of these persons.

The sisters in the room will please veil their faces. Each brother in the circle will take the sister at his left, by the right hand in the Patriarchal Grip. Each of you bring your left arm to the square, and rest it upon the shoulder or arm of the person at your left. ~~The brethren and sisters~~ **Those** in the circle will repeat the words of the prayer.

OFFICIATOR: *(The officiator kneels at the altar, and makes the Sign of the Second Token of the Aaronic Priesthood by bringing his right hand forward, with the hand in cupping shape, resting it upon the altar. His left arm is raised to the square. The prayer is spoken by the officiator, who decides its form and content. He speaks a few sentences at a time, which are repeated in unison by the patrons in the circle. After the prayer, the patrons in the circle release the grip, the officiator rises, and the audiotape resumes.)*

PETER: The sisters will unveil their faces, and the brethren and sisters in the circle will return to their seats. *(All patrons sit.)* We will now uncover the Veil.

THE VEIL OF THE TEMPLE

(A Veil segment is now displayed from behind the curtain that is in the front of the endowment room. The officiator takes a pointer in hand, and prepares to draw attention to the marks on the Veil as they are explained.)

At this point, a **Lecture At The Veil** was prepared for the participants. It was originally inserted to give an overview of the meaning of the endowment in plainness without symbolism, but without disclosing the *real truth* until the participants discover the mysteries on their own. The modern LDS Church has eliminated the Lecture for convenience. (What has been deleted will be given later.) The following is a pure, plain, and complete explanation of the mysteries that the symbolic endowment represents, which we are now authorized to receive.

Truly, there has never been an easier explanation of the Eternal Plan of Salvation revealed to humankind:

The temple Veil represents that which separates us from our Creators. The name "Elohim" was purposefully chosen by Joseph Smith for the presentation of the endowment because it is the plural form of the Hebrew word "Eloah," which refers to "God." "Elohim" expresses all concepts of divinity and includes a representation of all Celestial Beings. As it has been explained, these Celestialized Beings are simply human beings who have advanced in knowledge and technology to such a degree that They can create and control all aspects of life throughout the Universe.

Even if one does not believe in "God" (which is an easy conclusion to reach when presented with the explanations given, believed, and fostered throughout the world), it would be hard, logically, to reject the fact that human beings are advancing in knowledge and technology at a rapid pace. What will humans understand about life in the future? What about in a million years? Humans of the 21st century—who can can clone and heal themselves and other animals, create various plants and animals through science, and do what years ago would be considered a miracle only "God" could do—would be considered Creators and Gods by those who lived upon the earth when these technologies were not available.

There are no such beings as the "Gods" supposed and invented by the religions of the world and perpetuated by the spiritual leaders belonging to organizations or acting on their own (the *ministers of Lucifer*). "Elohim" are simply Advanced Human Beings acting within Their powers to continue what has been done in the worlds "heretofore created." The same way "Elohim" received Their power and knowledge and became perceived "Gods" to those who do not share Their abilities, is the same way all human beings have advanced and progressed throughout the Universe.

Even if one were to accept the notion that human life evolved from the most primitive forms of bacteria that have evolved over millions of years to become the human race, one still must consider (using *common sense*) that there are other advanced forms of bacteria in the Universe which have been around a lot longer than those found here in this relatively new solar system. What about that bacterium which has been around, evolved, and advanced millions of years ahead of those found in this solar system? What about a "Big Bang" that occurred millions of years before the *bang* that created our known Universe? If there was a "Big Bang," and this theorized creation process allowed for the creation of bacteria that eventually evolved into advanced humans, it is only reasonable to believe that there were other *bangs* somewhere else and that there will be still more in the future of the infinite Universe. These evolved and advanced bacteria, for the person who accepts this theory as scientific truth, are "Elohim."

There has never been a time when human beings have not existed. The concept of eternal is just that—without beginning and without end. There is no beginning or end to the Universe. What modern scientists (who are far from being considered "Gods" with their present power and knowledge) perceive as the expansion of the Universe is simply creation taking place where there once was nothing organized or created.

What else could possibly be expected from Advanced Human Beings who have learned through millions of years of experience how to love and respect each other's opinions and desires of happiness, who have all their needs provided for through their advanced knowledge and power, and can virtually create anything that they want? Would they just sit around all day and interact with their surroundings to continue to experience what they have created? Some do. These are those who are categorized as "Terrestrial Beings." Perhaps others take advantage of the technology and power of those who exist to serve them and are in a constant need to have some outside force, other than themselves, care for their every need and create and provide for them all that they need to experience happiness. Some do. These are those who are "Telestial Beings." But there are some who don't particularly enjoy doing things solely for themselves and using their powers, knowledge, and environments for their *own* happiness. Instead, They find a great amount of joy in making sure others experience life and the contentment it can bring to all the quintessential eternal creatures that act and are acted upon only by their free will—human beings. These are "Elohim."

In our mortal state, we know nothing about the Gods who live in another galaxy far from our own. We don't even have any knowledge of other beings who live in the solar system right next to ours! If we did associate with these Beings at one time in our existence, we have forgotten these experiences, or better, our inept brains cannot seem to remember anything about them. To our conscious knowledge, there are no other humans in our solar system other than those found upon this earth. And it is difficult for us to accept or rationalize that there exists anyone else <u>like us</u> in the Universe. Yet, when we look at a clear night sky and see with our own eyes billions upon billions of clusters of light, only the most narrowed-minded among us would assume that there are none like us *somewhere out there*.

In order for a free-thinking and free-learning human being to learn *difference*, there must be something that is different. If one were to eat only the fruit of a tree that produced the most delicious apples that could possibly grow, how would those apples be appreciated and known for their delicious taste if there existed nothing to create the comparative value? Even in mortality, those who live in luxury and riches cannot comprehend any other lifestyle. Likewise, those raised in abject poverty find it hard to comprehend why a person needs more than one pair of shoes at a time or more than a single bed and a simple but effective cover from the elements of weather. But when the poor person begins to experience what the wealthy person does, things begin to make a little more sense as to why *more* is better. Likewise also, when the wealthy lose what they have and experience a life of poverty, they learn to appreciate what they once took for granted. To appreciate *light*, we need to experience *dark*. To realize a *difference* in all things, we must experience the opposite.

If we as human beings are created in the image of Advanced Human Beings and placed in Their environment and exist in Their world of equality, plenty, and eternal joy, how would we ever come to an understanding of what we, as free-willed human beings, are all about? We need to experience the opposite of everything They are about. And since these Beings learned to know and experience joy from the absence of joy, it makes perfect sense that to bring us the same experience of joy, we must be allowed to go through the same process They went through in order to recognize the same experience.

"Elohim" planted the *Tree of Knowledge of **Good** and **Evil*** in Their environment and told us that if we ate of its fruit, we would be cast out of Their presence and environment. Yes, They planted a tree that produced "evil" fruit! In other words, these Advanced Beings showed us real-time advanced media connections to worlds in other parts of the Universe upon which were human beings going through their mortal state of existence. We saw the inequality, the wars, the hate, the poverty, the disease, and the death, even all things that we couldn't comprehend in the state in which we were created. "Why," we asked ourselves, "would anyone want to go through all that?"

After it had become apparent to us that we were not acting upon or reacting to our surroundings and existence the same way our Creators (Eternal Parents) were, we became frustrated because we saw Them and respected Them as the ultimate form of life. In other words, They appeared to enjoy Their existence and realized a value of happiness from it that we couldn't understand. We began to see that if we wanted to be like Them, we would have to do what They did to arrive at where They are at. We wanted our own world patterned after Theirs.

Once we arrived at this understanding through the experience on the planet of our Celestial Parents, we realized we had reached a point where we were no longer progressing. At this point, these Advanced Humans told us that They would create a solar system for us. They took into account what we had learned about ourselves during our time spent with Them. We each had developed different personalities and propensities for experiencing happiness. Taking all things into account, They created a solar system specifically designed for us in size and structure to accommodate each of our differing degrees and abilities to experience happiness. Because it would be *for us*, we gave our view and helped direct the organization of our own solar system based on what we had learned from observing what was done in other worlds.

Once our solar system was formed and patterned after the one where we were first created, and a world prepared that could support the life placed thereupon, we saw that everything was good and desired to be there. However, there was a problem: we could not take the materials of our Creators' earth and incorporate them with the elements of our new world. And since our bodies were created from the elements of Their world, we would have to leave our bodies behind and have ones created from the elements of our new world. Since the body is not really who we are, as all of our experiences are recorded and stored on our spiritual core, it was easy to understand that our spirits had to come out of the bodies created from the elements of our Creators' world and be placed in bodies created from the elements of the new one.

There was also a problem with the new solar system: there was only *one* of the planets prepared to sustain the type of bodies our spirits needed to begin to have experiences in our new environment. There were other planets (larger and smaller than the one that could support life) specifically created in our solar system for our "batch of siblings" that could not sustain life presently, but would one day be transformed into the places where each of us could exist according to our individual desires of happiness. So how were we all going to fit on just one planet? Our bodies would be somewhat cramped for space and we wouldn't have all that we would need to satisfy our individual desires for happiness. Our spirit entities, however, were microscopic in comparison to the mortal body required to house them, and could exist in mass in the atmosphere of this new world until bodies were created to accommodate them.

To respond to all of our needs, yet still maintain proper order so that we would not crowd each other out, only a few bodies were created from the elements of the new world, at first. However, we would soon discover that the natural effects of our new world created and destroyed bodies all the time. Therefore, our spirit entities exist in the atmosphere of the earth among the rest of the elements that makeup this atmosphere until a body arrives that can house it properly. The moment that a body is introduced into the world, the breath of life (our spirit entity) enters therein from the surrounding atmosphere. Thus, we experience birth; and our spirit does not come out of the body again until the last breath is exhausted as the normal course of our natural world forces it out through death.

The problem with our new bodies, on our new earth, is that the way in which they are formed is not like the *perfect* bodies we possessed in the old world where we used to live. These mortal bodies would not allow our spirit element to react properly so that we can remember anything beyond the life we experienced before our spirit entered one of these *imperfect* bodies. But since these less-than-desirable bodies grow old and give out, our spirits would have the opportunity to record experiences in many different bodies and life situations upon this new earth created for us. Some might refer to this as a continual process of reincarnation (rebirth).

Because "Elohim" wanted us to experience existence for a time that was different from what we were used to with Them, They knew that They needed to stay out of the way and allow us to exist without Their intervention. They would control things from a distance, or rather, without our knowing They were there. The *prime directive* of these Advanced Human Beings is: Do not allow Yourselves to be known to a civilization of human beings where the purpose of their existence is to learn what it is like <u>*not to be*</u> an Advanced Human Being. However, They knew that free-willed beings, who can't remember how to treat each other properly, would need some guidance. To provide this guidance, some of the Advanced Human Beings from our Creators' solar system became nomads who travel throughout the Universe and assure the *prime directive* is followed, so that the less advanced human race doesn't destroy itself. These are otherwise known to our Creators as, **A**dvanced **N**omads of **G**ods **E**ternal **L**ove and **S**ervice i.e., **ANGELS**.

This *prime directive* is what is known in the presentation of the temple endowment as the "Temple Veil" and will be explained in more detail later.

For all those going through the temple for the first time, Joseph thought it necessary to incorporate into the presentation of the endowment a *Lecture At The Veil* to summarize the endowment and repeat the basic principles presented therein. The mysteries of God are hidden in the symbolic nature of the presentation of the endowment. It was not intended for anyone to make the connection between the symbolism of the endowment and the eternal truths (*real truth*) that only Joseph knew in his day. It was not his calling to make these things known in their plainness. It was his job to give the people a *stumbling block* that would cause them to stumble further so that they could continue to experience life without knowing *real truth*. But in fairness, this *real truth* must be available and all must be given the opportunity to understand it through the proper channels.

The proper channel to receive an understanding of the endowment and all it figuratively represents is through this final work. The time has come to reveal all things to the understanding of the mortal mind so that no human is left with an excuse to say, "I just didn't understand!"

From a resurrected and now Advanced Human, these things are revealed to the world. Advanced Human Beings realize that modern-day Neanderthal-like humans (comparatively speaking), such as this author and those like him, cannot be given or receive proper instruction that they will understand except by the means of communication to which they are accustomed. Therefore, to avoid any duplicity in revealing the truth behind the symbolism of the endowment, a certain Advanced Human Being superseded the *prime directive* and visited this author and taught him with a natural voice, which consisted of vibrating words coming from His advanced physical mouth, which were then received in this author's eardrums. As a result, the meaning of the symbolism of the LDS Temple Endowment was revealed, remembered, and later written in this book. This was done in this way because of the vast amount of human beings (especially males) who believe that they can understand the symbolism simply by asking God and receiving an understanding through "revelation." They ask God by the *words of their mouth*, with their hands raised high above their heads; and they do indeed receive an answer from "revelation"—directly from *Lucifer*; i.e., their own mind. And their answers always lead to confusion and contention.

Based on the conversations between this author and the Advanced Human Being who presented himself as the man once known in mortality in one of his lives as Joseph Smith, this appropriate *Lecture At The Veil* is given in plainness to the world:

Up to this point in the endowment, the participants have been taken through three (**3**) different stages of human experience:

1) Our pre-mortal existence on the planet where our free-willed spirits were created and placed into bodies formed from the elements of that world. Our Eternal Mothers reared us in such a way that we established a strong *foundation of humanity*, or that which separates our behavioral patterns from those of other life forms that are preprogrammed to act in specified ways. This existence instituted our *human conscience* and was intended and necessary to maintain consistent order throughout the Universe. This is where we agreed to accept and obey the plan of the Father and the laws that have existed forever and which exist in every part of the Universe. This is the *eternal law* that all beings who have the power to act on their own accord (without perfunctory mandates [instincts] guiding them) must obey. This *Law* is presented in the endowment as the **Law of Obedience**.

In essence, the first experiences we encountered and stored in our spiritual core (subconscious) provided us with an emotional alignment that would guide our actions throughout the rest of eternity. Whenever our course of action deviates from this carefully-aligned axis of our primordial experience, we immediately sense that something is out of equilibrium and we automatically seek to adjust our actions to compensate for the feeling and bring us back into balance. This alignment is what we recognize as *happiness*. Any deviation from the experiences we have stored in our subconscious (spiritual core) creates an unsettling frustration, which we recognize as *unhappiness*.

It is impossible for a human to disobey the **Law of Obedience**. It is the only law that our free agency cannot ignore and act in opposition to; therefore, it is a law that <u>must</u> be *obeyed*, and is presented in the endowment separate from the other *laws* that we had to accept by covenant, or by exercising our free agency. Upon our refusal to obey these laws, we receive the consequence (*penalty*) associated with each one. The experiences of our existence with Celestial Beings, who we appropriately call our Eternal Mothers and Father, will always stay with us and were given to us without any choice of our own. We did not use our free agency to choose to exist. And because They created us and made us human beings instead of plants, animals, or other forms of life, preprogrammed to act and be acted upon, They are responsible to assure two things: First, that the **Law** is established correctly (thus only Celestial Beings associate with us while our spirits are being *aligned*), and second, that we are guaranteed that each and every one of us will be provided with an environment which will allow us to obey this eternal law. This **Law** is what guarantees eternal happiness.

2) The second stage of human experience is our mortal life, where this **Law** is the "enmity" placed between our spiritual natures (*seed of the woman*) and our flesh (*Lucifer*). We exist in the "lone and dreary world," an environment diametrically opposite to the Celestial world where we lived for eons of time developing our eternal human conscience. The fleshly bodies we possess in this mortal world are totally opposite from the bodies in which our newly-created and pure spirits were placed in the beginning. Because of this *fallen* state, our human nature acts contrary to the experiences that bring us happiness; thus, this life seems to be a struggle and a burden where the experience of happiness is short and fleeting.

Part of the law Celestial Beings must obey is to require us to go through mortality without Their intervention or assistance so that we will understand how wonderful it is living in a controlled environment. These rules and laws concerning mortality are what are symbolically presented in John the Beloved's Revelation as *The Book of Life*. God, who represents all Celestial Creators, male and female, must follow the eternal pattern that has always been followed throughout eternity. However, as free-willed beings Themselves, Celestial Beings have never been allowed complete control over Their creations and are subjected to the same eternal laws as each of us. Though it has not happened (as far as it has been revealed to the author of this work), a Celestial Being *could* use His or Her free agency to disobey the laws of creation set forth in *The Book of Life*. For this reason, a **Christ** (one "**anointed**" for this purpose) is created and prepared to oversee the actions of all free-willed beings. As humans progress to find their individual desires for happiness (within the *happiness* each has already established in their individual spirit), there will be some who want to become Gods and do what Gods do. These humans will be given the power and knowledge to create life and allow it to progress as it always has—the end thereof being eternal happiness for the new life created. However, an *anointed* Christ will be their ruler and the overseer of all of their works. Yes, our Eternal Father is subjected to the reign of *His* own Christ.

A Christ, meaning "anointed one," is a preprogrammed spirit that has been created by "Elohim" to assure that the eternal laws are always obeyed. A Christ does not have free agency and *cannot* fail or do the wrong thing. This Being is prepared before the foundation of any solar system and it's worlds. A Christ is placed in control of all aspects of creation, and there is not anything made that is made without his knowledge and control—worlds without end. With this understanding, John's words come alive:

In the beginning was the Word, and the Word was with God, and the Word was God. The same was in the beginning with God. All things were made by him; and without him was not any thing made that was made. (John 1:1–3)

A Christ's primary responsibility is to assure that all God's creations do exactly what they were created to do. On his way into the city of Bethany, so the story goes, Jesus approached a fig tree that should have been producing fruit as it was created to do. To give his disciples a better understanding of his purpose and power, Jesus stopped the fig tree from continuing to exist because it didn't fulfill the measure of its creation (see Matthew 21:17–21).

Human beings were created to experience happiness. It is a Christ's responsibility to make sure we fulfill the measure of our creation. Therefore, concerning us, he has only one desire: create the environment that exemplifies, in every way, the one in which we established our sense of happiness. In this way, he is our *savior* and the *only* way to salvation, or a guaranteed existence of eternal happiness.

While existing among our Eternal Parents, all things were provided for us freely and according to our desire to possess them. We were each treated with respect and equality regardless of what our personal desires of happiness were. Since all of us experienced the same existence of abundance, wanting for nothing, and were treated equally by our Creators, it was impossible for us to think of another less than ourselves—all were equally happy according to each of our individual desires for happiness. We didn't measure or judge what another was or did just because it didn't agree with what we chose for ourselves. We had no reason to disagree with another, as everyone's individual opinion was valued exactly the same by our Creators. They made sure everyone's opinions and desires were fulfilled. In this pre-mortal world, it was always done unto us what we would want done unto us in every situation. Thus, "Elohim" comply with the ever-lasting and never-changing gospel of <u>Their</u> **Christ**.

A Christ's purpose is to "redeem" us, or return us to the state of existence that we enjoyed with our Creators, but this time, in our own solar system, on our own planet according to our own individual desire and opinion of happiness. Unlike all free-willed beings, Christ has no opinion of happiness, but must provide the environment and all things that satisfy the desire of every single human being created and placed in this solar system. So when Christ teaches us how to act, he teaches one thing only: Do Unto Others What You Would Have Them Do Unto You.

A Christ sacrifices free will in order to make sure our needs of happiness are met. The **Law of Sacrifice** presented in the endowment represents the part of our existence where the Father prepares and presents our Christ to us; thus, the **Law** is administered by Elohim. We must each choose for ourselves to submit to the power and authority of Christ or we cannot fulfill the measure of our creation and be eternally happy. Though a Christ makes a *sacrifice* of "free will" by virtue of who he is, we also must choose to *sacrifice* the perfect world, on which we were brought into existence, for the imperfect world where we would learn by our own experience what "perfect" and "imperfect" actually mean. Therefore, the *penalty* for not accepting a Christ and submitting to his power and authority, is that we are no longer allowed to exist and will be cut off from the kingdom of God forever. This is the first law that we have a choice to follow or not. Though there are some who resist the challenge of an *imperfect* world, ultimately, all human beings come to realize they cannot achieve personal satisfaction unless they submit to the **Laws of Obedience** and **Sacrifice**. (This is figuratively represented in the endowment by Adam refusing to partake of the fruit at first, but then reluctantly doing so after finally realizing there was no other way.)

Our ability to act for ourselves is the power of our *priesthood*, as it has been presented in the endowment. When we place the *robes of the priesthood* upon us, it simply means that we act according to our free agency. After the plan of salvation and our "Savior" is presented to us, and we agree to submit to his power and authority, we are placed in a newly-created solar system upon a planet that is in opposition to our established happiness. In this "lone and dreary world" we are allowed the opportunity to experience many things that will help us realize that the happiness we have chosen for ourselves is indeed the right choice for each of us individually. In our pre-mortal state, we became who we will always be, as we established our individual foundation of happiness by existing there for eons of time. Mortality is the time to prove to ourselves who we have chosen to be.

Without the guidance of Celestial Beings, we are left to the influence of each other. We have vainly created values of beauty, prominence, wealth, and success among ourselves, whereas there were no such values created or needed in a world where everyone was valued equally. In an environment void of Celestial people, we each strive to find our happiness following the subconscious drive-train that steers us to our individual happiness. In a world of inequality where we must struggle to provide for ourselves the things upon which our happiness depends, we do what is best for us, regardless of what our actions do to another. We have no choice. We were created to be happy. Therefore, all of our actions will be based on the desires that will bring us, personally, this happiness.

If there was only one piece of fruit left that would save two of us from starvation, our flesh is going to desire that piece of fruit and value it over the life of the other. It is almost impossible to do unto another what you would have that person do unto you, when there is not equality in all things. If your conscience tells you to give the last piece of fruit to the other so he won't die, is this not what you would expect the other to do also? Yet, if you both did unto each other what you would want done unto you, one (or both) of you is still going to die regardless.

The *curse* of mortality is having to labor for things that bring us happiness, which we didn't have to work for before. Also, the sexual urges that we are allowed to have, which we didn't have before, cause us further pain and sorrow as we give in to them, create life, and then protect that life by taking another's life, or another's equality, in some way to support the ones we created (our families). Thus, the curses of mortality are presented as "*by the sweat of thy face you shall eat your bread*," and "*in sorrow you shall bring forth children*" all the days of your life.

To make the experience even more poignant so we could distinguish between the good things that make us happy and the bad things that do not, the bodies we inhabit in mortality don't allow our spirits to bring to remembrance our past experiences. We have the established conscience that leads us to desire what we *feel* will make us happy, but we are not allowed to remember what it was actually like to be happy. If we could remember what it was like to live in complete happiness, we would remember how to act and would act this way, not allowing ourselves the opportunity to experience an existence of opposition. This inability to remember is presented in the endowment as the "cherubim and the flaming sword," which keeps us from partaking of the fruit we once partook of at will in the *Garden of Eden*—this "garden" representing an environment of eternal happiness where all things are provided freely for our enjoyment and happiness.

Without the intervention of the Gods, we are subject to the craftiness and manipulation of other humans who can't remember either. They also want to be valued and praised for what they do. So as we search for the meaning of the sensations that arise from our consciences, or as we ponder on what life is all about, others step up to establish their value as individuals and create religion, philosophy, science, the arts, and many other human inventions that allow one human being to be placed above another in some way. It is not our fault that we desire what we had before. It is our *fallen* flesh-and-bone bodies that corrupt us and cause us to search for something that we will never get in this mortal environment. In other words, *Lucifer* rules and reigns over us in the "lone and dreary world." His influences (the desires of our flesh) cause all kinds of confusion as we seek to understand and satisfy our intrinsic desire to be happy. It is easier to follow *Lucifer* and give in to his (our fleshly) enticings than it is to follow our conscience (that which tells us what is right). Therefore, we learn to accept and justify inequality and the unequal values we place on everything (including each other) in this *fallen* state.

Since our conscience doesn't allow us to stop the pursuit of happiness, which is being valued as much as everyone else, we created "money." Money is the abstract measure of value we have placed upon everything we need for our happiness. It is abstract because it is something none of us can comprehend when we try to align it with our spiritual natures. Why do we have it? Who created it? Why is it we can buy anything we want in the world for money? The answer: *Lucifer*. It seems unfair that our Creators are forced to follow the eternal laws and place us in a situation such as mortality. IF we could only remember what was right and what brought us happiness, surely we would give up money and inequality to have it again. Wouldn't we?

In our pre-mortal state, we valued our Eternal Parents above all others. Though They valued us equally, we valued Them above ourselves and each other. We saw Their power and Their glory and wanted, each of us, to be valued in the eyes of others just as much as we valued Them. In other words, we all wanted to be Celestial Beings. However, it was quite apparent that most of us were not. Though we wanted Their power and glory (the way They are viewed by Their children), we did not want to sacrifice our own desire of happiness in order to serve others forever. We actually believed that, if given the chance, we could prove to ourselves and to others that we *could* possess Celestial power and glory and still be happy by using these powers appropriately. Our Parents explained to us that most of us were not going to be like Them, but that we would be happier in other states of glory. We were not easily convinced. But They knew mortality would be the probationary state, or the time for us to prove it to ourselves.

Most humans are prone to take advantage of others and do not serve the best interests of others in sacrifice of their own. They have power and glory upon the earth because of the flesh (*Lucifer*) and they misuse it for their own benefit and happiness, which is consistent with their eternal natures, but not consistent with Celestial propensities. However, our free will creates our intelligence and logical mind. And there will be many who make the complaint:

> *If I would have just known what it was like to be Celestial, I would have done it in the flesh! If Celestial Beings, or any like them, were to have come to me in the flesh, I would have listened to them for sure!*

Thereby, these have an excuse and a reason to claim that their inability to use power and glory for the sake of others, instead of themselves, was caused by them not having the opportunity to choose between the two. Keep in mind, in the pre-mortal state there was no "bad fruit"—all was good. And in mortality, because we can't remember what the good fruit tasted like, there seems to be no "good fruit." "So how can it be fair when one is not given the fair chance to choose between the two (good and bad fruit)?"

To make sure that there would be no excuses, prophets were chosen upon the earth, and even Christ came as a mortal, to teach the people and give them a choice of the two different fruits. Alas, the majority of human beings have always rejected Christ and his prophets. Nevertheless, the **Law of the Gospel** is given to humankind by *true messengers of God* so that there would be no excuses. This law has been and always will be: Do Unto Others As You Would Have Them Do Unto You.

When enough time has passed in mortality where humankind has had the opportunity to accept "*Lucifer and his ministers*" over what our conscience tells us is happiness—even after we have purchased what we desire for our happiness with *money*—it will be time for God to send *true messengers* to cast *Lucifer* out and to allow us in our *fallen* state, to once again interact with Celestial Beings. This will take place during the Millennial period.

3) The third stage of human development and experience is known as the Millennium. During this Millennial period, it is necessary that we have all of our physical and emotional needs provided for. This is so that no other excuse can affect the unconditional acceptance that most of us *are not*, nor ever will be, Celestial in nature. Before this stage, one might make the excuse:

I didn't believe Christ, Christopher, or others like them, because they were just men like me! I have believed men before and have been deceived by their cunning ways. I disparaged him and refused to listen to what he had to say because of my previous experiences of being deceived. How was I supposed to know he was a true messenger when he was as fleshly of a man as I am? If I had heard it for myself from the mouth of a Celestial Being, I would have believed, accepted it, and acted differently!

This excuse will be eliminated when all mortals have the opportunity to interact with Those who come here from another planet and who are indeed Celestial Servants. During this Millennial state, presented in the endowment as the *Terrestrial World*, there will be no more excuses. Christ will reign solely upon the earth and take away the curses associated with mortality. All things will be provided freely for everyone equally, and only Celestial mothers will have children (conforming to the **Law of Chastity**). Throughout the earth, everyone's opinion of and desire for happiness will be fulfilled. However, the human race will still not be able to remember all that is recorded in their spiritual essence—this so that none have an excuse. Both the "good and bad" fruit will be allowed to grow upon the earth until the good overcomes the bad.

When all the mysteries of God are presented to us (the understanding of *Pay*, *Lay*, *Ale* in association with the Celestial **Law of Consecration**) and we are able to interact with Those who know these mysteries and teach us all we need to know about our existence, even after we have determined for ourselves that we are not Celestial, we will be ready to accept our individual desire for happiness in the kingdom of our own choosing. Finally, at that time, the Veil will be lifted from our minds and all things will be brought back to our remembrance, and we will be prepared to enter into our desired eternal kingdoms. The time just before we will be able to remember all of our experiences *perfectly* is figuratively presented in the endowment as the *Ceremony at the Veil*:

10
SALVATION IN THE KINGDOM OF GOD

PETER: Brethren and sisters, **this is the Veil of the temple;** I will now explain the marks on the Veil. These four marks are the marks of the Holy Priesthood, and corresponding marks are found in your individual garment.

~~This one~~ on the right is the mark of the square. It is placed in the garment over the right breast, suggesting to the mind exactness and honor in keeping the covenants entered into this day.

~~This one~~ on the left is the mark of the compass. It is placed in the garment over the left breast, suggesting to the mind an undeviating course leading to Eternal Life; a constant reminder that desires, appetites, and passions are to be kept within the bounds the Lord has set; and that all truth may be circumscribed into one great whole.

This is the navel mark. It is placed in the garment over the navel, suggesting to the mind the need of constant nourishment to body and spirit.

This is the knee mark. It is placed in the right leg of the garment, so as to be over the kneecap, suggesting that every knee shall bow and every tongue confess that Jesus <u>is</u> the Christ.

These other three marks are for convenience in working at the Veil. Through this one, the person representing the Lord puts forth his right hand, to test our knowledge of the tokens of the Holy Priesthood. Through the one on the right, he asks us certain questions; through the one on the left, we give our answers.

(As the officiator, who now represents Peter, steps to the front of the Veil, another male worker steps behind it to represent the Lord. A small mallet hangs on the metal frame that supports the Veil.)

PETER: As all of you will have to pass through the Veil, we will show you how this is to be done. The person is brought to this point, and the worker gives three distinct taps with the mallet *(the officiator raps the mallet three times)*, whereupon the Lord parts the Veil, and asks:

LORD: What is wanted?

PETER: Adam, having been true and faithful in all things, desires further light and knowledge by conversing with the Lord through the Veil.

LORD: Present him at the Veil, and his request shall be granted.

PETER: The person is then brought to this point, whereupon the Lord puts forth his right hand, gives the First Token of the Aaronic Priesthood, and asks:

LORD: What is that?

PETER: The First Token of the Aaronic Priesthood.

LORD: Has it a name?

PETER: It has.

LORD: Will you give it to me?

PETER: I will, through the Veil.

PETER: The person then gives, through the Veil, the name of this token, which is the New Name received in the temple today. The Lord then gives the Second Token of the Aaronic Priesthood and asks:

LORD: What is that?

PETER: The Second Token of the Aaronic Priesthood.

LORD: Has it a name?

PETER: It has.

LORD: Will you give it to me?

PETER: I will, through the Veil.

PETER: The person then gives the name of this token, which is his first given name, if he is going through the temple for his own endowment, or if he is going through for the dead, it is the first given name of the person for whom he is officiating. The Lord then gives the First Token of the Melchizedek Priesthood, or Sign of the Nail, and asks:

LORD: What is that?

PETER: The First Token of the Melchizedek Priesthood, or Sign of the Nail.

LORD: Has it a name?

PETER: It has.

LORD: Will you give it to me?

PETER: I will, through the Veil.

PETER: The person then gives the name of this token, which is "the Son," meaning, the Son of God. The Lord then gives the Second Token of the Melchizedek Priesthood, the Patriarchal Grip, or Sure Sign of the Nail, and asks:

LORD: What is that?

PETER: The Second Token of the Melchizedek Priesthood, the Patriarchal Grip, or Sure Sign of the Nail.

LORD: Has it a name?

PETER: It has.

LORD: Will you give it to me?

PETER: I cannot. I have not yet received it. For this purpose I have come to converse with the Lord through the Veil.

LORD: You shall receive it ~~upon the Five Points of Fellowship~~, through the Veil.

~~(The officiator demonstrates the Five Points of Fellowship through the Veil with the temple worker, who represents the Lord, as each point is mentioned.)~~

~~PETER: The Five Points of Fellowship are: inside of right foot by the side of right foot, knee to knee, breast to breast, hand to back, and mouth to ear.~~

PETER: **It is received as left arms are placed upon right shoulders through the Veil.** The Lord then gives the name of this token, and asks:

LORD: What is that?

PETER: The Second Token of the Melchizedek Priesthood, the Patriarchal Grip, or Sure Sign of the Nail.

LORD: Has it a name?

PETER: It has.

LORD: Will you give it to me?

PETER: I will, ~~upon the Five Points of Fellowship,~~ through the Veil.

The person then repeats back to the Lord the name of this token, as he received it, whereupon the Lord says:

LORD: That is correct.

PETER: The person is again brought to this point, and the worker gives three distinct taps with the mallet. The Lord parts the Veil and asks:

LORD: What is wanted?

PETER: Adam, having conversed with the Lord through the Veil, desires now to enter his presence.

PETER: The Lord puts forth his right hand, takes the person by the right hand, and says:

LORD: Let him enter.

PETER: He is admitted into the presence of the Lord.

We will now report.

Jehovah, we have been down to ~~the man~~ Adam **and Eve** and ~~his~~ **their** posterity in the Terrestrial World, and have given unto them the Law of Consecration, and have caused them to receive it by covenant. We have given unto them the Second Token of the Melchizedek Priesthood, the Patriarchal Grip, or Sure Sign of the Nail, with its accompanying sign, and have taught them the Order of Prayer. They are now ready to converse with the Lord through the Veil. This is our report.

JEHOVAH: It is well, Peter, James, and John.

Elohim—Peter, James, and John have been down to ~~the man~~ Adam **and Eve** and ~~his~~ **their** posterity in the Terrestrial World and have done all that they were commanded to do.

ELOHIM: It is well. Jehovah, instruct (go down with) Peter, James, and John to introduce ~~the man~~ Adam **and Eve** and ~~his~~ **their** posterity (in the Terrestrial World. Introduce them) at the Veil, where we will give unto them the name of the Second Token of the Melchizedek Priesthood, the Patriarchal Grip, or Sure Sign of the Nail, preparatory to their entering into our presence (the Kingdom of God).

JEHOVAH: It shall be done, Elohim.

Peter, James, and John, you will introduce the man Adam **and Eve** and his their posterity at the Veil (let us go down to the man Adam and his posterity in the Terrestrial World, where we will introduce them at the Veil, and), where we will give unto them the name of the Second Token of the Melchizedek Priesthood, the Patriarchal Grip, or Sure Sign of the Nail, preparatory to their entering into our presence (the Kingdom of God).

PETER: It shall be done, Jehovah. Come, James and John; we will introduce them at the Veil. (Let us go down with Jehovah and do all things for the man Adam and his posterity in the Terrestrial World that Elohim has commanded us.)

The text added in black, above, indicates Joseph's original intent of how the presentation of the endowment should have been given. During the Millennial reign of Christ, the Savior himself will personally be here upon the earth working with those chosen to help him prepare humankind for entrance to each one's chosen planet ("Kingdom of God"). This preparatory state has been previously explained as the *Millennium*.

"Peter" instructing the patrons at the Veil is a figurative representation of properly chosen and "true messengers of the Father" explaining all things in their correct order and unfolding all the mysteries of God to the people of the earth *before* Christ's reign upon the earth. All human beings will have the opportunity to know the truth of all things pertaining to who they are and why they exist. They will be given a clear, simple, and concise explanation of how they were created, why they were created, and how each of them as individual, free-willed human beings will choose what makes each happy. This opportunity is what has been coined correctly as a *marvelous work and a wonder*.

This *marvelous work and a wonder* consists of these books: Sacred, Not Secret—The Official Guide In Understanding the LDS Temple Endowment, The Sealed Portion—The Final Testament of Jesus Christ, 666, The Mark of America—Seat of the Beast; The Apostle John's New Testament Revelation Unfolded, Human Reality—Who Are We and Why Do We Exist, The Light of the Moon—The Plain and Precious Words of the Ancient Prophets, and the other books associated with this work, which will provide a way for all humans to come to a complete understanding of *real truth*. (The contents of these books will be available without charge on the Worldwide Internet at www.thesealedportion.com.) The *truth* contained within these books will set the people free from all organized religion and erroneous spiritual indoctrination administered by those who *think* they know the truth, but are in reality the *ministers of Lucifer* as it has been explained throughout this book. When this work is complete and published (by 2012), the people of the earth will not have the excuse that they did not have access to the fullness of the mysteries of God and a correct understanding of the Eternal Plan of Salvation. Whether one accepts this work as *real truth* or not, will not negate the fact that it has been *made available* to all humans equally, "*through the Veil*." This work gives one the chance to understand all things withheld from the foundation of the earth. This is in fulfillment of what the Lord told the world through Moroni:

> *Come unto me, O ye house of Israel, and it shall be made manifest unto you how great things the Father hath laid up for you, from the foundation of the world; and it hath not come unto you, because of unbelief. Behold, when ye shall rend that veil of unbelief which doth cause you to remain in your awful state of wickedness, and hardness of heart, and blindness of mind, then shall the great and marvelous things which have been hid up from the foundation of the world from you—yea, when ye shall call upon the Father in my name, with a broken heart and a contrite spirit, then shall ye know that the Father hath remembered the covenant which he made unto your fathers, O house of Israel. And then shall my revelations which I have caused to be written by my servant John be unfolded in the eyes of all the people. Remember, when ye see these things, ye shall know that the time is at hand that they shall be made manifest in very deed. Therefore, when ye shall receive this record ye may know that the work of the Father has commenced upon all the face of the land. Therefore, repent all ye ends of the earth, and come unto me, and believe in my gospel, and be baptized in my name; for he that believeth and is baptized shall be saved; but he that believeth not shall be damned; and signs shall follow them that believe in my name.* (Ether 4:14–18)

The "Kingdom of God" is nothing more or less than the eternal existence of humankind in the environment of their own choosing, after all choices have been presented to them. These choices and understandings are given, first, "*through the Veil*" by "Peter." Again, "Peter" represents the chosen prophet who teaches the people by "disclosing his true identity as an apostle of Jesus Christ" (through this *marvelous work and wonder*) *before* Advanced Human Beings come to the earth. This last chosen prophet proves he is a *true messenger* by giving "Adam" (the people of the world) the "sign and token" (real truth of things as they were, as they are, and as they are to come) he received in the *Garden of Eden*. The second way that humankind will receive the choices and understanding necessary to enable them to choose their proper kingdom of glory, is when Christ personally comes back to the earth (during the Millennium). He will present to the people of the earth, in person, the very *same things* that they had the opportunity to receive or reject from the holy prophets.

During the Millennium, human beings will still be restricted in their ability to remember their past lives and all other things that are recorded in their spirits that they have not experienced during their present mortal life. This is why this part of the endowment is given *at the Veil*—which again, is nothing more than a human's inability to remember anything beyond the current mortal life in which one is participating, and the lack of intercession and involvement of the Gods who created them. Though Christ will come to this earth and be accepted as an Advanced Human Being from a nearby solar system, humans will still act with their free will without having a clear recollection of all things. They will continue to suffer because of their choices until they come to an understanding of what it takes to live peacefully and in happiness with other free-willed beings.

This *real truth* was illustrated beautifully by Jacob as he related Zenos' allegory of the olive tree. It was the prophet Zenos' way of presenting the *real truth* without "disclosing his true identity," as was explained relating to all "true messengers of God." It was his form of the Holy Endowment. It's beauty and profundity is unmatched. The allegory presents, through figurative expression, how the Lord is involved in helping humankind. But no matter what the Lord does by allowing his servants to labor in his vineyard, and their doing exactly what he tells them, they all fail. It doesn't matter to which group of humans (the *tame* or the *wild* olive trees) the *real truth* is revealed through the prophets, for while there might have been some good fruit for a time, eventually the Lord is left to weep over the whole of humanity:

> *And it came to pass that the Lord of the vineyard wept, and said unto the servant: What could I have done more for my vineyard? Behold, I knew that all the fruit of the vineyard, save it were these, had become corrupted. And now these which have once brought forth good fruit have also become corrupted; and now all the trees of my vineyard are good for nothing save it be to be hewn down and cast into the fire. ...And now, behold, notwithstanding all the care which we have taken of my vineyard, the trees thereof have become corrupted, that they bring forth no good fruit; and these I had hoped to preserve, to have laid up fruit thereof against the season, unto mine own self. But, behold, they have become like unto the wild olive-tree, and they are of no worth but to be hewn down and cast into the fire; and it grieveth me that I should lose them. But what could I have done more in my vineyard? Have I slackened mine hand, that I have not nourished it? Nay, I have nourished it, and I have digged about it, and I have pruned it, and I have dunged it; and I have stretched forth mine hand almost all the day long, and the end draweth nigh. And it grieveth me that I should hew down all the trees of my vineyard, and cast them into the fire that they should be burned. Who is it that has corrupted my vineyard?*
> (Jacob 5:41–2, 46–7)

The Lord decides to go personally into the vineyard and labor with his servants and allow the good and the bad fruit to grow together:

And as they begin to grow ye shall clear away the branches which bring forth bitter fruit, according to the strength of the good and the size thereof; and ye shall not clear away the bad thereof all at once, lest the roots thereof should be too strong for the graft, and the graft thereof shall perish, and I lose the trees of my vineyard. For it grieveth me that I should lose the trees of my vineyard; wherefore ye shall clear away the bad according as the good shall grow, that the root and the top may be equal in strength, until the good shall overcome the bad, and the bad be hewn down and cast into the fire, that they cumber not the ground of my vineyard; and thus will I sweep away the bad out of my vineyard. (Ibid., 65–6)

Jesus Christ will not appear and destroy the world and the choices humans have made for themselves. He will use the opportunity to teach us the proper way to live by allowing us to compare *his way* with the myriads of other ways we have developed and become accustomed to throughout our human, free-willed evolution. In just one of many hypothetical examples that could be used, the Advanced Beings who come with Christ will set up medical kiosks throughout the world in which technologies far more advanced than anything ever known will be introduced. At these *Celestial Health Clinics*, one will be healed of all infirmities without cost and according to the desire of the person. Doctors and hospitals and pharmaceuticals set up for profit which put one human of more education above another, will not be forcefully eliminated. A person will have a choice of free, *highly-advanced*, medical care and treatment verses their loyal family doctor, who will continue to accept payment in money. What human is going to choose the Neanderthal tactics of seemingly primitive doctors and their medicine over being healed almost instantaneously without cost? As the "good fruit" grows, the "bad fruit" of the doctors, their pride, their glory, and their means will be "hewn down and cast into the fire"; not by the will of the Lord, but by the free choice of the people, as it has always been done—worlds without end.

When the people of the earth find that Advanced Beings from another solar system are here to help and provide all that any person could possibly need for all of their physical and emotional needs (for FREE), money and the values and inequality it represents will soon become obsolete. Then will the prophecies of John begin to unfold concerning the merchants, kings, and exalted (successful) of the earth, who are the *only* ones prophesied to suffer upon Christ's return:

Revelation

(Plain and Precious parts shown in ***bold italics***.)

18:1 And after these things I saw another angel come down from heaven, having great power ***over fire; that by the flame of his fire*** the earth ***might be*** lightened with ***the*** glory ***of God***.

18:2 And he cried mightily with a strong voice, saying, Babylon the great is fallen, is fallen, and is become the habitation of devils, and the hold of every foul spirit, and a cage of every unclean and hateful bird.

18:3 For all nations have drunk of the wine of the wrath of her fornication, and the kings of the earth have committed fornication with her, and the merchants of the earth are waxed rich through the abundance of her delicacies.

18:4 And I heard another voice ***as if it came*** from heaven, saying, Come out of her, my people, that ye be not partakers of her sins, and that ye receive not of her plagues.

18:5 For her sins have reached ***even*** unto ***the*** God ***of*** heaven, and ***she shall remember*** her iniquities ***in the Day of Judgment***.

18:6 ***For when the Lamb cometh he shall*** reward her even as she rewarded you, and ***recompense*** double unto her according to her works: in the cup which she hath filled, ***it shall be filled*** to her double.

18:7 How much she hath glorified herself, and lived deliciously, so much torment and sorrow give her: for she saith in her heart, I sit a queen, and am no widow, and shall see no sorrow.

18:8 Therefore shall her plagues ***be manifested*** in ***the*** day ***of the Lord***, death, and mourning, and famine; and she shall be utterly burned with fire: for strong is the Lord God who judgeth her.

18:9 And the kings of the earth, who have committed fornication and lived deliciously with her, shall bewail her, and lament for her, when they shall see the smoke of her burning,

18:10 ***And these shall stand*** afar off ***fearing*** her torment, saying, Alas, alas that great city Babylon, that mighty city! for in one ***day*** is thy judgment come.

18:11 And the merchants of the earth shall weep and mourn over her; for no man buyeth their merchandise any more:

18:12 The merchandise of gold, and silver, and precious stones, and of pearls, and fine linen, and purple, and silk, and scarlet, and all thyine wood, and all manner vessels of ivory, and all manner vessels of most precious wood, and of brass, and iron, and marble,

18:13 And cinnamon, and odours, and ointments, and frankincense, and wine, and oil, and fine flour, and wheat, and beasts, and sheep, and horses, and chariots, and slaves, and souls of men.

18:14 And the fruits that thy soul lusted after are departed from thee, and all things which were dainty and goodly are departed from thee, and thou shalt find them no more at all.

18:15 The merchants of these things, which were made rich by her, shall stand afar off for the fear of her torment, weeping and wailing,

18:16 And saying, Alas, alas, that ***great harlot*** that was clothed in fine linen, and purple, and scarlet, and decked with gold, and precious stones, and pearls; ***yea, even that great city which reigneth over the kings of the earth.***

18:17 For in one ***day*** so great riches is come to nought. And every shipmaster, and all the company in ships, and sailors, and as many as trade by sea, stood afar off,

18:18 And cried when they saw the smoke of her burning, saying, What city is like unto this great city!

18:19 And they cast dust on their heads, and cried, weeping and wailing, saying, Alas, alas, that great city, wherein were made rich all that had ships in the sea by reason of her costliness! for in one ***day*** is she made desolate.

18:20 And ***I saw in the likeness of things upon earth*** a mighty angel ***in heaven take*** up a stone like a great millstone ***and hang it about her neck***, and cast ***her*** into the sea, saying, ***because of her*** violence shall that great city Babylon be thrown down, and shall be found no more at all.

18:21 And the voice of harpers, and musicians, and of pipers, and trumpeters, shall be heard no more at all in thee; and no craftsman, of whatsoever craft he be, shall be found any more in thee; and the sound of a millstone shall be heard no more at all in thee;

18:22 And the light of a candle shall shine no more at all in thee; and the voice of the bridegroom and of the bride shall be heard no more at all in thee: for thy merchants were the great men of the earth; for by thy sorceries were all nations deceived.

18:23 And in her was found the blood of prophets, and of saints, and of all that were slain upon the earth.

18:24 Rejoice over her, ***all ye who are in*** heaven, and ***all*** ye ***upon the earth who have heeded the words of the*** holy apostles and prophets; for God ***shall avenge*** you on her.

In the presentation of the endowment, although "Peter" *introduces* the patrons at the Veil, he is *not* the one who will present them to converse with the Father through the Veil—Christ is. Furthermore, Brigham Young incorporated into the presentation of the endowment a part that supports and furthers his agenda, but is far from what was originally intended. He has the *husband* act as God and the one who stands on the other side of the Veil conversing with the wife before bringing her into the "presence of the Lord." Little did Young realize the vast numbers of LDS single women who would eventually go through the temple (without a husband) to receive their endowment. At first, single women could not go through the temple unless they were to be married. The LDS leadership soon realized the mistake, not that their false prophet Brigham had made it, but because of their own erroneous belief in order to justify that the *eternal* God changes from time to time to suit the fancies of men. Just so they are now informed correctly: an Eternal God does the *same thing* yesterday, today, and forever. Men change. Our Creators and truth do not.

The following *Lecture At The Veil* has been explained appropriately above. The lecture is very good, and follows, figuratively, what Joseph intended for it. Though it can now be understood properly in context of everything revealed symbolically about the endowment, its exclusion in modern-day endowments was purposefully allowed to make the presentation more convenient for modern-day, fast-paced living. And the way the powerful LDS Church is presently building temples and changing the original, there might soon be a "drive-up/*fast food-type*" endowment for those patrons wanting to assure their worthiness and fulfillment of temple-attendance requirements, but without the long wait.

PETER: Brethren and sisters, we are instructed to introduce you at the Veil, where you will receive the name of the Second Token of the Melchizedek Priesthood, the Patriarchal Grip, or the Sure Sign of the Nail, preparatory to your entering into the presence of the Lord.

~~Introduction~~

~~**NARRATOR:** Brethren and sisters, the ordinances of the endowment as here administered, long withheld from the children of men, pertain to the dispensation of the fullness of time and have been revealed to prepare the people for exaltation in the Celestial Kingdom, where God and Christ dwell. The deep meaning of the eternal truths constituting the endowment has been set forth in brief instructions and by symbolic representation. If you give prayerful and earnest thought to the Holy Endowment, you will obtain the understanding and spirit of the work done in the temples of the Lord. The privilege of laboring here for the dead permits us to enter the temple frequently, and to refresh our memories, and to enlarge our understanding of the endowment.~~

~~The Initiatory~~

~~You were first washed and anointed, a garment was placed upon you, and a New Name was given you. This name you should always remember; but you must never reveal it to any person, except at the Veil.~~

The Creation

You then entered this room. Here you heard the voices of persons representing a council of the Gods: Elohim, Jehovah, and Michael. Elohim said, "See, yonder is matter unorganized; go ye down and organize it into a world, like unto the other worlds that we have heretofore formed." As the creation of the earth progressed, you heard the commands and the reports of the persons representing the Gods.

If we are faithful, we shall enter the Celestial Kingdom and there hear and know the Gods of heaven. They are perfect; we are imperfect. They are exalted; we may attain exaltation.

Our spirits at one time lived with the Gods; but each of us was given the privilege of coming upon this earth to take upon himself a body, so that the spirit might have a house, in which to dwell.

Michael, one of the council of the Gods, became the man Adam, to whom was given the woman Eve. However, as Adam, he did not remember his life and labors in the council. It is so with us all. We came into the world with no memory of our previous existence.

The Garden

We then followed Adam and Eve into the garden, where Elohim provided that they might eat freely of all kinds of fruit of the garden, except the fruit of the Tree of Knowledge of Good and Evil. He forbade them to partake of this fruit, saying that in the day they did so, they should surely die. When Adam and Eve were left alone in the garden, Satan appeared and tempted them. Eve yielded to the temptation, partook of the fruit, and offered it to Adam. Adam had resisted the temptation of Satan, but when Eve offered him the forbidden fruit, he partook of it that they might continue together and perpetuate the human race. Adam and Eve now understood that it was Lucifer who had tempted them. They became self conscious. Discovering their nakedness and hearing the voice of the Lord, they made aprons of fig leaves and hid themselves. They had learned that everything has its opposite, such as good and evil, light and darkness, pleasure and pain.

The Lord again entered the garden. Adam and Eve confessed their disobedience. The Lord cursed Satan and cast him out of the Garden of Eden, and the Lord commanded, "Let cherubim and a flaming sword be placed to guard the way of the Tree of Life, lest Adam put forth his hand, and partake of the fruit thereof, and live forever in his sins."

Before their departure, however, instructions were given them. Addressing Eve, the Lord said, "Because thou hast hearkened to the voice of Satan, and hast partaken of the forbidden fruit, and given unto Adam, I will greatly multiply thy sorrow and thy conception. In sorrow shalt thou bring forth children; nevertheless, thou mayest be preserved in childbearing. Thy desire shall be to thy husband, and he shall rule over thee in righteousness."

To Adam, the Lord said, "Because thou hast hearkened to the voice of thy wife, and hast partaken of the forbidden fruit, the earth shall be cursed for thy sake. Instead of producing fruits and flowers spontaneously, it shall bring forth thorns, thistles, briars, and noxious weeds to afflict and torment man; and by the sweat of thy face shalt thou eat thy bread all the days of thy life, for dust thou art, and unto dust shalt thou return."

Having been commanded, Jehovah provided Adam and Eve with coats of skins for a covering. The garment which was placed upon you after you had been washed and anointed represents the coat of skins, or covering, of Adam and Eve. They were also promised that further light and knowledge would be given them.

The Law of Obedience and Sacrifice

The Law of Obedience was then taught Adam and Eve and accepted by them. Eve covenanted with Adam that thenceforth she would obey the law of her husband and abide by his counsel in righteousness; and Adam covenanted with the Lord that he would obey the Lord and keep his commandments. You likewise covenanted to comply with the Law of Obedience.

The Law of Sacrifice, accompanying the Law of Obedience, as contained in the Old and New Testaments of the Bible, was next presented to Adam; and you were all placed under covenant to observe it. The Law of Obedience and Sacrifice includes the promise of the Savior, the Only Begotten of the Father, who is full of grace and truth, and who, by his sacrifice, has become the Redeemer of mankind. All things should be done in the name of the Son. An angel of the Lord explained this to Adam, who was given the privilege of showing his obedience by offering sacrifices to the Lord in similitude of the sacrifice of Jesus Christ. Later, the people of Israel lived under this law, which continued in force until the death of Jesus Christ.

The First Token of the Aaronic Priesthood, with its accompanying name, sign, and penalty was given you; and you were told that the name of this token is your New Name or the New Name of the dead, if officiating for the dead. The sacred nature of the tokens of the Priesthood was carefully explained at this time. You were placed under solemn covenant never to reveal these tokens, with their accompanying names, signs, and penalties, even at the peril of your life. You were told that the execution of the penalties indicate different ways in which life may be taken.

The Telestial World

Then Adam and Eve were driven out of the garden into the Telestial Kingdom, or the lone and dreary world, the world in which we are now living. There Adam offered a prayer saying, "Oh God, hear the words of my mouth," repeating it three times.

Satan entered, and claiming to be the god of this world, asked Adam what he desired. Adam replied that he was waiting for messengers from his Father. Satan declared that a preacher would soon arrive. A man representing a sectarian minister entered and preached doctrine, which Adam did not accept.

Peter, James, and John were sent down by the Lord, to learn, without disclosing their identity, if the man Adam had been faithful to his covenants. They found that he had been faithful and so reported. They were sent down again, this time in their true character as apostles of the Lord Jesus Christ, to visit and to instruct Adam and his posterity in the Telestial World. Before so teaching the people, they cast Satan out.

The Law of the Gospel

The Law of the Gospel, as contained in the Book of Mormon and the Bible, was then given Adam and his posterity. You were placed under covenant to obey the Law of the Gospel, and to avoid all lightmindedness, loud laughter, evil speaking of the Lord's anointed, and taking the name of the Lord in vain. The Robe of the Holy Priesthood was placed upon your left shoulder, according to the order of the Aaronic Priesthood. The Second Token of the Aaronic Priesthood was given you, with its name, sign, and penalty; and you were informed that the name of this token is your first given name, or the first given name of the person for whom you are officiating. The Robe of the Holy Priesthood was then changed to the right shoulder, as was done anciently when officiating in the ordinances of the Melchizedek Priesthood. With the robe on the right shoulder, you have authority also, if called to the Bishopric, to act in the Aaronic Priesthood.

The Terrestrial World – The Law of Chastity

You were then introduced, with the Robe of the Holy Priesthood on the right shoulder, into the Terrestrial Kingdom. The Law of Chastity was there explained to you in plainness, and you were placed under covenant to obey this law. The First Token of the Melchizedek Priesthood, or Sign of the Nail, with its accompanying name, sign, and penalty, was next given you. You were told that the name of the First Token of the Melchizedek Priesthood is, "the Son," meaning the Son of God.

The book of Doctrine and Covenants, in connection with the Book of Mormon and the Bible, was presented to you; and the Law of Consecration, as contained in the book of Doctrine and Covenants, was explained to you; and you received this law by covenant.

The Second Token of the Melchizedek Priesthood, the Patriarchal Grip, or Sure Sign of the Nail, or the Nail in the Sure Place, was given you, together with its sign. The name of this token will be given you at the Veil.

This token has reference to the crucifixion of the Savior. When he was placed upon the cross, the crucifiers drove nails through the palms of his hands; then, fearing that the weight of his body would cause the nails to tear through the flesh of his hands, they drove nails through his wrists. Hence, in the palm is the Sign of the Nail, and in the wrist is the Sure Sign of the Nail, or the Nail in the Sure Place.

~~The Veil~~

~~You have now progressed so far in the endowment that you are ready to receive the name of the Second Token of the Melchizedek Priesthood and to pass through the Veil into the Celestial Kingdom.~~

~~The sisters in this company who are to be married and sealed for time and eternity should be taken through the veil by their intended husband. Others will be taken through the Veil by the regular temple workers.~~

~~Conclusion~~

~~Brethren and sisters, you will have received this day the sacred ordinances of the endowment. The Eternal Plan of Salvation for man, as he journeys from his pre-existent state to his future high place in the Celestial Kingdom, has been presented to you. You have covenanted to obey all the laws of the gospel, including the Laws of Obedience, Sacrifice, Chastity, and Consecration, which make possible an exaltation with the Gods; and you have received the First and Second Tokens of the Aaronic Priesthood, and the First and Second Tokens of the Melchizedek Priesthood, with the names, signs, and penalties of these tokens, except the name of the Second Token of the Melchizedek Priesthood, which will be given you at the Veil. All this is done for the glory, honor, and endowment of the children of Zion.~~

~~Brethren and sisters, strive to comprehend the glorious things presented to you this day. No other people on earth have ever had this privilege, except as they have received the keys of the Priesthood given in the endowment. These are what are termed "the mysteries of Godliness," — that which will enable you to understand the expression of the Savior, made just prior to his betrayal, "This is life eternal, that they might know thee, the only true God, and Jesus Christ, whom thou has sent." May God bless you all. Amen.~~

CEREMONY AT THE VEIL

The *Ceremony At The Veil* represents the time when all of us will be given the eternal, exalted (resurrected) body that we will choose for ourselves based on what we have learned from life in mortality living upon this planet. The choice will be made according to the degree of happiness that we have learned best suits our individual desires. This is preparatory for our placement on the planet that will provide us with everything we need to enjoy our lives in happiness forever—this is known as Eternal Salvation, or Eternal Joy.

Jehovah's (the Christ's) responsibility is to assure that all of us understand the purpose of our existence—which is to experience happiness. He assures that we have been given every opportunity to choose for ourselves, and that we have been treated fairly and according to the plan of salvation outlined in *The Book of Life*. He will assure that there will be no excuses for anyone. All Celestial Beings follow this *book* in creating new human life and assuring that this creation process is carried out properly with order and for the benefit of the new life created.

Jehovah figuratively presents us to "Elohim," whose role as our Creators mandates that They assure that we have all been given everything we needed to ascertain what makes us happy. Keep in mind, "man is that he might have joy," or human creation has only one purpose: to provide the opportunity for happiness.

This presentation and conversation with Elohim, wherein He asks each of us questions, does not *actually* occur for every person. It would reasonably take a God thousands of years just to speak to each of the billions of human beings placed in this solar system for a few seconds. The *Ceremony At The Veil* is symbolic of our Creators' direct involvement in assuring fairness, equality, and completion in purpose of our mortal state. Again, this mortal state precedes the final state in which we will exist forever.

The asking of questions and answering them, along with presenting each *sign* and *token* with its accompanying *name*, simply refers to God verifying that we have not missed a step and that we have understood each phase of our creation. If we miss anything, or say anything incorrectly, the worker representing "Elohim" on the other side of the Veil will pause and not respond or allow the ceremony to proceed until we get it right. The worker representing Jehovah is there at our side to make sure we say the right things.

We were created as individual spirits with the capability of exercising free will. This is possible because of the nature of our spirit makeup, which has no pre-mandated or pre-recorded instructions or commands as does the makeup of all other life forms. In the beginning, we were created to become unique individuals who react to different environments and situations according to our own choice.

The first environment in which we were placed was among Celestial Mothers, who chose this role because it brought the greatest amount of happiness to Them. They could not become these Mothers unless it was proven that in every way They would raise Their children properly and provide the appropriate example from which free-willed beings could establish the first experiences that would be recorded in their spirit memory banks. The experience with *perfect* Mothers established a human foundation by which all of our future actions and experiences would be measured. It became our conscience. This conscience makes us feel good and in balance when we are experiencing things that correlate to or mirror what our Mother's taught us through example. On the other hand, this conscience can also cause us stress, imbalance, frustration, and confusion when what we experience is out of line with our first memories of life.

The spirit part of us is *holy*, in that all of us were created equally and given the same opportunity and power to control our own destinies. This is what is referred to as the *Holy Ghost*. When we listen to our *common sense*, that is, if it has not been corrupted by doctrines, philosophies, and ideas generated in mortality, we make choices consistent with the *Holy Ghost* inside our heads; in other words, we are listening to and being guided by what our Eternal Mothers taught us by example and deed in the beginning. As taught previously in the presentation of the endowment, "Michael" was the third member of the Godhead (the Holy Ghost) and became the man Adam and the woman Eve, which represents all of us.

"Lucifer" represents our natural desire to seek to become like our First Parents:

I want you to eat of the fruit of the Tree of Knowledge of Good and Evil, that your eyes may be opened; for that is the way Father gained His knowledge. You must eat of this fruit so as to comprehend that everything has its opposite: good and evil, virtue and vice, light and darkness, health and sickness, pleasure and pain; and thus your eyes will be opened and you will have knowledge.

We desire to be like Them, even though we learn from making our own choices that very few of us can be trusted with the power that They possess. We come to know this from our experiences in "the lone and dreary world," where it is properly presented that "Lucifer" rules and reigns.

The two main purposes of this world are: **1.** To experience an environment and situation where all things act contrary to our ability to exercise our free will in attaining self-fulfillment, which is happiness. In other words, to experience a condition of existence that is opposite to that which we experienced when we lived on another planet with other Human Beings far more advanced than we are here upon this planet; and where those first experiences set a measure that foundationalized what we consider to be normal and self-fulfilling (who we are)—happiness. **2.** To prove that most of us are not capable of being trusted with the power and knowledge that some Advanced Human Beings possess. This Celestial knowledge and power allows a human being the ability to do anything he or she wants with one's free will. This power includes the ability to create life and enjoy the reward associated with creating it, which is the ability to achieve, experience, and enjoy the greatest spiritual and physical feeling possible to a human being—a sexual orgasm.

In mortality, the *real truth* has been withheld from us so that we can experience what happens without it. Without *real truth*, mortals invent their own religions and paradigms of thought, contrary to their own consciousness, but determined by their innate desire to make sense of the things that confuse them because of their inability to remember anything beyond their current mortal state. Those who are *like* our First Parents, or those who are Celestial, would never create a religion or *lead* us in any way. They do not judge us, nor do They establish any measure of righteousness for us based on <u>Their</u> personal preferences; except for one established paradigm upon which is based all the laws and commandments that govern all human beings: Love other free-willed beings as you do yourself.

Therefore, any human being who has experienced mortality and has become a religious leader, a political leader, business leader, a dominant husband, wife, or partner, teacher or parent, and has acted with his or her free agency to control the actions of another in any way, or in any way profited (monetarily or ego-based) personally therefrom *without regard for the happiness of the other*, can rest assured that their innate propensities preclude them from ever having the power of a Celestial Human.

Thus was it proclaimed by the original author of the endowment:

> *Behold, there are many called* (many spirits created), *but few are chosen. And why are they not chosen? Because their hearts are set so much upon the things of the world, and aspire to the honors of men, that they do not learn this one lesson—That the rights of the priesthood* (or the power of being a God) *are inseparably connected with the powers of heaven* (what is mandated in "The Book of Life"), *and that the powers of heaven* (Celestial power) *cannot be controlled nor handled only upon the principles of righteousness. That they may be conferred upon us* (here in mortality to prove us), *it is true; but when we undertake to cover our sins, or to gratify our pride, our vain ambition, or to exercise control or dominion or compulsion upon the souls of the children of men, in any degree of unrighteousness, behold, the heavens withdraw themselves; the Spirit of the Lord is grieved; and when it is withdrawn, Amen to the priesthood or the authority of that man.* (D&C 121:34–7)

Mortality is a proving ground to allow us the opportunity to get to know ourselves better. We all want the best possible human condition, but do not realize that what might be the best for us is not the best for others. We will learn in mortality that the *only way* we will ever experience peace and happiness is to allow Celestial Humans complete control and power over our lives. With this power, They do not "lead" us; They "serve" us. We become Their masters and They exist to assure that we are provided everything we need to experience happiness.

The human problem of being happy is largely due to the two purposes of mortality mentioned above. We have already experienced what we consider beautiful, peaceful, and all the things which we now equate with happiness. But our foundation for recognizing these things was acquired around *Perfect Human Beings who only use Their power for our sakes*. We are unhappy here in mortality because we are left to deal with people who *are not* like Them, and who use their worldly power over us to take away our free agency and enforce their own will upon us. Furthermore, since we all have the ability to create life and enjoy the reward (sex) associated with it, we find that there are just as many feelings of sorrow associated with this power as with the reward itself. Because of this power, we experience possessiveness, jealousy, dissatisfaction with our physical bodies because they are not attractive enough, or we are not fulfilled in our efforts to satiate the urge of this power.

Regardless of the fact that mortality makes us miserable most of the time, it is our human nature to seek to have power and be valued (seen by others) as one who successfully utilizes power for good. We get this propensity because this is what we saw, but can't remember, when we were reared among those Advanced Humans who had power and always used it for "good." We seek to succeed in the world, and if we fail there, we seek to succeed in our families. If we fail in the family situation, we seek to succeed in our personal relationships with the one we choose to share the power to produce life and experience its reward (the one with whom we have sex). And if we fail there, we seek to succeed as an individual, which usually leads us into all kinds of personal religious and spiritual experiences, which help maintain the confidence instilled in us from the beginning of our creation that we are just as equal and valued as everyone else.

What does one do who is given power over the life of another? Does that one use this power for the benefit and the "good" of the person over whom he or she has authority, or does that one use their power for their own desire to satisfy their *own* happiness? There has never been, there is not currently, nor will there ever be a mortal *leader* who will use his or her power for the benefit of those over whom he or she exercises power and authority. This includes world leaders, religious leaders, business leaders, supervisors, team leads, law enforcement officials, husbands, wives, sexual partners, mothers, and fathers. World leaders use power to support their political agendas and the laws of *their* "land." Religious leaders use power to support their religious agendas and the laws of *their* "God." Business leaders (from CEOs to low-level team leads) use power to make themselves more valuable in the economy in an effort to earn more money for themselves. Law enforcement officials use their power to support and enforce the "laws of the land" created by the world leaders, and in so doing, attempt to make themselves more valuable, thereby increasing their earning potential. Husbands, wives, and sexual partners use their power to dominate the other and assure that *their* individual needs are met; therefore, being "in love" means that the other person meets the expectations and needs of the one "in love." When these expectations and needs are not met, humans fall "out of love." Finally, the grossest use of this power is that of mothers and fathers who use their power and influence *to control* the lives of their children. They do this, not for their children's sake, but so that others will value them personally as successful parents, judging them by how successful their children are as world leaders, religious leaders, business leaders, supervisors, team leads, law enforcement officials, husbands, wives, sexual partners, mothers, and fathers.

There is a big difference between those who "lead" us and those who "serve" us. Those who "lead" us, use their power and influence to entice us down the path that *they* have already chosen for us, hoping that we will be just like them and experience happiness as they do. Those who "serve" us, recognize that we are just as valued and just as free-willed as they are, and that we have the agency to choose our own path and pursue it according to our *own* desire of happiness, which in most cases is much different than their own. "Servants" serve the desires of others. "Leaders" tell others what their desires should be.

No free-willed human creature wants to be told what to do. It is contrary to our nature. We want to do what we want to do. We do not want someone to lead us. We want the power to act as we desire and do what we will determine on our own makes us the happiest. We acquired this "nature" from our foundational experiences with *true Servants*, who *did not* set a course for who we were to become, but allowed us the free will to set our own course. They provided us with everything we needed to do this. They did not tell us what to do. They told other life forms (plants and animals) what to do—that's why these live instinctually with perfunctory commands that they are not aware of; flora and fauna follow these commands because they have no choice in the matter. We have a choice.

Servants do not tell a Master what to do. The Master tells the servants what the Master needs. It was customary for the Jews to call their teachers and leaders "Master." The Jews who saw Jesus this way often referred to him as "Master." But in private, Jesus would not allow his disciples to see him or treat him as such (though oftentimes they did because they did not yet understand the role of a Christ):

Neither be ye called masters: for one is your Master, even Christ. But he that is greatest among you shall be your servant. (Matthew 23:10–11)

And there was also a strife among them, which of them should be accounted the greatest. And he said unto them, The kings of the Gentiles exercise lordship over them; and they that exercise authority upon them are called benefactors. But ye shall not be so: but he that is greatest among you, let him be as the younger; and he that is chief, as he that doth serve. For whether is greater, he that sitteth at meat, or he that serveth? is not he that sitteth at meat? but I am among you as he that serveth. (Luke 22:24–7)

Finally, during the Millennium period of mortality, "the heavens will be opened" and we will have access to the knowledge and power of Celestial Humans who will intervene in our world on our behalf. These "servants" will assure that every human is provided with an equal opportunity to experience existence in a yet-imperfect body, without the capability of remembering all of one's past experiences, but also without having to spend most of one's mortal experience worrying about money and how one is going to survive. At this time, all things will be provided for the human race—free of charge. These Advanced Beings will bring with Them the technology that will assure that a human can be a man *or* a woman depending on one's individual choice. Even as our current technology provides the opportunity for a male to become a female through various transsexual operations, Celestial Beings will have the ability to perfect the operation and reverse it at any time according to the desire of the individual. The purpose is to allow all humans the free will to *be who they want to be*.

The gospel of Jesus Christ will spread throughout the earth. This gospel teaches us to love and accept each other no matter what one chooses, as long as the choices do not affect another's free will. A government will be established upon this earth with powers that will assure peace and equality for all. It will eventually eliminate borders, nations, religions, philosophies, and other mortal paradigms, travel restrictions, and all other prejudicial boundaries established by the nonsense of selfish mortals who once had power in the world. *REAL TRUTH* will reign supreme throughout the earth.

At this time, *Telestial* people will gather in "telestialized" parts of the world, *Terrestrial* in "terrestrialized,"

Celestial in "celestialized." (These words are symbolic as far as degrees of glory are concerned—all are equal in the eyes of our righteous Creators.) All humans will have the opportunity to travel to these different parts of the world and ascertain if they are happy with these kinds of people and cultures or not. We will come to know who we *truly* are and what *truly* makes us happy without the excuse that, "We were never given a fair opportunity, so how could we possibly know?"

It is understood that at the end of the Millennium, "Lucifer" will be released and reign for a short time, once again turning some from the truth. This is symbolic of human beings coming to an understanding that when they choose to take upon them the body that they will possess forever (the body that will have the capacity to finally remember all of their past-life experiences), most of them *will not be* Celestial. This includes the inability to experience sexual pleasure. Nothing is more desired than this ability. Nothing brings more joy than this power. But now, *The Book of Life* demands that it be taken from all those who are not Celestial Servants. It just doesn't make sense to the free-willed mind, and will cause the flesh to argue:

> *Why can't the Gods continue to allow all humans to experience this pleasure and eliminate the bad that comes with the good? Since Celestial partners (male and female) will have bodies where Their DNA only allows Them to be attracted to Their Eternal Mate, thus eliminating any lust or jealousy, why can't the Gods give these types of bodies to Terrestrial and Telestial human beings? We have been experiencing sex all throughout mortality, and now technology allows us to do it without producing children, and we agree that we should not rear and provide a foundation upon which these children will judge themselves forever; but why not allow us the tremendous joy of sex? It doesn't make any sense!*

To the natural, logical mind, it doesn't make sense now, and it will not make sense at the time of the "Ceremony At The Veil" when we are about to receive our eternal bodies. But thus it is, and thus it has always been. The only reward outside of the joy Celestial Beings receive in serving others' needs, is in the ultimate, natural, sensory experience allowed through the sexual contact that creates life. Since no other beings will be allowed the power to create life, none other will be allowed to experience it—worlds without end.

At this time, we will have to make a choice: receive the body we have determined is the best-suited for our happiness, or cease to exist. "Ceasing to exist" is the symbolic "Second Death" that will come upon those who do not agree with the rules and laws written in *The Book of Life*. Their spirit entities will be taken apart and this individual will no longer experience anything. This is merciful and just. This is the way order is maintained in the Universe. If it were not so, then free-willed beings could become enemies of peace and happiness (as they so often do in mortality), and there would literally exist the fantasized human creations characterized as "Alien Invaders" who seek to destroy life and continue war throughout the Universe.

Those who have proven to themselves and to the rest of us that they can be trusted with the power and knowledge of a God, will receive the **name** of the *token* associated with the Celestial Kingdom. These will be embraced by Elohim upon the "Five Points of Fellowship" and given all the power and authority They and Those like Them possess to create future posterity:

Health in the navel, marrow in the bones, strength in the loins and in the sinews, power in the Priesthood be upon me, and upon my posterity through all generations of time, and throughout all eternity.

The modern LDS Church, because of its lack of proper authority and understanding, deleted the "Five Points of Fellowship" upon which the Celestial *token* is given. The way it is given is paramount to it's acceptance. Those who are Celestial Humans now *share* these powers with other Celestial Beings. The Celestial individual speaks as a God would speak (*mouth to ear*), has the same support as all Gods have (*hand to back*), has the same desires and propensities as all Gods (*breast to breast*), submits to, honors, and obeys the Eternal Laws of heaven and earth contained in *The Book of Life* (*knee to knee*), and follows side by side along the same path of action as the rest of the Gods (*inside of right foot by inside of right foot*).

These individuals, though very, very few in comparison with the rest of humanity, will become the next generation of Gods who will go to other parts of the endless Universe and repeat what has been done for *us* in this solar system.

The rest of the human race will be placed variously on one of the several other prepared planets of this solar system that they have chosen for themselves, where each will enjoy living in the *Kingdom of God* forever. There they will add new experience to new experience and always enjoy the eternal gift of life granted to them by their Eternal Servants—Our Eternal Parents and Their Only Begotten Son (he who was created or "begotten" to serve us), even he who was known in mortality as Jesus, the Christ. And with the *Holy Ghost* (as it has been explained throughout this book) as our constant companion, we will experience the purpose of the Eternal Plan of Salvation of God forever.

We will experience ETERNAL HAPPINESS!

Thus, given with the glory and the power of a God, *Elohim's* final words in the symbolic presentation of the Temple Endowment—the most beautiful symbolic representation of all that is written in *The Book of Life*—are:

Let him enter.

(At this point, a temple worker motions to the patrons, row by row, directing them to the various veil segments. A worker (representing Jehovah) stands at each segment to introduce the patron to (Elohim) who is on the other side of the veil. The worker gives three distinct taps with the mallet.)

(ELOHIM): What is wanted?

(JEHOVAH): Adam, having been true and faithful in all things, desires further light and knowledge, by conversing with (Elohim), through the Veil [for and in behalf of _____, *(patron and then temple worker read name of deceased)* who is dead].

(ELOHIM): Present him at the Veil, and his request shall be granted.

(Elohim) gives the First Token of the Aaronic Priesthood through the opening in the Veil.)

(ELOHIM): What is that?

PATRON: The First Token of the Aaronic Priesthood.

(ELOHIM): Has it a name?

PATRON: It has.

(ELOHIM): Will you give it to me?

PATRON: I will, through the Veil. *(The patron gives the New Name).*

(Elohim) gives the Second Token of the Aaronic Priesthood.)

(ELOHIM): What is that?

PATRON: The Second Token of the Aaronic Priesthood.

(ELOHIM): Has it a name?

PATRON: It has.

(ELOHIM): Will you give it to me?

PATRON: I will, through the Veil.

(The patron gives their first given name, or the first given name of the person for whom the temple work is being done). [Elohim] gives the First Token of the Melchizedek Priesthood.)

(ELOHIM): What is that?

PATRON: The First Token of the Melchizedek Priesthood, or Sign of the Nail.

(ELOHIM): Has it a name?

PATRON: It has.

(ELOHIM): Will you give it to me?

PATRON: I will, through the veil—the Son.

([Elohim] gives the Second Token of the Melchizedek Priesthood.)

(ELOHIM): What is that?

PATRON: The Second Token of the Melchizedek Priesthood, the Patriarchal Grip, or Sure Sign of the Nail.

(ELOHIM): Has it a name?

PATRON: It has.

(ELOHIM): Will you give it to me?

PATRON: I cannot. I have not yet received it. For this purpose I have come to converse with (Elohim) through the Veil.

(ELOHIM): You shall receive it ~~upon the Five Points of Fellowship~~ through the Veil.

([Elohim] and the patron, still holding the grip, ~~embrace upon the Five Points of Fellowship~~ by placing their left arms through the marks of the compass and square, which are cut through the Veil. The patron's left arm goes through the mark of the compass, and [Elohim's] left arm goes through the mark of the square.)

(ELOHIM): This is the name of the token—"Health in the navel, marrow in the bones, strength in the loins and in the sinews, power in the Priesthood be upon me, and upon my posterity, through all generations of time, and throughout all eternity."

(ELOHIM): What is that?

PATRON: The Second Token of the Melchizedek Priesthood, the Patriarchal Grip, or Sure Sign of the Nail.

(ELOHIM): Has it a name?

PATRON: It has.

(ELOHIM): Will you give it to me?

PATRON: I will, ~~upon the Five Points of Fellowship~~ through the Veil. Health in the navel, marrow in the bones, strength in the loins and in the sinews, power in the Priesthood be upon me, and upon my posterity, through all generations of time, and throughout all eternity.

(ELOHIM): That is correct.

([Elohim] and patron break the ceremonial embrace, and the temple worker [representing Jehovah] gives three distinct taps with the mallet.)

(ELOHIM): What is wanted?

(JEHOVAH): Adam, having conversed with (Elohim) through the Veil, desires now to enter his presence.

(ELOHIM): Let him enter.

(The Veil is now parted and [Elohim] takes the patron by the right hand, and pulls him gently through the veil into the Celestial Room.)

Yea,

Let him enter the kingdom of his own choosing.

Worlds without end.

Epilogue

Joseph Smith said the following to some of his closest friends:

Christ was in the beginning with the Father, and was the only one born of God; even the only one prepared for us, that all those who are begotten through him shall be partakers of the same glory with him; these are they who are the church of the Firstborn. All of you were also in the beginning with the Father and with Christ. In the beginning you were created as that which is Spirit; and your Spirit is full of truth, even that truth that you shared with Christ and the Father. For truth is a pure knowledge of things as they are, and as they were, and as they are to come; and this truth you learned with the Father with a fullness; and this same fullness is brought forth through the Spirit, even the Spirit of truth. And whatsoever is more or less than the fullness of this truth is from the spirit of the flesh, which is that wicked one who has lied to you from the beginning. For the flesh cannot remember the truth of God. But the Spirit is full of truth because it is of God. Christ came among us to bring to our remembrance the Spirit of truth, and John bore record of him, saying: I, John, received a fullness of truth, yea, even of all truth through Christ; And no man can receive of his fullness unless he keepeth his commandments. He that keepeth his commandments receiveth truth and light, until he is glorified in truth and knoweth all things, even those things as they are, as they were, and as they are to come. For all these things were given to man in the beginning, as man was also in the beginning with God. And this truth is the intelligence of man, or the light of truth which dwells within him, which was not created or made, neither indeed can it be, because it is the experience of each man. And this truth is independent in that sphere in which

God has placed man, to act for himself, and his Spirit became the intelligence or the experience of man; otherwise there is no existence. Behold, here is the agency of man, and here is the condemnation of man: even that his experiences are the truth of who he is. And that which he has experienced is that which he has done from the beginning and shall be plainly manifest unto him through the Spirit of truth within him. And in the flesh they receive not the light of truth which dwells within man. And every man whose Spirit receiveth not the light is under condemnation. For man shall be known by his spirit. And the Spirit is made of elements that are eternal, even as the body is made of element; and the spirit and body, inseparably connected, receive a fullness of joy; And when separated, man cannot receive a fullness of joy. These elements inseparably connected make up the tabernacle of God; yea, and man was created in the image of the tabernacle of God, even temples; and whatsoever temple is defiled, God shall destroy that temple. The glory of God is intelligence, or, in other words, light and truth. And this glory or intelligence is the same as that which was given to man in the beginning. This light and truth forsake that which is evil, even that which keepeth not the commandments given to us in the beginning. For every spirit of man was innocent in the beginning, having received of the glory of God through his grace. And because of the flesh, man has fallen. But by the same grace, Christ came into the world and gave us in the flesh the commandments we received, yea, even the light and truth we received in the beginning from God. Therefore, God having redeemed man from the fall, man can again become innocent before God and partake of his glory.

Present when he spoke these incredible truths, were scribes who took notes and transcribed to the best of their memory what Joseph had said. (This incomplete rendition is recorded and accepted by millions of LDS faithful as D&C 93:21–38.) Joseph edited most of the content that he allowed his scribes to publish as doctrine, deleting and changing many of the *plain and precious* explanations of the mysteries of God that he had explained in private, but was not allowed to give in public. Because he did this, some of his closest friends, many of whom were prominent men and leaders of the early LDS Church, turned against him, branded him a false prophet, deceiver, and manipulator, and renounced their belief in his prophetic mission. These men could not reconcile the eternal truths (mysteries of God) Joseph was revealing to them in private with their inbred religious traditions and prejudices they had acquired throughout their life.

One of his closest friends, who was also a counselor in the First Presidency of the LDS Church, Frederick G. Williams, became one of Joseph's most ardent critics after Joseph revealed the above related mystery that man has the potential to become equal with God in all things. Joseph told Williams that the cause of his inability to accept such doctrine was because he could not remember the "light and truth" within his own spirit. The scribes wrote what Joseph told Williams as D&C 93:39–42:

And that wicked one cometh and taketh away light and truth, through disobedience, from the children of men, and because of the tradition of their fathers. But I have commanded you to bring up your children in light and truth. But verily I say unto you, my servant Frederick G. Williams, you have continued under this condemnation; You have not taught your children light and truth, according to the commandments; and that wicked one hath power, as yet, over you, and this is the cause of your affliction. And now a commandment I give unto you—if you will be delivered you shall set in order your own house, for there are many things that are not right in your house.

Each time Joseph made a *private* attempt to explain some part of the mysteries of God, he was rejected and mocked for it by those who looked to him for understanding. The simple truths (reality) of God were not accepted by most, because these real truths did not support the misunderstood and misinterpreted Holy Scriptures and contradicted the traditions that the people were accustomed to. The people looked **"beyond the mark"** and despised the words of plainness and sought for things that they could not understand. Joseph knew his calling did not require him to reveal such things in public, but it did require him to give the people what they desired:

But behold, the Jews were a stiffnecked people; and they despised the words of plainness, and killed the prophets, and sought for things that they could not understand. Wherefore, because of their blindness, which blindness came by looking beyond the mark, they must needs fall; for God hath taken away his plainness from them, and delivered unto them many things which they cannot understand, because they desired it. And because they desired it God hath done it, that they may stumble. (Jacob 4:14)

What was the "mark" that the Jews looked beyond? What was the cause of the blindness that made the early Latter-day Saints stumble and fall from the grace (truth) of God? It is the same "mark" of which Ezekiel spoke figuratively to ancient Israel:

*And the glory of the God of Israel was gone up from the cherub, whereupon he was, to the threshold of the house. And he called to the man clothed with linen, which had the writer's inkhorn by his side; And the LORD said unto him, Go through the midst of the city, through the midst of Jerusalem, and **set a mark upon the foreheads of the men** that sigh and that cry for all the abominations that be done in the midst thereof. And to the others he said in mine hearing, Go ye after him through the city, and smite: let not your eye spare, neither have ye pity: Slay utterly old and young, both maids, and little children, and women: but come not near any man upon whom is the mark; and begin at my sanctuary.* (Ezekiel 9:3–6)

The "mark" is the symbol of the lamb of God. It was the "mark" that Moses commanded the Jews to: "*Draw out and take you a lamb according to your families, and kill the passover. And ye shall take a bunch of hyssop, and dip it in the blood that is in the bason, and strike the lintel and the two side posts with the blood that is in the bason; and none of you shall go out at the door of his house until the morning*" (see Exodus 12:21–2). It was the "mark" that saved the children of Israel. It is the same "mark" figuratively used by Ezekiel and then borrowed by John the Beloved as he described those of the latter-days who, "*shall see his face; and his name shall be in their foreheads.*" (Revelation 22:4)

The "**mark**" is the simple gospel of Jesus Christ, the **Royal Law** on which hang all the law and the prophets:

Love Thy Neighbor As Thyself

As was the case with each and every prophet called before him, even in the case of Jesus Christ himself, Joseph could not get the people to LIVE THE FULLNESS OF THE GOSPEL OF JESUS CHRIST. Because the LDS people "looked beyond the mark," Joseph gave them what they wanted. He gave them a church. He gave them leaders instead of servants. He gave them church responsibilities and outward ordinances. He gave them tithes and offerings. He gave them priesthood and authority over each other. And to finalize the *stumbling block* he was required to put before them so that they may stumble, Joseph Smith gave them the Temple Endowment, which until this day, has been held **SECRET** by those who are *blind*, but is now understood only as **SACRED** to those who have regained their sight.

—Christopher, "Bearer of Christ"

a practical plan to end poverty...

wwunited.org
888.499.9666

www.ingramcontent.com/pod-product-compliance
Lightning Source LLC
Chambersburg PA
CBHW041122300426
44113CB00002B/25